Cracking the

AP®

ENGLISH LANGUAGE & COMPOSITION EXAM

2016 Edition

Richard Hartzell, PhD,
and the Staff of The Princeton Review

PrincetonReview.com

Penguin
Random
House

The Princeton Review
24 Prime Parkway, Suite 201
Natick, MA 01760
E-mail: editorialsupport@review.com

Published in the United States by Penguin Random House LLC, New York, and in Canada by Random House of Canada, a division of Penguin Random House Ltd., Toronto.

Terms of Service: The Princeton Review Online Companion Tools ("Student Tools") for retail books are available for only the two most recent editions of that book. Student Tools may be activated only twice per eligible book purchased for two consecutive 12-month periods, for a total of 24 months of access. Activation of Student Tools more than twice per book is in direct violation of these Terms of Service and may result in discontinuation of access to Student Tools Services.

"On Dumpster Diving" by Lars Eighner. From *Travels with Lizbeth*. Copyright © 1994. Reprinted by permission of Steven Saylor.

"The Hairy Maid at the Harpsichord: Some Speculations on the Meaning of *Gulliver's Travels*" by Dennis Todd. Copyright © 1992 by the University of Texas Press. Reprinted by permission of the University of Texas Press.

Farewell to Manzanar by James D. Houston and Jeanne Wakatsuki Houston. Copyright © 1973 by James D. Houston. Reprinted by permission of Houghton Mifflin Harcourt Publishing Company. All rights reserved.

The End of Education by Neil Postman. Copyright © 1995 by Neil Postman. Used by permission of Alfred A. Knopf, a division of Random House, Inc.

"Phenomenal Woman," copyright © 1978 by Maya Angelou, from *And Still I Rise* by Maya Angelou. Used by permission of Random House, Inc.

The Second Sex by Simone De Beauvoir, translated by H.R. Parshley, copyright 1952 and renewed 1980 by Alfred A. Knopf, a division of Random House, Inc. Used by permission of Alfred A. Knopf, a division of Random House, Inc.

ISBN: 978-0-8041-2616-8
ISSN: 1558-9676

AP and Advanced Placement Program are registered trademarks of the College Board, which does not sponsor or endorse this product.

The Princeton Review is not affiliated with Princeton University.

Editor: Meave Shelton
Production Editor: Emily Epstein White
Production Artist: Craig Patches

Printed in the United States of America on partially recycled paper.

10 9 8 7 6 5 4 3 2 1

2016 Edition

Editorial

Rob Franek, Senior VP, Publisher
Casey Cornelius, VP Content Development
Mary Beth Garrick, Director of Production
Selena Coppock, Managing Editor
Meave Shelton, Senior Editor
Colleen Day, Editor
Sarah Litt, Editor
Aaron Riccio, Editor
Orion McBean, Editorial Assistant

Random House Publishing Team

Tom Russell, Publisher
Alison Stoltzfus, Publishing Manager
Melinda Ackell, Associate Managing Editor
Ellen Reed, Production Manager
Kristin Lindner, Production Supervisor
Andrea Lau, Designer

Acknowledgments

Even though there is only one author, a team of people contributed to the creation of this book.

First of all, I want to thank Paul Tipton for his sage counsel and Kamilla Khaydarov and Rachel Newman, who wrote the student essays. Also, thanks go to my assistant, Kathryn Lee. Her cheerful manner and professional support proved invaluable; I could not have completed the text without her help.

Thanks to Dawn Shepherd Wolfe and Jeff Soules, who updated and reviewed this book.

I cannot fail to mention both my wife, Susana, and Laura, who for months on end allowed me to replace them with my computer screen and tolerated the very, very occasional bouts of bad humor that resulted from my sequestration.

And finally I'd like to thank my colleague and friend Robb Cutler for suggesting that I take on this project; I have forgiven him.

–Richard Hartzell

Special thanks to Linda Kelley, Gina Donegan, David Stoll, John Moscatiello, and Lisa Liberati for their invaluable contributions to the recent editions of this book.

Contents

Register Your

1 Go to **PrincetonReview.com/cracking**

2 You'll see a welcome page where you can register your book using following ISBN: 9780804126168.

3 After placing this free order, you'll either be asked to log in or to answer a few simple questions in order to set up a new Princeton Review account.

4 Finally, click on the "Student Tools" tab located at the top of the screen. It may take an hour or two for your registration to go through, but after that, you're good to go.

NOTE: If you are experiencing book problems (potential content errors), please contact EditorialSupport@review.com with the full title of the book, its ISBN number (located above), and the page number of the error.

Experiencing technical issues? Please email TPRStudentTech@review.com with the following information:

- your full name
- e-mail address used to register the book
- full book title and ISBN
- your computer OS (Mac or PC) and Internet browser (Firefox, Safari, Chrome, etc.)
- description of technical issue

Book Online!

Once you've registered, you can...

- Find any late-breaking information released about the AP English Language and Composition Exam

- Take a full-length practice PSAT, SAT, and ACT

- Get valuable advice about the college application process, including tips for writing a great essay and where to apply for financial aid

- Sort colleges by whatever you're looking for (such as Best Theater or Dorm), learn more about your top choices, and see how they all rank according to *The Best 380 Colleges*

- Access comprehensive study guides and a variety of printable resources, including the bubble sheets and scoring worksheets for the practice tests in this book

- Check to see if there have been any corrections to this edition

Look For These Icons Throughout The Book

 Online Articles

 Proven Techniques

 More Great Books

 Applied Strategies

The Princeton Review®
Your Goals. Our Expertise.™

Part I
Using This Book
to Improve Your
AP Score

- Preview: Your Knowledge, Your Expectations
- Your Guide to Using This Book
- How to Begin

PREVIEW: YOUR KNOWLEDGE, YOUR EXPECTATIONS

Your route to a high score on the AP English Language and Composition Exam depends a lot on how you plan to use this book. Respond to the following questions.

1. Rate your level of confidence about your knowledge of the content tested by the AP English Language and Composition Exam.

    A. Very confident—I know it all
    B. I'm pretty confident, but there are topics for which I could use help
    C. Not confident—I need quite a bit of support
    D. I'm not sure

2. Circle your goal score for the AP English Language and Composition Exam.

    5   4   3   2   1   I'm not sure yet

3. What do you expect to learn from this book? Circle all that apply to you.

    A. A general overview of the test and what to expect
    B. Strategies for how to approach the test
    C. The content tested by this exam
    D. I'm not sure yet

YOUR GUIDE TO USING THIS BOOK

This book is organized to provide as much—or as little—support as you need, so you can use this book in whatever way will be most helpful to improving your score on the AP English Language and Composition Exam.

- The remainder of **Part I** will provide guidance on how to use this book and help you determine your strengths and weaknesses.

- **Part II** of this book contains Practice Test 1, its answers and explanations, and a scoring guide. (Bubble sheets can be found in the very back of the book for easy tear-out.) We strongly recommend that you take this test before going any further, in order to realistically determine:
    ◦ your starting point right now
    ◦ which question types you're ready for and which you might need to practice
    ◦ which content topics you are familiar with and which you will want to carefully review

    Once you have nailed down your strengths and weaknesses with regard to this exam, you can focus your test preparation, build a study plan, and be efficient with your time.

- **Part III** of this book will:
    ◦ provide information about the structure, scoring, and content of the AP English Language and Composition Exam
    ◦ help you to make a study plan
    ◦ point you toward additional resources

- **Part IV** of this book will explore various strategies:
  - how to attack multiple-choice questions
  - how to write effective essays
  - how to manage your time to maximize the number of points available to you

- **Part V** of this book is a review of the terms and rhetorical modes that will give you an edge on the AP English Language and Composition Exam.

- **Part VI** of this book contains Practice Test 2, its answers and explanations, and a scoring guide. (Bubble sheets can be found in the very back of the book for easy tear-out.) If you skipped Practice Test 1, we recommend that you do both (with at least a day or two between them) so that you can compare your progress between the two. Additionally, this will help to identify any external issues: if you get a certain type of question wrong both times, you probably need to review it. If you only got it wrong once, you may have run out of time or been distracted by something. In either case, this will allow you to focus on the factors that caused the discrepancy in scores and to be as prepared as possible on the day of the test.

Once you register your book online, you can print out the bubble sheets and scoring worksheets for both practice tests!

You may choose to use some parts of this book over others, or you may work through the entire book. This will depend on your needs and how much time you have. Let's now look at how to make this determination.

HOW TO BEGIN

1. Take a Test
Before you can decide how to use this book, you need to take a practice test. Doing so will give you insight into your strengths and weaknesses, and the test will also help you create an effective study plan. If you're feeling test-phobic, remind yourself that a practice test is a tool for diagnosing yourself—it's not how well you do that matters but how you use information gleaned from your performance to guide your preparation.

So, before you read further, take Practice Test 1 starting at page 7 of this book. Be sure to do so in one sitting, following the instructions that appear before the test.

2. Check Your Answers
Using the answer key on page 34, count how many multiple-choice questions you got right and how many you missed. Don't worry about the explanations for now, and don't worry about why you missed questions. We'll get to that soon.

3. Reflect on the Test
After you take your first test, respond to the following questions:
- How much time did you spend on the multiple-choice questions?
- How much time did you spend on each essay?
- How many multiple-choice questions did you miss?
- Do you feel you had the knowledge to address the subject matter of the essays?
- Do you feel you wrote well-organized, thoughtful essays?

4. Read Part III of this Book and Complete the Self-Evaluation

As discussed in the Guide section above, Part III will provide information on how the test is structured and scored. As you read Part III, re-evaluate your answers to the questions above. At the end of Part III, you will revisit and refine the questions you answer above. You will then be able to make a study plan, based on your needs and time available, that will allow you to use this book most effectively.

5. Engage with Parts IV and V as Needed

Notice the word *engage*. You'll get more out of this book if you use it intentionally than if you read it passively, hoping for an improved score through osmosis.

The Strategy chapters will help you think about your approach to the question types on this exam. Part IV will open with a reminder to think about how you approach questions now and then close with a reflection section asking you to think about how or whether you will change your approach in the future.

The Terms and Modes chapters are designed to provide a review of the terminology you are likely to encounter on the exam, and will help you to identify the rhetorical fallacies and modes used in both test passages and student essays. You will have the opportunity to assess your mastery of the content of each chapter through test-appropriate questions and a reflection section.

6. Take Practice Test 2 and Assess Your Performance

Once you feel you have developed the strategies you need and gained the knowledge you lacked, you should take Practice Test 2, which starts at page 199 of this book. You should do so in one sitting, following the instructions at the beginning of the test.

When you are done, check your answers to the multiple-choice sections against the Answer Key on page 226. See if a teacher will read your essays and provide feedback.

Once you have taken the test, reflect on what areas you still need to work on, and revisit the chapters in this book that address those deficiencies. Through this type of reflection and engagement, you will continue to improve.

7. Keep Working

As we will discuss in Part III, there are other resources available to you, including a wealth of information on AP Central. You can continue to explore areas that can stand to improve and engage in those areas right up to the day of the test.

Part II
Practice Test 1

- Practice Test 1
- Practice Test 1: Answers and Explanations

Practice Test 1

AP® English Language and Composition Exam

DO NOT OPEN THIS BOOKLET UNTIL YOU ARE TOLD TO DO SO.

At a Glance

Total Time
1 hour
Number of Questions
54
Percent of Total Grade
45%
Writing Instrument
Pencil required

Instructions

Section I of this examination contains 54 multiple-choice questions. Fill in only the ovals for numbers 1 through 54 on your answer sheet.

Indicate all of your answers to the multiple-choice questions on the answer sheet. No credit will be given for anything written in this exam booklet, but you may use the booklet for notes or scratch work. After you have decided which of the suggested answers is best, completely fill in the corresponding oval on the answer sheet. Give only one answer to each question. If you change an answer, be sure that the previous mark is erased completely. Here is a sample question and answer.

Sample Question   Sample Answer

Chicago is a   Ⓐ ● Ⓒ Ⓓ Ⓔ
(A) state
(B) city
(C) country
(D) continent
(E) village

Use your time effectively, working as quickly as you can without losing accuracy. Do not spend too much time on any one question. Go on to other questions and come back to the ones you have not answered if you have time. It is not expected that everyone will know the answers to all the multiple-choice questions.

About Guessing

Many candidates wonder whether or not to guess the answers to questions about which they are not certain. Multiple choice scores are based on the number of questions answered correctly. Points are not deducted for incorrect answers, and no points are awarded for unanswered questions. Because points are not deducted for incorrect answers, you are encouraged to answer all multiple-choice questions. On any questions you do not know the answer to, you should eliminate as many choices as you can, and then select the best answer among the remaining choices.

GO ON TO THE NEXT PAGE.

This page intentionally left blank.

ENGLISH LANGUAGE AND COMPOSITION
SECTION I
Time—1 hour

Directions: This part consists of selections from prose works and questions on their content, form, and style. After reading each passage, choose the best answer to each question and completely fill in the corresponding oval on the answer sheet.

Note: Pay particular attention to the requirement of questions that contain the words NOT, LEAST, or EXCEPT.

Questions 1-10. Read the following passage carefully before you choose your answers.

(The following passage is from Jonathan Swift's 1729 essay "A Modest Proposal.")

There only remains one hundred and twenty thousand children of poor parents annually born. The question therefore is, how this number shall be reared and provided
Line for, which, as I have already said, under the present situation
5 of affairs, is utterly impossible by all the methods hitherto proposed. For we can neither employ them in handicraft or agriculture; we neither build houses (I mean in the country) nor cultivate land: they can very seldom pick up a livelihood by stealing, till they arrive at six years old, except where
10 they are of towardly parts, although I confess they learn the rudiments much earlier, during which time, they can however be properly looked upon only as probationers, as I have been informed by a principal gentleman in the county of Cavan, who protested to me that he never knew above one or two
15 instances under the age of six, even in a part of the kingdom so renowned for the quickest proficiency in that art.
I am assured by our merchants, that a boy or a girl before twelve years old is no salable commodity; and even when they come to this age they will not yield above three
20 pounds, or three pounds and half-a-crown at most on the exchange; which cannot turn to account either to the parents or kingdom, the charge of nutriment and rags having been at least four times that value.
I shall now therefore humbly propose my own thoughts,
25 which I hope will not be liable to the least objection.
I have been assured by a very knowing American of my acquaintance in London, that a young healthy child well nursed is at a year old a most delicious, nourishing, and wholesome food, whether stewed, roasted, baked, or boiled;
30 and I make no doubt that it will equally serve in a fricassee or a ragout.
I do therefore humbly offer it to public consideration that of the hundred and twenty thousand children already computed, twenty thousand may be reserved for breed,
35 whereof only one-fourth part to be males; which is more than we allow to sheep, black cattle or swine; and my reason is, that these children are seldom the fruits of marriage, a circumstance not much regarded by our savages, therefore one male will be sufficient to serve four females. That the
40 remaining hundred thousand may, at a year old, be offered

in the sale to the persons of quality and fortune through the kingdom; always advising the mother to let them suck plentifully in the last month, so as to render them plump and fat for a good table. A child will make two dishes at an
45 entertainment for friends; and when the family dines alone, the fore or hind quarter will make a reasonable dish, and seasoned with a little pepper or salt will be very good boiled on the fourth day, especially in winter.
I have reckoned upon a medium that a child just born
50 will weigh 12 pounds, and in a solar year, if tolerably nursed, increaseth to 28 pounds.
I grant this food will be somewhat dear, and therefore very proper for landlords, who, as they have already devoured most of the parents, seem to have the best title to
55 the children.

1. This text can best be described as

   (A) scientific
   (B) satirical
   (C) forthright
   (D) humanitarian
   (E) sadistic

2. In the first, second, and fourth paragraphs the author relies on dubious

   (A) similes
   (B) *ad hominem* arguments
   (C) extended metaphors
   (D) arguments from authority
   (E) appeals to ignorance

GO ON TO THE NEXT PAGE.

3. It can be inferred that the "merchants" (line 17) and the "American" (line 26) represent

   (A) cannibals who routinely eat children
   (B) the author's fictional acquaintances
   (C) aristocrats who exploit the poor
   (D) businessmen well-versed in commerce
   (E) typical Londoners

4. The phrase "the charge of nutriment and rags having been at least four times that value" (lines 22-23) is ironic chiefly because

   (A) food was relatively cheap at that time
   (B) "four times" is a mere approximation
   (C) twelve pounds is a very small sum of money
   (D) the parents could not support their children without the aid of the kingdom
   (E) there is no evidence that the children were wearing rags

5. The word "fricassee" (line 30) is best interpreted to mean

   (A) animal
   (B) child
   (C) dish
   (D) place
   (E) master

6. Which of the following rhetorical devices does the author employ in lines 32-39?

   (A) process analysis
   (B) example
   (C) cause and effect
   (D) deductive reasoning
   (E) analogy

7. The phrase "always advising the mother to let them suck plentifully in the last month" (lines 42-43) extends the comparison between the children and

   (A) properly nourished mammals
   (B) poor and ruthless parents
   (C) savages
   (D) animals raised for slaughter
   (E) the poor treatment of animals

8. In line 52, "dear" means

   (A) expensive
   (B) sweet
   (C) cherished
   (D) unforgettable
   (E) unhealthy

9. In context, "devoured" (line 54) is an effective word choice because

   (A) it fits both figuratively and literally
   (B) it is appropriate only literally
   (C) it is indicative of the landlords' plight
   (D) it works as a sentimental appeal
   (E) it reveals the author's point of view

10. The author mentions "sheep, black cattle, or swine" (line 36) in order to convey which of the following ideas?

   (A) Animals are often treated more humanely than are children.
   (B) Large numbers of animals should be kept for breeding purposes.
   (C) Male animals are often more effective for breeding than female animals.
   (D) The poor are often used as commodities to profit their owners.
   (E) Marriage is not universally valued in all cultures.

GO ON TO THE NEXT PAGE.

Questions 11-22. Read the following passage carefully before you choose your answers.

(The following passage is excerpted from a contemporary article in a scholarly journal.)

The most obvious joke in the title of Swift's *Travels into Several Remote Nations of the World* is that what purports to be a chronicle of several excursions to remote nations
Line turns out to be a satiric anatomy of specifically English
5 attitudes and values. But there is a second joke. Many of the supposedly unfamiliar and exotic sights Gulliver sees in his sixteen years and seven months of wandering in remote nations, and even the radically altered perspectives from which he sees them (as diminutive landscapes, giant
10 people, intelligent animals, etc.), could have been seen or experienced in a few days by anyone at the tourists sights, public entertainments, shows, spectacles, and exhibitions in the streets and at the fairs of London.

It is not surprising that *Gulliver's Travels* should be
15 filled with the shows and diversions of London. All the Scriblerians were fascinated with popular entertainments; collectively and individually, they satirized them in many of their works. Swift shared this fascination with his fellow Scriblerians, and he transforms the sights and shows of
20 London into an imaginative center of *Gulliver's Travels*.

1

Gulliver himself senses that the wonders he sees in remote nations resemble popular entertainments back home in England when he notes that the capital city of Lilliput "looked like the painted Scene of a City in a Theatre."[1] And
25 other popular entertainments would allow Londoners to see many of the same sights Gulliver saw in Lilliput. A Londoner could experience what a miniature city looked like to the giant Gulliver by going to see the papier-mâché and clay architectural and topographical models displayed at fairs and
30 in inns, some of which were extraordinarily elaborate and detailed, such as the model of Amsterdam exhibited in 1710, which was twenty feet wide and twenty to thirty feet long, "with all the Churches, Chappels, Stadt house, Hospitals, noble Buildings, Streets, Trees, Walks, Avenues, with the
35 Sea, Shipping, Sluices, Rivers, Canals &c., most exactly built to admiration."[2]

Miniature people, as well as miniature landscapes, could be seen in one of the most popular diversions in London, the peepshows, which were enclosed boxes containing scenes
40 made out of painted board, paper flats, and glass panels and given the illusion of depth by mirrors and magnifying glasses. All of this was seen through a hole bored in one side. Among the most popular scenes were interiors, particularly palace interiors of European royalty, and so there is a direct
45 analogy between peering in the hole of a peepshow and

Gulliver's looking into the palace in Lilliput: "I applied my Face to the Windows of the middle Stories, and discovered the most splendid Apartments that can be imagined. There I saw the Empress, and the young Princes in their several
50 Lodgings. Her Imperial Majesty was pleased to smile very graciously upon me, and gave me out the window her Hand to kiss." The queen's movements could have been seen in the peepshows, too, for clockwork animating the figures was introduced early in the century. And much the same illusion
55 of a living, miniature world could be found in another popular diversion, the "moving picture," a device in which cutout figures were placed within a frame and activated by jacks and wheels. This curiosity fascinated contemporary Londoners: "The landscape looks as an ordinary picture till
60 the clock-work behind the curtain be set at work, and then the ships move and sail distinctly upon the sea till out of sight; a coach comes out of town, the motion of the horses and wheels are very distinct, and a gentleman in the coach that salutes the company; a hunter also and his dogs keep
65 their course till out of sight." Swift saw this same moving picture, or one very much like it, and was impressed.

From the article "The Hairy Maid at the Harpsichord: Some Speculations on the Meaning of *Gulliver's Travels*," by Dennis Todd, originally published in *Texas Studies in Literature and Language* Volume 34 Issue 2, pp. 239-283.

11. The purpose of the passage is most likely to

   (A) describe the cultural landscape in *Gulliver's Travels*
   (B) draw a comparison between the fictional world Gulliver experienced and the similar imaginative elements of eighteenth-century London
   (C) point out the superfluous nature of entertainment in Swift's London
   (D) provide evidence that Swift's satire is derived from the natural curiosity of European royalty
   (E) discredit the notion that *Gulliver's Travels* is a wholly original work

---

1 *Gulliver's Travels*, in *The Prose Works of Jonathan Swift*, ed. Herbert Davis, 14 vols. (Oxford: B. Blackwell, 1939–68), XI:13

2 Quoted in John Ashton, *Social Life in the Reign of Queen Anne* (New York: Chatto and Windus, 1883), 219–20

GO ON TO THE NEXT PAGE.

12. In the passage, the author's overall attitude toward *Gulliver's Travels* can best be described as

    (A) cleverly subversive
    (B) bitingly sarcastic
    (C) generally appreciative
    (D) halfheartedly engaged
    (E) insistently dismissive

13. "Scriblerians" (line 16) refers to

    (A) book craftsmen in London
    (B) characters in Swift's novels
    (C) English politicians and aristocrats
    (D) historians of popular entertainment
    (E) a circle of English authors

14. It can be inferred from the second paragraph that Jonathan Swift was

    (A) a citizen of London
    (B) a producer of public entertainments
    (C) a member of the Scriblerians
    (D) a painter as well as an author
    (E) a traveling salesman

15. The stylistic feature most evident in the first two paragraphs (lines 1-20) is the use of

    (A) repeated syntactical patterns
    (B) shifts in tense and person
    (C) historical allusions
    (D) a series of extended metaphors
    (E) didactic analogies and asides

16. In describing miniature people and landscapes in the final paragraph, the author emphasizes their

    (A) size
    (B) obscurity
    (C) magnificence
    (D) commonness
    (E) transience

17. In the fourth paragraph, the author includes long quotes primarily in order to

    (A) refute the claims of his detractors that *Gulliver's Travels* was purely imaginative
    (B) document the connection between *Gulliver's Travels* and popular entertainments
    (C) challenge the prevailing scholarship on the miniature people and landscapes in *Gulliver's Travels*
    (D) highlight the inconsistencies within *Gulliver's Travels* regarding miniature people and landscapes
    (E) inform the reader of the sources for the study of miniature people and landscapes in *Gulliver's Travels*

18. Which of the following best describes the relationship between the first section (lines 1-20) and the second section (lines 21-66) of the passage?

    (A) The second section answers the series of questions raised in the first section.
    (B) The second section challenges the prevailing picture detailed in in the first section.
    (C) The second section undermines the positions of scholars introduced in the first section.
    (D) The second section expands on a technical definition introduced in the first section.
    (E) The second section provides evidence for the claims introduced in the first section.

19. The footnote 1 in line 24 indicates that

    (A) the article first appeared as an addendum to *Gulliver's Travels*
    (B) *Gulliver's Travels* was first published in 1939
    (C) the quotation "looked like the…Theater" was excerpted from *Gulliver's Travels*, part of a 14 volume set of Swift's works
    (D) the quotation "looked like the…Theater" was originally written by Herbert Davis
    (E) *Gulliver's Travels* was reprinted in its entirety in 1939, and credited to Herbert Davis instead of Swift

GO ON TO THE NEXT PAGE.

20. The footnote 2 in line 36 indicates

    (A) the quotation was taken from a professional journal

    (B) the quotation refers to a 1710 exhibit in Amsterdam

    (C) the quotation originally appeared in *Gulliver's Travels* in 1883

    (D) the quotation, describing a miniature exhibition of Amsterdam, first appeared in a book by John Ashton

    (E) the quotation was originally published in a newspaper

21. The detail in lines 46-52 suggest the scene is viewed by which of the following?

    (A) an impartial anthropologist

    (B) an intrigued visitor

    (C) a critical literary scholar

    (D) an argumentative architect

    (E) a struggling writer

22. The speaker's tone might best be described as

    (A) emphatic and insistent

    (B) scholarly and enthusiastic

    (C) dejected but hopeful

    (D) erudite and cynical

    (E) intransigent yet competent

GO ON TO THE NEXT PAGE.

Questions 23-33. Read the following passage carefully before you choose your answers.

(The following passage is from A Vindication of the Rights of Women *by Mary Wollstonecraft in 1792.)*

My own sex, I hope, will excuse me, if I treat them like rational creatures, instead of flattering their fascinating graces, and viewing them as if they were in a state of
Line perpetual childhood, unable to stand alone. I earnestly
5   wish to point out in what true dignity and human happiness consists—I wish to persuade women to endeavour to acquire strength, both of mind and body, and to convince them that the soft phrases, susceptibility of heart, delicacy of sentiment, and refinement of taste, are almost synonymous
10   with epithets of weakness, and that those beings who are only the objects of pity and that kind of love, which has been termed its sister, will soon become objects of contempt.

Dismissing then those pretty feminine phrases, which the men condescendingly use to soften our slavish dependence,
15   and despising that weak elegancy of mind, exquisite sensibility, and sweet docility of manners, supposed to be the sexual characteristics of the weaker vessel, I wish to show that elegance is inferior to virtue, that the first object of laudable ambition is to obtain a character as a human being,
20   regardless of the distinction of sex; and that secondary views should be brought to this simple touchstone.

This is a rough sketch of my plan; and should I express my conviction with the energetic emotions that I feel whenever I think of the subject, the dictates of experience
25   and reflection will be felt by some of my readers. Animated by this important object, I shall disdain to cull my phrases or polish my style;—I aim at being useful, and sincerity will render me unaffected; for, wishing rather to persuade by the force of my arguments, than dazzle by the elegance of my
30   language, I shall not waste my time in rounding periods, nor in fabricating the turgid bombast of artificial feelings, which, coming from the head, never reach the heart—I shall be employed about things, not words!—and, anxious to render my sex more respectable to members of society, I
35   shall try to avoid that flowery diction which has slided from essays into novels, and from novels into familiar letters and conversation.

These pretty nothings—these caricatures of the real beauty of sensibility, dropping glibly from the tongue, vitiate
40   the taste, and create a kind of sickly delicacy that turns away from simple unadorned truth; and a deluge of false sentiments and overstretched feelings, stifling the natural emotions of the heart, render the domestic pleasures insipid, that ought to sweeten the exercise of those severe duties,
45   which educate a rational and immortal being for a nobler field of action.

The education of women has, of late, been more attended to than formerly; yet they are still reckoned a frivolous sex, and ridiculed or pitied by the writers who endeavour by
50   satire or instruction to improve them. It is acknowledged that they spend many of the first years of their lives in acquiring a smattering of accomplishments: meanwhile strength of body and mind are sacrificed to libertine notions of beauty, to the desire of establishing themselves—the only way women
55   can rise in the world—by marriage. And this desire making mere animals of them, when they marry they act as such children may be expected to act—they dress; they paint, and nickname God's creatures—Surely these weak beings are only fit for a seraglio!—Can they govern a family, or take
60   care of the poor babes whom they bring into the world?

23. In the initial paragraph, the author employs both

   (A) apology and classification
   (B) irony and exposition
   (C) analogy and extended metaphor
   (D) flattery and epithets
   (E) induction and persuasion

24. In the initial paragraph, the author decries

   (A) traditional feminine attributes
   (B) traditional male attributes
   (C) modern sexuality
   (D) the importance of love
   (E) the importance of sentiments

25. In the initial paragraph, the author suggests that

   (A) men prefer strong women
   (B) a man will never truly love a strong woman
   (C) men never respect strong women
   (D) women need emotional and physical strength
   (E) women need intellectual and physical strength

26. The author ties the second paragraph to the first by using the words

   (A) "vessel" and "touchstone"
   (B) "soften" and "inferior"
   (C) "laudable" and "sex"
   (D) "slavish" and "virtue"
   (E) "soften" and "weak"

GO ON TO THE NEXT PAGE.

27. The word "vessel" (line 17) is a metaphor for

    (A) sex
    (B) woman
    (C) man
    (D) phrase
    (E) character

28. The author suggests that a woman's worth may be best judged by

    (A) comparing her with a praiseworthy man
    (B) examining the elegance of her writing
    (C) evaluating the strength of her character
    (D) evaluating her physical beauty
    (E) examining her manners

29. The author proposes to write in a manner that is both

    (A) cogent and emotional
    (B) polished and intellectual
    (C) ornate and rhetorical
    (D) elegant and cerebral
    (E) convincing and flowery

30. The words "pretty nothings" (line 38) are a reprise of

    (A) "letters and conversation" (lines 36-37)
    (B) "essays" and "novels" (line 36)
    (C) "flowery diction" (line 35)
    (D) "rounding periods" (line 30)
    (E) "members of society" (line 34)

31. With the phrase "dropping glibly from the tongue" (line 39) the author begins

    (A) a caricature of women
    (B) a critique of turgid bombast
    (C) a panegyric of sugary writing
    (D) an analysis of sentimental writing
    (E) an extended metaphor

32. One can infer from the passage that to become strong human beings, rather than mere children, young women need

    (A) an education different from that of young men
    (B) more understanding husbands
    (C) obliging husbands
    (D) a good marriage
    (E) the same education as that of young men

33. The tone of the final paragraph is

    (A) sardonic
    (B) lyrical
    (C) condescending
    (D) frivolous
    (E) reserved

GO ON TO THE NEXT PAGE.

Questions 34-44. Read the following passage carefully before you choose your answers.

(The following passage is from Neil Postman's 1995 book, The End of Education.*)*

But it is important to keep in mind that the engineering
of learning is very often puffed up, assigned an importance it
does not deserve. As an old saying goes, *There are one and*
Line *twenty ways to sing tribal lays, and all of them are correct.*
5 So it is with learning. There is no one who can say that this
or that is the best way to know things, to feel things, to see
things, to remember things, to apply things, to connect things
and that no other will do as well. In fact, to make such a
claim is to trivialize learning, to reduce it to a mechanical
10 skill.

Of course, there are many learnings that are little else
but a mechanical skill, and in such cases, there well may
be a best way. But to become a different person because of
something you have learned—to appropriate an insight, a
15 concept, a vision, so that your world is altered—that is a
different matter. For that to happen, you need a reason. And
this is the metaphysical problem I speak of.

A reason, as I use the word here, is different from a
motivation. Within the context of schooling, motivation
20 refers to a temporary psychic event in which curiosity is
aroused and attention is focused. I do not mean to disparage
it. But it must not be confused with a reason for being
in a classroom, for listening to a teacher, for taking an
examination, for doing homework, for putting up with school
25 even if you are not motivated.

This kind of reason is somewhat abstract, not always
present in one's consciousness, not at all easy to describe.
And yet for all that, without it schooling does not work. For
school to make sense, the young, their parents, and their
30 teachers must have a god to serve, or, even better, several
gods. If they have none, school is pointless. Nietzsche's
famous aphorism is relevant here: "He who has a *why* to
live can bear with almost any *how*." This applies as much to
learning as to living.

35 To put it simply, there is no surer way to bring an end to
schooling than for it to have no end.

34. The "engineering of learning" (lines 1-2) most nearly means

   (A) development of schools
   (B) building of schools
   (C) educational methodology
   (D) building up of knowledge
   (E) study of engineering

35. The "old saying" (line 3) serves as

   (A) an analogy to the sentences that follow
   (B) a contrast to the sentences that follow
   (C) an illustration of the first sentence
   (D) a historical interlude
   (E) a tribute to tribal lays

36. The series of infinitives in the initial paragraph emphasizes that the learning process is

   (A) long and tedious
   (B) multifaceted and impersonal
   (C) active and varied
   (D) difficult and trivial
   (E) mechanical and complicated

37. According to the author, motivation is

   (A) not important
   (B) synonymous with reason
   (C) abstract and fleeting
   (D) momentary and concrete
   (E) psychological and enduring

38. Both the first and third paragraphs contain

   (A) aphorisms
   (B) ironical statements
   (C) syllogistic reasoning
   (D) *ad hominem* arguments
   (E) notable parallelism

39. In line 30, "god" most nearly means

   (A) religion
   (B) deity
   (C) reason
   (D) person
   (E) Nietzsche

GO ON TO THE NEXT PAGE.

40. The author employs the argument from authority as

    (A) a contrast to his point of view
    (B) a relevant concrete example
    (C) an apt analogy
    (D) an example of cause and effect
    (E) an illustration of the cruelty in schools

41. The paradox in the final sentence rests on

    (A) different meanings of "end"
    (B) a crass simplification
    (C) the comparison between schooling and learning
    (D) the eternal process of learning
    (E) a new way of bringing schooling to an end

42. The principal contrast employed by the author in the passage is between

    (A) education and wisdom
    (B) theory and practice
    (C) knowledge and literacy
    (D) ignorance and religion
    (E) motivation and purpose

43. Which of the following best states the subject of the passage?

    (A) The historical development of educational institutions
    (B) The necessity of higher purpose in education
    (C) The challenges of educational reform in the United States
    (D) The lack of scientific rigor in educational theory
    (E) The separation of church and state in American education

44. The passage as a whole is best described as

    (A) an objective analysis
    (B) an impassioned plea
    (C) a linear narrative
    (D) a dramatic monologue
    (E) a reasoned argument

GO ON TO THE NEXT PAGE.

Questions 45-54. Read the following passage carefully before you choose your answers.

(The following passage is from Plessy v. Ferguson, 1896.)

It is one thing for railroad carriers to furnish, or to be required by law to furnish, equal accommodations for all whom they are under a legal duty to carry. It is quite another
Line thing for government to forbid citizens of the white and
5 black races from traveling in the same public conveyance, and to punish officers of railroad companies for permitting persons of the two races to occupy the same passenger coach. If a state can prescribe, as a rule of civil conduct, that whites and blacks shall not travel as passengers in the same
10 railroad coach, why may it not so regulate the use of the streets of its cities and towns as to compel white citizens to keep on one side of a street, and black citizens to keep on the other? Why may it not, upon like grounds, punish whites and blacks who ride together in street cars or in open vehicles
15 on a public road or street? Why may it not require sheriffs to assign whites to one side of a court room, and blacks to the other? And why may it not also prohibit the commingling of the two races in the galleries of legislative halls or in public assemblages convened for the consideration of the political
20 questions of the day? Further, if this statute of Louisiana is consistent with the personal liberty of citizens, why may not the state require the separation in railroad coaches of native and naturalized citizens of the United States, or of Protestants and Roman Catholics?
25 The white race deems itself to be the dominant race in this country. And so it is, in prestige, in achievements, in education, in wealth, and in power. So, I doubt not, it will continue to be for all time, if it remains true to its great heritage, and holds fast to the principles of constitutional
30 liberty. But in view of the constitution, in the eye of the law, there is in this country no superior, dominant, ruling class of citizens. There is no caste here. Our constitution is color-blind, and neither knows nor tolerates classes among citizens. In respect of civil rights, all citizens are
35 equal before the law. The humblest is the peer of the most powerful. The law regards man as man, and takes no account of his surroundings or of his color when his civil rights as guaranteed by the supreme law of the land are involved. It is therefore to be regretted that this high tribunal, the final
40 expositor of the fundamental law of the land, has reached the conclusion that it is competent for a state to regulate the enjoyment by citizens of their civil rights solely upon the basis of race.
In my opinion, the judgment this day rendered will, in
45 time, prove to be quite as pernicious as the decision made by this tribunal in the Dred Scott Case.
It was adjudged in that case that the descendants of Africans who were imported into this country, and sold

as slaves, were not included nor intended to be included
50 under the word "citizens" in the constitution, and could not claim any of the rights and privileges which that instrument provided for and secured to citizens of the United States; that, at the time of the adoption of the constitution, they were "considered as a subordinate and inferior class of beings,
55 who had been subjugated by the dominant race, and, whether emancipated or not, yet remained subject to their authority, and had no rights or privileges but such as those who held the power and the government might choose to grant them." The recent amendments of the constitution, it was supposed,
60 had eradicated these principles from our institutions.
I am of opinion that the state of Louisiana is inconsistent with the personal liberty of citizens, white and black, in that state, and hostile to both the spirit and letter of the constitution of the United States. If laws of like character
65 should be enacted in the several states of the Union, the effect would be in the highest degree mischievous. Slavery, as an institution tolerated by law, would, it is true, have disappeared from our country; but there would remain a power in the states, by sinister legislation, to interfere
70 with the full enjoyment of the blessings of freedom, to regulate civil rights, common to all citizens, upon the basis of race, and to place in a condition of legal inferiority a large body of American citizens, now constituting a part of the political community, called the "People of the United
75 States," for whom, and by whom through representatives, our government is administered. Such a system is inconsistent with the guaranty given by the constitution to each state of a republican form of government, and may be stricken down by congressional action, or by the courts in the discharge
80 of their solemn duty to maintain the supreme law of the land, anything in the constitution or laws of any state to the contrary notwithstanding.
For the reason stated, I am constrained to withhold my assent from the opinion and judgment of the majority.

45. The speaker in this passage is
    (A) delivering a political speech
    (B) rendering a legal judgment
    (C) reminiscing about the past
    (D) a state governor
    (E) involved with the railroad company

GO ON TO THE NEXT PAGE.

46. In the first paragraph, the series of rhetorical questions serves the speaker's strategy of reasoning by

    (A) appeals to authority
    (B) analogy
    (C) description
    (D) induction
    (E) deduction

47. In line 28, "it" refers to

    (A) "white race" (line 25)
    (B) "country" (line 26)
    (C) "prestige" (line 26)
    (D) "power" (line 27)
    (E) "time" (line 28)

48. Which of the following best describes the rhetorical function of the sentence "There is no caste here." (line 32)?

    (A) It reiterates the claim of the previous sentence with a different the syntactical structure.
    (B) It clarifies the author's attitude toward the caste system through analogy.
    (C) It specifies the author's preference for the best social system for the United States.
    (D) It refutes the claims of his opponents by using a simple syntactical structure.
    (E) It documents the claims introduced in the first paragraph by appealing to a comparison to the caste system.

49. Based on the passage, the speaker holds that

    (A) racial equality will become a reality in America
    (B) civil equality is guaranteed by the Constitution
    (C) racial equality is guaranteed by the Constitution
    (D) both civil and racial equality are guaranteed by the Constitution
    (E) neither civil nor racial equality is guaranteed by the Constitution

50. In line 45, "pernicious" most nearly means

    (A) just
    (B) unjust
    (C) useful
    (D) propitious
    (E) harmful

51. In the speaker's opinion, the Louisiana law is subject to censure by

    (A) either the United States Congress or the United States Supreme Court
    (B) Louisiana legislation only
    (C) United States legislation only
    (D) the people of Louisiana only
    (E) neither the United States Congress nor the United States Supreme Court

52. In line 66, "mischievous" is best interpreted to mean

    (A) whimsical
    (B) insubordinate
    (C) troublemaking
    (D) pernicious
    (E) disgraceful

53. The final paragraph functions as

    (A) an exception to the rule offered in the first two paragraphs
    (B) a critique of the claims of his political and ideological opponents
    (C) a definitive statement of dissent from the claims of the court
    (D) a contrast to the claims of the previous paragraph
    (E) an acknowledgement of an objection the author's central thesis

54. The style of the entire passage can be best described as

    (A) ornate and whimsical
    (B) dry and objective
    (C) abstract and legalistic
    (D) terse and opinionated
    (E) probing and subtle

END OF SECTION I

AP® English Language and Composition Exam

DO NOT OPEN THIS BOOKLET UNTIL YOU ARE TOLD TO DO SO.

At a Glance

Total Time
2 hours, plus a 15-minute reading period

Number of Questions
3

Percent of Total Grade
55%

Writing Instrument
Pen required

Instructions

Section II of this examination requires answers in essay form. To help you use your time well, the coordinator will announce the time at which each question should be completed. If you finish any question before time is announced, you may go on to the following question. If you finish the examination in less than the time allotted, you may go back and work on any essay question you want.

Each essay will be judged on its clarity and effectiveness in dealing with the requirements of the topic assigned and on the quality of the writing. After completing each question, you should check your essay for accuracy of punctuation, spelling, and diction; you are advised, however, not to attempt many longer corrections. Remember that quality is far more important than quantity.

Write your essays with a pen, preferably in black or dark blue ink. Be sure to write CLEARLY and LEGIBLY. Cross out any errors you make.

The questions for Section II are printed in the green insert. You are encouraged to use the green insert to make notes and to plan your essays, but be sure to write your answers in the pink booklet. Number each answer as the question is numbered in the examination. Do not skip lines. Begin each answer on a new page in the pink booklet.

GO ON TO THE NEXT PAGE.

ENGLISH LANGUAGE AND COMPOSITION
SECTION II
Reading Period—15 minutes
Time—2 hours

Question 1

(Suggested writing time—40 minutes. This question counts for one-third of the total essay section score.)

Directions: The following prompt is based on the accompanying six sources.

This questions requires you to synthesize a variety of source into a coherent, well-written essay. When you synthesize sources you refer to them to develop your position and cite them accurately. *Your argument should be central; the sources should support this argument. Avoid merely summarizing sources.*

Remember to attribute both direct and indirect citations.

Introduction

In democratic nations today, the ability to vote is presumed. Many consider this right a "natural right," while others consider it a privilege or even a civic duty.

Assignment

Read the following sources (including the introductory information) carefully. **Then, in an essay that synthesizes at least three of the sources for support, take a position on the most important consideration in granting suffrage to women in America.**

You may refer to the sources by their titles (Source A, Source B, etc.) or by the descriptions in parentheses.

Source A	(Anthony lecture)
Source B	(*Daily Graphic*)
Source C	(Hunt)
Source D	(66th Congress)
Source E	(*Minor v. Happersett*)
Source F	(*Woman's Sphere*)

GO ON TO THE NEXT PAGE.

Source A

Anthony, Susan B. "Is It a Crime for a Citizen of the United States to Vote?" 3 April 1873.

The following passage is the opening of a speech given by Susan B. Anthony, who in 1872 was arrested and charged with voting illegally.

Friends and Fellow-citizens: I stand before you to-night, under indictment for the alleged crime of having voted at the last Presidential election, without having a lawful right to vote. It shall be my work this evening to prove to you that in thus voting, I not only committed no crime, but, instead, simply exercised my citizen's right, guaranteed to me and all United States citizens by the National Constitution, beyond the power of any State to deny.

Our democratic-republican government is based on the idea of the natural right of every individual member thereof to a voice and a vote in making and executing the laws. We assert the province of government to be to secure the people in the enjoyment of their unalienable rights. We throw to the winds the old dogma that governments can give rights. Before governments were organized, no one denies that each individual possessed the right to protect his own life, liberty and property. And when 100 or 1,000,000 people enter into a free government, they do not barter away their natural rights; they simply pledge themselves to protect each other in the enjoyment of them, through prescribed judicial and legislative tribunals. They agree to abandon the methods of brute force in the adjustment of their differences, and adopt those of civilization.

Nor can you find a word in any of the grand documents left us by the fathers that assumes for government the power to create or to confer rights. The Declaration of Independence, the United States Constitution, the constitutions of the several states and the organic laws of the territories, all alike propose to protect the people in the exercise of their God-given rights. Not one of them pretends to bestow rights.

"All men are created equal, and endowed by their Creator with certain unalienable rights. Among these are life, liberty and the pursuit of happiness. That to secure these, governments are instituted among men, deriving their just powers from the consent of the governed."

Here is no shadow of government authority over rights, nor exclusion of any from their full and equal enjoyment. Here is pronounced the right of all men, and "consequently," as the Quaker preacher said, "of all women," to a voice in the government. And here, in this very first paragraph of the declaration, is the assertion of the natural right of all to the ballot; for, how can "the consent of the governed" be given, if the right to vote be denied. Again:

"That whenever any form of government becomes destructive of these ends, it is the right of the people to alter or abolish it, and to institute a new government, laying its foundations on such principles, and organizing its powers in such forms as to them shall seem most likely to effect their safety and happiness."

Surely, the right of the whole people to vote is here clearly implied. For however destructive in their happiness this government might become, a disfranchised class could neither alter nor abolish it, nor institute a new one, except by the old brute force method of insurrection and rebellion. One-half of the people of this nation to-day are utterly powerless to blot from the statute books an unjust law, or to write there a new and a just one.

GO ON TO THE NEXT PAGE.

Source B

Wust, Thomas. Untitled political cartoon.
The Daily Graphic. 1873.

The following is a political cartoon.

Source C

<u>United States v. Susan B. Anthony</u> (1873).

The following passage is excerpted from Judge Ward Hunt's instructions to the jury.

The right of voting, or the privilege of voting, is a right or privilege arising under the Constitution of the State, and not of the United States. The qualifications are different in the different States. Citizenship, age, sex, residence, are variously required in the different States, or may be so. If the right belongs to any particular person, it is because such person is entitled to it by the laws of the State where he offers to exercise it, and not because of citizenship of the United States. If the State of New York should provide that no person should vote until he had reached the age of 31 years, or after he had reached the age of 50, or that no person having gray hair, or who had not the use of all his limbs, should be entitled to vote, I do not see how it could be held to be a violation of any right derived or held under the Constitution of the United States. We might say that such regulations were unjust, tyrannical, unfit for the regulation of an intelligent State; but if rights of a citizen are thereby violated, they are of that fundamental class derived from his position as a citizen of the State, and not those limited rights belonging to him as a citizen of the United States. (…)

If she believed she had a right to vote, and voted in reliance upon that belief, does that relieve her from the penalty? It is argued that the knowledge referred to in the act relates to her knowledge of the illegality of the act, and not to the act of voting; for it is said that she must know that she voted. Two principles apply here: First, ignorance of the law excuses no one; second, every person is presumed to understand and to intend the necessary effects of his own acts. Miss Anthony knew that she was a woman, and that the constitution of this State prohibits her from voting. She intended to violate that provision—intended to test it, perhaps, but certainly intended to violate it. The necessary effect of her act was to violate it, and this side is presumed to have intended. There was no ignorance of any fact, but all the facts being known, she undertook to settle a principle in her own person. She takes the risk, and she cannot escape the consequences. It is said, and authorities are cited to sustain the position, that there can be no crime unless there is a culpable intent; to render one criminally responsible a vicious will must be present. A commits a trespass on the land of B, and B, thinking and believing that he has a right to shoot an intruder on his premises, kills A on the spot. Does B's misapprehension of his rights justify his act? Would a Judge be justified in charging the jury that if satisfied that B supposed he had a right to shoot A he was justified, and they should find a verdict of not guilty? No Judge would make such a charge. To constitute a crime, it is true that there must be a criminal intent, but it is equally true that knowledge of the facts of the case is always held to supply this intent. An intentional killing bears with it evidence of malice in law. Whoever, without justifiable cause, intentionally kills his neighbor is guilty of a crime. The principle is the same in the case before us, and in all criminal cases. (…)

Upon this evidence I suppose there is no question for the jury and that the jury should be directed to find a verdict of guilty.

GO ON TO THE NEXT PAGE.

Source D

Joint resolution of the 66th Congress,
May 19, 1919.

Sixty-sixth Congress of the United States of America;

At the First Session,

Begun and held at the City of Washington on Monday, the nineteenth day of May,
one thousand nine hundred and nineteen.

JOINT RESOLUTION

Proposing an amendment to the Constitution extending the right of suffrage
to women.

Resolved by the Senate and House of Representatives of the United States
of America in Congress assembled (two-thirds of each House concurring therein),
That the following article is proposed as an amendment to the Constitution,
which shall be valid to all intents and purposes as part of the Constitution when
ratified by the legislatures of three-fourths of the several States.

"ARTICLE ————.

"The right of citizens of the United States to vote shall not be denied or
abridged by the United States or by any State on account of sex.

"Congress shall have power to enforce this article by appropriate
legislation."

F. H. Gillett

Speaker of the House of Representatives.

Thos. R. Marshall

Vice President of the United States and
President of the Senate.

GO ON TO THE NEXT PAGE.

Source E

Minor v. Happersett, 88 U.S. 162 (1874)

The following passage is excerpted from the Opinion of the Court.

In October, 1874, the Supreme Court voted unanimously that the Constitution of the United States does not confer on women the right to vote in federal elections.

When the Federal Constitution was adopted, all the States, with the exception of Rhode Island and Connecticut, had constitutions of their own. These two continued to act under their charters from the Crown. Upon an examination of those constitutions we find that in no State were all citizens permitted to vote. Each State determined for itself who should have that power. Thus, in New Hampshire, "every male inhabitant of each town and parish with town privileges, and places unincorporated in the State, of twenty-one years of age and upwards, excepting paupers and persons excused from paying taxes at their own request," were its voters; in Massachusetts "every male inhabitant of twenty-one years of age and upwards, having a freehold estate within the commonwealth of the annual income of three pounds, or any estate of the value of sixty pounds"; in Rhode Island "such as are admitted free of the company and society" of the colony; in Connecticut such persons as had "maturity in years, quiet and peaceable behavior, a civil conversation, and forty shillings freehold or forty pounds personal estate," if so certified by the selectmen. (…)

Certainly, if the courts can consider any question settled, this is one. For nearly ninety years the people have acted upon the idea that the Constitution, when it conferred citizenship, did not necessarily confer the right of suffrage. If uniform practice long continued can settle the construction of so important an instrument as the Constitution of the United States confessedly is, most certainly it has been done here. Our province is to decide what the law is, not to declare what it should be.

We have given this case the careful consideration its importance demands. If the law is wrong, it ought to be changed; but the power for that is not with us. The arguments addressed to us bearing upon such a view of the subject may perhaps be sufficient to induce those having the power, to make the alteration, but they ought not to be permitted to influence our judgment in determining the present rights of the parties now litigating before us. No argument as to woman's need of suffrage can be considered. We can only act upon her rights as they exist. It is not for us to look at the hardship of withholding. Our duty is at an end if we find it is within the power of a State to withhold.

Being unanimously of the opinion that the Constitution of the United States does not confer the right of suffrage upon any one, and that the constitutions and laws of the several States which commit that important trust to men alone are not necessarily void, we affirm the judgment.

GO ON TO THE NEXT PAGE.

Source F

Nineteenth-century political cartoon.

Woman Devotes Her Time to Gossip and Clothes Because She Has Nothing Else to Talk About. Give Her
Broader Interests and She Will Cease to Be Vain and Frivolous.

GO ON TO THE NEXT PAGE.

Question 2

(Suggested time—40 minutes. This question counts for one-third of the total essay section score.)

The passages that follow were published shortly after the appearance of Mary Shelley's *Frankenstein* (1818). At that time, very few people knew the identity of the author. The first passage has been extracted from an anonymous piece from *The Quarterly Review*. The second passage is part of (Sir) Walter Scott's review of *Frankenstein* in *Blackwood's Edinburgh Magazine*.

Read the passages carefully. Then write an essay in which you compare and contrast the manner in which each critic uses language to convey a point of view.

Passage 1

On board this ship poor Frankenstein, after telling his story to Mr. Walton, who has been so kind to write it down for our use, dies of cold, fatigue, and horror; and soon after,
Line the monster, who had borrowed (we presume from the
5 flourishing colony of East Greenland) a kind of raft, comes alongside the ship, and notwithstanding his huge bulk, jumps in at Mr. Walton's cabin window, and is surprised by that gentleman pronouncing a funeral oration over the departed Frankenstein; after which, declaring that he will go back to
10 the Pole, and there burn himself on a funeral pyre (of ice, we conjecture) of his own collecting, he jumps again out the window into his raft, and is out of sight in a moment.

Our readers will guess from this summary, what a tissue of horrible and disgusting absurdity this work presents. It
15 is piously dedicated to Mr. Godwin, and is written in the spirit of his school. The dreams of insanity are embodied in the strong and striking language of the insane, and the author, notwithstanding the rationality of his preface, often leaves us in doubt whether he is not as mad as his hero. Mr.
20 Godwin is the patriarch of a literary family, whose chief skill is in delineating the wanderings of the intellect, and which strangely delights in the most affecting and humiliating of human miseries. His disciples are a kind of out pensioners of Bedlam, and like "Mad Bess" or "Mad Tom," are
25 occasionally visited with paroxysms of genius and fits of expression, which makes sober-minded people wonder and shudder.

But when we have thus admitted that *Frankenstein* has passages which appall the mind and make the flesh creep,
30 we have given it all the praise (if praise it can be called) which we dare to bestow. Our taste and our judgment alike revolt at this kind of writing, and the greater the ability with which it may be executed the worse it is—it inculcates no lesson of conduct, manners, or morality; it cannot mend,
35 and will not even amuse its readers, unless their taste have been deplorably vitiated—it fatigues the feelings without interesting the understanding; it gratuitously harasses the sensations. The author has powers, both of conception and language, which employed in a happier direction might,
40 perhaps (we speak dubiously), give him a name among these whose writings amuse or amend their fellow-creatures; but we take the liberty of assuring him, and hope that he may be in a temper to listen to us, that the style which he has

adopted in the present publication merely tends to defeat his
45 own purpose, if he really had any other object in view than that of leaving the wearied reader, after a struggle between laughter and loathing, in doubt whether the head or the heart of the author be the most diseased.

GO ON TO THE NEXT PAGE.

Passage 2

Exhausted by his sufferings, but still breathing vengeance against the being which was at once his creature and his persecutor, this unhappy victim to physiological discovery
Line expires just as the clearing away of the ice permits Captain
5 Walton's vessel to hoist sail for the return to Britain. At midnight, the daemon, who had been his destroyer, is discovered in the cabin, lamenting over the corpse of the person who gave him being. To Walton he attempts to justify his resentment towards the human race, while, at the same
10 time, he acknowledges himself a wretch who had murdered the lovely and the helpless, and pursued to irremediably ruin his creator, the select specimen of all that was worthy of love and admiration.

"Fear not," he continues, addressing the astonished
15 Walton, "that I shall be the instrument of future mischief. My work is nearly complete. Neither yours nor any man's death is needed to consummate the series of my being, and accomplish that which must be done; but it requires my own. Do not think that I shall be slow to perform this sacrifice.
20 I shall quit your vessel on the ice-raft which brought me hither, and shall seek the most northern extremity of the globe; I shall collect my funeral pile and consume to ashes this miserable frame, that its remains may afford no light to any curious and unhallowed wretch, who would create such
25 another as I have been…."

"He sprung from the cabin-window, as he said this, upon the ice-raft which lay close to the vessel. He was soon borne away by the waves, and lost in darkness and distance."

Whether this singular being executed his purpose or not
30 must necessarily remain an uncertainty, unless the voyage of discovery to the north pole should throw any light on the subject.

So concludes this extraordinary tale, in which the author seems to us to disclose uncommon powers of
35 poetic imagination. The feeling with which we perused the unexpected and fearful, yet, allowing the possibility of the event, very natural conclusion of Frankenstein's experiment, shook a little even our firm nerves; although such and so numerous have been the expedients for exciting terror
40 employed by the romantic writers of the age, that the reader may adopt Macbeth's words with a slight alteration:

"We have supp'd full with horrors
Direness, familiar to our 'callous' thoughts,
Cannot once startle us."

45 It is no slight merit in our eyes that the tale, though wild in incident, is written in plain and forcible English, without exhibiting that mixture of hyperbolical Germanisms with which tales of wonder are usually told, as if it were necessary that the language should be as extravagant as the fiction.
50 The ideas of the author are always clearly as well as forcibly expressed; and his descriptions of landscape have in them the choice requisites of truth, freshness, precision, and beauty.

GO ON TO THE NEXT PAGE.

Question 3

(Suggested time—40 minutes. This question counts for one-third of the total essay section score.)

Read carefully the passage below. Then write an essay that examines the extent to which the claim that a "neutral" stand on race perpetuates racial imbalance holds true today. Use appropriate evidence to support your argument.

> *I am saying that sometimes colorblindness is racism. I know that sounds counterintuitive, but let me go on.*
>
> *Think of society as comprised of lots of different groups of people, identified by their race, gender, etc. Neutrality in our society is supposed to be the great equalizer because we believe that, if we don't favor any one group, things will work themselves out and become more equal. But the thing is this: neutrality has this effect only if there is no previous social or historical context. But that's not how the real world is. There is, in fact, a social and historical context for every situation. So if I were being "neutral" and viewing everyone as being the same, ignoring personal contexts, I wouldn't be promoting equality because I would be ignoring the differences that exist and allowing the inequalities to continue to exist, given that I wouldn't do anything to help change them. Identifying problems and actively promoting solutions are necessary to effect useful change; being neutral is consenting to the status quo.*

STOP

END OF EXAM

Practice Test 1:
Answers and Explanations

ANSWER KEY

1. B	28. C
2. D	29. A
3. B	30. C
4. C	31. E
5. C	32. E
6. A	33. A
7. D	34. C
8. A	35. A
9. A	36. C
10. D	37. D
11. B	38. E
12. C	39. C
13. E	40. C
14. C	41. A
15. A	42. E
16. D	43. B
17. B	44. E
18. E	45. B
19. C	46. B
20. D	47. A
21. C	48. A
22. B	49. B
23. B	50. E
24. A	51. A
25. E	52. D
26. E	53. C
27. A	54. D

Once you have checked your answers, remember to return to page 3 and respond to the Reflect questions.

EXPLANATIONS FOR THE MULTIPLE-CHOICE QUESTIONS

1. **B**   This first passage, taken from Jonathan Swift's "A Modest Proposal" is a relatively easy one. If you take the author's proposal seriously, then four of the answers [(A), (C), (D), and (E)] are plausible; of course, the key is to understand that the author is not making a serious proposal, but, rather, he is satirizing other so-called scientific studies that, under the guise of humanitarianism, tend to offer cruel (if not sadistic) "solutions" to poverty. Therefore, (B) is the only acceptable answer.

2. **D**   Even if you are not familiar with the term "arguments from authority," you can easily guess the meaning. The authorities cited are "a principal gentleman in the county of Cavan" (paragraph 1), "our merchants" (paragraph 2), and "a very knowing American of my acquaintance in London" (paragraph 4). These are, of course, dubious authorities, indeed, which is one of the sources of humor in the passage.

    The easiest and fastest way to use POE in this case is to examine the shortest of the paragraphs, the fourth. Clearly, there are no similes (A) or extended metaphors (C) in the fourth paragraph, so there is no need to check the first or second paragraphs for these rhetorical devices. The other two answers are more esoteric, but logic leads you to eliminate them, even if you do not fully understand them as rhetorical terms. There is nothing approximating an appeal in paragraph four, so you can eliminate that answer easily; there is also no attempt to argue a point (B).

3. **B**   The "merchants" and the "American" both seem to believe the prospect of selling and eating children is feasible. The entire piece is a satire, though, so (A) and (B) are far too literal. The merchant is not necessarily an aristocrat, so rule out (C). We have no evidence to suggest that their sentiments are typical of all Londoners, so rule out (E). Since the author is satirizing, the merchants and American are no doubt fictional, so (B) is the best choice.

4. **C**   The irony comes from the clever juxtaposition of the phrase "nutriment and rags" with the sum of money, twelve pounds (four times three pounds). Twelve pounds is a paltry sum and indicative of the abject poverty of the children and their families, so (C) most accurately captures the irony of the statement. We have no idea what the price of food was at that time (A), nor what the children are wearing (E). Approximation is not ironic (B), and most likely the parents are NOT being aided by the kingdom (D), thus their poverty.

5. **C**   You may or may not be familiar with this word, but when you read it in context, the answer to this question becomes apparent—the entire paragraph is about food, and certainly you understand the other terms (*stewed, roasted, baked, boiled*). Reading the term in context allows you to eliminate the other choices: "animal," "child," "place," and "master."

6. **A**   The best approach to this question is to use POE. You can eliminate answers (B) and (C) right away. If you remember that "deductive reasoning" means starting with a generality and working logically to a specific conclusion, you can see that answer (D) is way off base too. Answer (E) may be tempting because of the existence of the phrase "which is more than we allow to sheep, black cattle, or swine" in the paragraph, but this paragraph is not dominated by analogy. Although this comparison is extended, it is not really a pattern. "Process analysis" (A) is the best answer; in this paragraph, the author analyzes a problem and proposes a process that will bring about a solution. The proposal describes the process for breeding, fattening, and preparing this very unusual source of protein.

7. **D** This question is related to the previous one. The proposal is to fatten the children for slaughter, just as if they were livestock (sheep, cattle, or pigs).

8. **A** By using POE, you should be able to narrow your choices down to (A) and (C) very quickly. The author says that the new meat will be expensive, and only the rich landlords will be able to afford it.

9. **A** By this point, you must have digested (forgive the pun) the satire, so you understand that the landlords have "devoured" the parents by charging unreasonably high rents and that, according to the author, they may as well literally devour (eat) their poor tenants' children. It is understandable that answer (E) may tempt you, but the diction in this sentence is hardly a revelation. We have understood the point of view all along; behind the comical satire is the rage of a man disgusted by the exploitation of the poor by the rich.

10. **D** The reference to farm animals serves to show that the poor and their children are being treated like chattel, similar to the way animals are treated by their owners. Choice (D) captures the point of this analogy. Breeding is not the point, so eliminate (B) and (C). Marriage is not the point, either, so eliminate (E). Humane treatment is not mentioned, so rule out (A).

11. **B** To answer this question, you need to think in terms of main idea. This is a fairly straightforward question that asks you to consider the type of material you are reading and what the author is saying within that context. In this piece of literary criticism, the author is making a connection between what Gulliver experienced and what an eighteenth-century Londoner might have seen exhibited in fairs and inns.

12. **C** The author does describe Swift's achievement in *Gulliver's Travels* in generally positive terms, thus choice (C) is correct. If the author were "cleverly subversive" (A), he would have attempted to undercut his generally positive portrayal of Swift in some way, but he never does. Authors on the AP exam are rarely only "halfheartedly engaged," so answer (D) can also be eliminated. Both (B) and (E) are both wrong and cannot be substantiated in the passage.

13. **E** This is a challenging question because the author provides no explicit definition for the "Scriblerians" in the passage. We do know that they were "fascinated with popular entertainments" (line 16) and that they "satirized them in many of their works" (lines 17-18), which means they are authors, not book craftsmen (A) or literary characters (B). We have no evidence that they worked as either historians or politicians, so we can also eliminate answer (C) and answer (D).

14. **C** In lines 18-19, we learn that Swift "shared this fascination with his fellow Scriblerians," which makes him a member of the circle. Thus answer (C) is correct. While he does have a distinct interest in public entertainments, he is not necessarily a "producer" of one himself, so answer (B) can be eliminated. There is simply no evidence in the passage for any of the other answer choices.

15. **A** The first two paragraphs maintain a consistent tense and person, so answer (B) can be eliminated. The author does not invest time in drawing historical allusions (C) or extended metaphors (D), so both of those choices can also be eliminated. He does make some claims that could be considered "asides," but they are hardly for "didactic" (i.e., educational) purposes and they are not the "most evident" stylistic feature, so we can eliminate (E) as well. The correct answer is (A) because the author does use a parallel, consistent syntactical structure throughout these paragraphs.

16. **D** The author wants us to see the connection between miniature people and landscapes in *Gulliver's Travels* and the common public entertainments of Swift's London. Thus, he is emphasizing their "commonness" (D) over other features. This directly contradicts "obscurity" in answer (B), which can be eliminated. He is also not emphasizing merely the fact they are small, so we can eliminate answer (A) as well. "Transcience" (E), which emphasizes their fleeting nature, is not discussed in the final paragraph; neither is "magnificence" (C), so both answers can be ruled out.

17. **B** The series of quotes in the final paragraph substantiate the author's claim that *Gulliver's Travels* was at least somewhat based on the kinds of popular entertainments that people often saw in London. Thus answer (B) is the correct answer. The author does not really aim his argument at other scholars or at claims that "*Gulliver's Travels* was purely imaginative," so we can eliminate answers (A) and (C). While he certainly does include information from other sources, his primary purpose is not to "inform readers of the sources," so we can eliminate answer (E).

18. **E** The first section of the essay introduces readers to the connection between *Gulliver's Travels* and popular entertainments, while the second section provides evidence to support that claim. Thus, answer (E) is correct. There really are no "series of questions" (A), "positions of scholars" (C), or "technical definition" (D), so these choices can be eliminated. It is not accurate at all the second choice "challenges" claims made in the first, so (B) is wrong as well.

19. **C** Footnote questions were added to the test in response to concerns raised by colleges and universities. In these days of easy access to information via the Internet, colleges are becoming increasingly concerned that students do not take seriously the intellectual property of authors and end up plagiarizing, wittingly or not. Footnotes give information about authorship and publication place and date and can also provide hints as to the purpose of a piece of writing or its context. This particular footnote simply indicates that the quote about Lilliput does, indeed, come from *Gulliver's Travels*, part of a 14-volume set of works by Swift.

20. **D** This quote from *Social Life in the Reign of Queen Anne* helps to set an elaborate scene, and the footnote helps to lend credibility to Todd's purpose in describing the imaginative miniature worlds of Swift's day.

21. **C** By paying attention to the title, the author, the subject matter, and the footnotes you should be able to use POE to weed out (B) and (C), and while the subject matter of this essay might be of interest to an anthropologist (A), the content and format is consistent with literary criticism.

22. **B** The tone of this passage is somewhat hard to detect because the author is so scholarly and generally positive, which is harder to detect than more overtly negative tones. Thus (B) is correct. He does support his claims, but not frantically, so answer (A) is incorrect. He is not "dejected" (i.e, sad), so answer (C) cannot be correct either. "Intransigent" basically means stubborn, so we can eliminate answer (E). And while this passage certainly is "erudite" (i.e., learned), he does not show any signs of cynicism, so answer (D) is incorrect.

23. **B** Again, POE is the best way to approach this question. Answers (A), (C), (D), and (E) are at least half wrong (therefore completely wrong). Take a look at (B). The author is being ironic when she says in the first line, "My own sex, I hope, will excuse me, if I treat them like rational creatures…." The second part of choice (B), "exposition," is defined as "a setting forth of meaning or intent," and that is exactly what the author is doing in this first paragraph. Answer choice (B) is correct. For the record, note that, in this context, the author's "apology" has nothing to do with being sorry; it most nearly means "defense of an idea."

24. **A** The author addresses women directly and pretends to excuse herself for addressing them as strong, confident people, instead of the weak, overly sentimental creatures that society wants (and expects) them to be.

25. **E** Your choice should boil down to (D) and (E). When the author says, "I wish to persuade women to endeavour to acquire strength, both of mind and body," she means intellectual and physical strength. Had she wanted to stress emotional strength, she would have replaced mind with heart.

26. **E** *Soften* and *weak* are important adjectives of both paragraphs; the author uses them in the second paragraph to tie this paragraph in with the first one.

27. **A** No doubt you can narrow your choices to (A) and (B). The best way to approach this type of question is to substitute in the answer choices for the original word and see which one makes the most sense. Try (A): "…supposed to be the sexual characteristics of the weaker <u>sex</u>.…" This seems great, but try (B) too, just in case: "…supposed to be the sexual characteristics of the weaker <u>woman</u>." Not as good. Naturally, in this case, the weaker sex is woman, but you are asked to find the meaning for "vessel" only. Choice (A) is the best answer.

28. **C** Again, there are only two reasonable answers: (A) and (C). The author states that "the first object of laudable ambition is to obtain a character as a human being, regardless of the distinction of sex." Thus, one must eliminate answer (A) because she is not suggesting that a comparison be made between a man and woman.

29. **A** The author wishes to convince the reader by the force of her cogent arguments and the sincerity of her emotions, so the answer is (A). If you don't have "cogent" on your vocabulary list, put it on now. It means "appealing to the intellect or powers of reasoning; convincing." You can eliminate the other choices: The author states unequivocally that she does not wish to polish her style, to employ the bombast and periodic sentences of a rhetorical style, to write elegantly, or to use flowery diction.

30. **C** The author points out—and rightfully so—that the flowery diction expected of women relegated them to a world outside of that of men. The difference in the social level of men and women was reflected in the way they used language. Only men could use the crude words that attempt to express the crude realities of life. Women were not supposed to know those same crude realities and, therefore, could not use the crude words that fit with those realities.

31. **E** The sugary diction becomes associated with the taste of a cloyingly sweet delicacy; this is an extended metaphor so POE allows you to eliminate (A), (B), and (D). This is not a caricature of women, nor is it a critique of bombast (remember, pompous speech or writing). If you do not know the meaning of "panegyric," then add it to your list of vocabulary. Panegyric means "statement of high praise." It should be clear that the author does not sing the praises of sugary writing.

32. **E** Since, in this passage, the author suggests that women have the capacity to be independent equals of men, she is most likely to agree that if women are educated in the same manner as men, then they would be more likely to be equals with men in the eyes of the world.

33. **A**   Use POE, especially if you don't know what choice (A) means. (Sardonic means "harsh, bitter, or caustic.") Lyrical is far too positive, so rule out (B). Frivolous (D) is a trap, since the women are perceived as frivolous, but that is not the author's tone. The author is quite passionate and not at all reserved, so rule out (E). Condescending (C) is a good trap, since lines 55-59 seem to convey this mood, but directly contradicts the message of line 2 ("rational creatures") and the title of the passage (see the blurb). The last line of the passage betrays Wollstonecraft's true purpose: to point out the illogic of assuming that women are helpless, useless creatures unfit for positions of responsibility.

34. **C**   What is the entire passage about? It is about learning and, most importantly, the reason for learning. This is simply a big-picture question in disguise. In this passage, the writer claims that teaching methodologies are overrated because there are many ways to teach and learn; what is important is having a reason for learning.

35. **A**   The phrase "So it is with learning," which follows the example of the ways to learn tribal lays, is a big clue that should tell you that an analogy is being used here. Besides, none of the other answers is plausible; POE can lead you with certainty to the correct answer.

36. **C**   Don't be thrown off by the use of the term "infinitives" in this question. Infinitives are simply verb forms that function as substantives, while retaining some verb characteristics. Some examples of infinitives are "We want him to win the lottery," or "To go willingly will prove that you are innocent." So this question specifically refers to the line "There is no one who can say that this or that is the best way to know things, to feel things, to see things, to remember things, to apply things, to connect things and that no other will do as well." From the context—and from your own experience, one hopes—learning is a positive experience, so any answer choice that uses a negative adjective should be eliminated. Learning is (not supposed to be) "tedious" (A), "impersonal" (B), "trivial" (D), or even "mechanical" (E); using POE leaves us with only (C). In fact, learning is an active and a varied process.

37. **D**   If you understand the passage, you should be able to quickly narrow your choices to (C) and (D); motivation, in the author's words, is fleeting (or momentary). Although the author does not say outright that a motivation is concrete, he does set up a clear rhetorical contrast between motivation and reason. Given that he describes reason as abstract, it figures that motivation should be roughly the opposite—or at least not the same. The only textual clue that tells us motivation is concrete is the word *event*.

38. **E**   We have already drawn attention to the string of infinitives in the first paragraph; in the third paragraph, you may have already noticed the parallel series of prepositional phrases (in which the preposition "to" is repeated). Choice (E), or "notable parallelism," is correct.

Let's go through the other choices. An "aphorism" is a pithy saying or proverb. "Syllogistic reasoning" proceeds along the lines of a syllogism: a major premise, a minor premise, and a conclusion. Here is an example of syllogistic reasoning: All Princeton Review books are useful; this is a Princeton Review book; therefore, this book is useful. *Ad hominem* arguments consist of attacks against a person's character. If you were to say, "This book must be awful because you wrote it," you would be adducing an *ad hominem* argument to prove your point.

39. **C**   Answers (A) and (B) are snares for the careless reader who fails to consider the context in which the word is used; "god" in this case has nothing to do with religion. The entire second half of the text is about the reason for education. One big clue that the author isn't using the word "god" literally, is the phrase "…must have a god to serve, or, even better, several gods." If this were a literal use of "god," then the term would not have been pluralized later.

40. **C**   In this case, the authority is Nietzsche, and the author gives us a clear rhetorical statement of his use of analogy in the sentence that follows the quote: "This applies as much to learning as to living."

41. **A**   Perhaps this is a good time to review two terms that are closely related: *oxymoron* and *paradox*. An oxymoron is an apparent contradiction of terms; a paradox is an apparent contradiction of ideas. The important word here is *apparent*.

    In this case, the last sentence is built on an apparent contradiction of terms: Schooling will be brought to an end if it has no end. Nonsense? No. We are supposed to understand that, in context, the second "end" is synonymous with reason (or goal or objective).

42. **E**   In this passage, Postman insists that education must serve a higher purpose or else it has no meaning for students, thus the contrast is between motivation—which Postman defines as temporary and superficial—and purpose—which gives meaning to everything a student can do in a classroom. Therefore, answer (E) is correct. He alludes to religion, but it hardly the "principal contrast," so answer (D) can be eliminated. Answers (A), (B), and (C) are all appealing because they refer to education in one way or another, but are wrong because they do not represent the central distinction in the passage.

43. **B**   As we saw in the question above, Postman is arguing that students need more than temporary motivation to succeed in education, so answer (B) is correct. Postman does not really examine the "historical development of educational institutions," so answer (A) is incorrect. And while the circumstances are "challenges" (C) and he does lament a "lack" (D) of something in education, neither answer (C) nor answer (D) is correct in its full form, so we can eliminate those choices as well.

44. **E**   Overall, this is a reasoned (and reasonable) argument rather than a "dramatic" (D) or "impassioned" (B) work, so we can eliminate choices (D) and (B), then select choice (E) as the correct answer. There is neither evidence of a "narrative" (C), in the sense of a story, nor of objectivity (A), so these choices can be ruled out as well.

45. **B**   If you missed the implications of the final statement, then you could eliminate (C) and (E) and guess. Choices (A) and (D) are similar in meaning, and both imply that the speaker is a politician—of which we have no proof. Choice (B) is your best bet. Of course, if you noticed the allusions to law in the body of the text and the judgment of the final statement, then you may have realized that the passage is the dissenting opinion of a judge in a federal case—and you would have been correct to assume that this was a case that went before the Supreme Court.

46. **B**   Perhaps the biggest clue that tells us analogy is being employed is the phrase "upon like grounds." Naturally, almost everyone would agree that it would be unthinkable, for example, to segregate passengers by religion (Catholic and Protestant). If we agree that this (and the other examples) are analogous to the case before the court (segregation of passengers by race), then we are forced to agree with this judge.

47. **A**   The "it" in this instance refers to the "white race" mentioned much earlier in line 25, thus choice (A) is the correct answer. If you think about the verb "remains" that follows immediately after "it" in line 28, follow the story back to its source. "It" is remaining "true to its great heritage." Whose great heritage? Keep working backward through the passage until you find out he is speaking about the "white race" in line 25 and its future.

48.   **A**   The brief sentence "There is no caste here" has the effect of changing the syntactical style of the sentence to restate the point made in earlier sentences. Thus, answer (A) is true. He is not primarily concerned with the caste system as such, so answers (B) and (E) are both incorrect. He does use "a simple syntactical structure," so answer (D) is appealing, but not correct because his primary purpose in this sentence is not to refute "the claims of his opponents" *per se.*

49.   **B**   Were you tempted to choose (C)? Did you choose (C)? If so, you fell into a trap. Today, it would be normal to expect this judge to propose both civil and racial equality, but the judge bases his arguments solely on the issue of civil rights. In fact, the judge says that the white race is the dominant one "in prestige, in achievements, in education, in wealth, and in power. So, I doubt not, it will continue to be for all time, if it remains true to its great heritage, and holds fast to the principles of constitutional liberty." Based on the passage, the speaker appears to believe that racial equality will never be a reality, although civil equality exists.

50.   **E**   If you do not know the meaning of the word, begin with POE. Immediately, you will see that (A) and (C) can be eliminated; they mean things that are opposite to the speaker's tone and meaning. If you know that "propitious" is roughly equivalent to (C), "useful," you can eliminate that choice as well. As for choice (B), although "unjust," like "harmful," fits the context, the latter choice is the better synonym for the original term ("pernicious"). Of course, as long as you can narrow the choices down to two or three, you should take a guess even if you are not sure. The definition of pernicious is: "causing great harm."

51.   **A**   In this passage, the phrases "may be stricken down by congressional action, or by the courts" and "duty to maintain the supreme law of the land" provide the answer; the Louisiana law is subject to censure by either the United States Congress or the United States Supreme Court.

52.   **D**   We often associate the word "mischievous" with playful mischief, which is why the test writers included choices like answer (A) and answer (C). But in this context, the meaning of "mischievous" is closer to harmful and thus answer (D) is correct. Always be sure to go back to read the word in its context so that you are not distracted by the most common meanings of the word or by the wrong answer choices.

53.   **C**   The final paragraph of this decision outlines why the author will dissent from the majority opinion of the court. This makes answer (C) the correct choice. The author is not describing objections to his argument or contrasts to earlier claims, thus answers (A), (D), and (E) can both be eliminated. The author is not primarily interested in his opponents in this paragraph, so answer (B), while appealing in some respects, is also incorrect.

54.   **D**   POE is the way to go on this one. Remember to look for one inappropriate word in each answer. Neither adjective in answer (A) is really appropriate, so you can eliminate (A). Try (B). Although one may argue that the style is "dry," it is not "objective"—the speaker is arguing only one side of an issue; so (B) is out. How about (C)? Of course, the passage could be thought of as "legalistic," but it is not at all "abstract"—so get rid of (C). As for (E), the passage is "probing," but it is certainly not "subtle." The speaker comes right out and says what he believes, calling this decision as pernicious as the Supreme Court's judgment of the Dred Scott Case. (In the Dred Scott case, the Supreme Court upheld a lower court ruling that the state of Louisiana could fine the railroad company for letting African Americans ride in the same carriages as whites, a situation that was prohibited by Louisiana state law.)

EXPLANATIONS FOR THE FREE-RESPONSE QUESTIONS

Question 1

Synthesis Essay

Although it is not perfect, this essay below merits an 8. Its use of language is skilled and it is reasonably well constructed. However, several of its assertions stray from the sources, particularly in the end of the second body paragraph and in the final paragraph. As often happens, this goes hand-in-hand with reliance on repetition rather than evidence to make a point; the author repeats several times that full citizenship requires voting rights, without leaning on anything more than the Anthony argument for support.

Embracing responsibility is an essential step on the path toward maturity. No group of people can become full, contributing members of their community if they are systematically denied the chance to be responsible for matters affecting that community. Equal responsibilities and equal citizenship do not necessarily imply identical roles. In theory, that responsibility need not include voting for everyone, and well-intentioned arguments have been made in this direction. But in practice, no other responsibility is equal to or could substitute for this one; someone denied the responsibility of voting cannot be considered an equal citizen. Thus, women's suffrage is a right that springs directly from equal citizenship; it is not a gift of the legislature.

Susan B. Anthony made precisely this argument in her 1872 defense against the charges of unlawful voting. She grounded her defense in the Constitution's acknowledgment of "the natural right of every individual member" of the country "to a voice and a vote." Per Anthony, the Constitution acknowledges rights; it does not claim "the power to create or to confer" them. This is ultimately the meaning of the Constitutional amendment granting women the right to vote, which says that "the right of citizens…to vote shall not be denied or abridged…on account of sex." This amendment follows the form of the rest of the Bill of Rights: it does not lay out a right explicitly, but rather states that the right exists, and that neither Congress nor the states could restrict it.

As Susan B. Anthony and the 66th Congress both saw, it is essential that all people be given the right to vote so that they may be full, responsible citizens. This point had earlier been made in the cartoon printed as Source F, which illustrates the way a lack of civic participation confines women to trivial matters. People do not tend to engage thoughtfully in issues in which they are legally forbidden from having any influence. It is only by acknowledging women's voting rights that the government acknowledges their complete citizenship, for without the responsibility of voting, women would not be involved in the political process, as required of all full citizens.

Arguments to the contrary, such as Source B (a cartoon showing men confined to gossip and child-rearing, and women in positions of authority and political power), miss the point. No one claims that all citizens are the same, or that granting the vote will turn women into men (or vice versa, probably more terrifying for the male population of the time). Roles within a society can be "separate but equal." But in terms of being responsible citizens of a state or of this country, the right to vote is sacrosanct.

Question 2

Rhetorical Analysis Essay

The following sample essay is a strong one; the writer could expect to receive a score of 8 with this work. One important thing to note about this essay is the structure. The writer avoids the common error made in comparison and contrast essays; he or she does NOT write first about one review in one paragraph and another in a second paragraph. That said, inside each paragraph, the discussion of the articles is clearly segregated; this could have been handled more deftly, but this organization gets the job done. The introduction is a bit on the long side, but it provides a clear outline of the material and engages the reader thoroughly.

Mary Shelley's Frankenstein is, in modern times, heralded as a classic, great work of art. However, when it was first published in 1818, few people regarded it as a worthy work of literary art. As seen in the two passages taken from the critics' reviews of the novel, Frankenstein inspired extreme sentiments and reactions—readers either loved and enjoyed it or abhorred it and were disgusted by it. The two reviews presented convey the two contrasting emotions, as if in response to each other. The first, an anonymous piece from The Quarterly Review, criticizes Mary Shelley's work, using vernacular and plain (yet grotesque) language and popular culture allusions and standards to illustrate the author's condemnation of Frankenstein. Conversely, Sir Walter Scott's review from Blackwood's Edinburgh Magazine is itself written in a worthy literary manner, using heightened terms, literary terms, and quotations from other works to demonstrate his positive point of view. In the 1800s, there were many magazines available for the literate to purchase and indulge in, some were professional journals intended for those who worked in a particular industry (like science or literature), while others were broader publications for the general public. The difference between the two kinds was always (and still is) readily apparent in the type of language used by the authors of the magazine's articles. It can be surmised that Blackwood's Edinburgh Magazine was intended for those immersed in literature, or at least those who were highly educated. Scott's writing is romantic, mentioning "daemons," "the lovely and helpless" and "creature" and "persecutor." All these words and phrases are characteristic of a gothic or a romantic novel, in which the reader is presented with a tortured hero who is persecuted in some form and is faced with something lovely (usually a female). Phrases such as "resentment toward the human race," "expedients for exciting terror," and "uncommon powers of poetic imagination" are meant for a reader with a heightened vocabulary; one capable of understanding Scott's references and intentions. However, juxtaposed with Sir Walter Scott's review, the anonymous review from The Quarterly Review (a seemingly plain publication) is straightforward and simple. Instead of embellishing or elaborating, the author uses language like "strong and striking language," "tissue of horrible and disgusting absurdity," and "fatigues the feelings" to criticize the novel. Overall, the article has a condescending tone; in summarizing the conclusion of the novel, the author adds in his own commentary, sarcastically remarking on the implausibility of the entire situation. All his opinions are presented in a clear, plain manner, which serves to make very clear his utter loathing of Mary Shelley's work.

Both Scott and the anonymous author make use of popular conventions, standards, and allusions of their time period. However, their references again establish a distinct difference between the two articles. Scott, in his piece, quotes Macbeth, by William Shakespeare, to illustrate his point that Frankenstein, while shocking, cannot shock an already jaded audience. Furthermore, he speaks of terror being "employed by the romantic writers of the age" mentioning literary conventions. Another convention is brought up when he states that Shelley does not utilize "hyperbolic Germanisms" with which tales of wonder are usually told. The anonymous author, on the other hand, never quotes another literary work to support his ideas. He alludes to Bedlam, "Mad Bess," and "Mad Tom" as popular cultural figures. Continuing with his appeal to the masses, the anonymous author points out that <u>Frankenstein</u> "inculcates no lessons of conduct, manners or morality." Unlikely popular literature of the time, Shelley's novel disregards the conventions of morals and lessons learned.

Though the two reviews were written in highly different forms of language, both convey their point of view clearly. Scott's review was a positive one, meant for an elite readership. The anonymous author, however, wrote a disgusted condemnation for the pious masses.

Question 3

Argumentative Essay

The following sample essay is very strong. The one noticeable flaw is the discussion of Switzerland; this detour pertains to neutrality, but it is not clear how it relates to racism. It is difficult to gauge just how deleterious the flaw may be. Certainly, the essay would earn a score of at least 7 and may get an 8.

Often, it is believed that if one ignores an issue or a problem, it will merely disappear. Mothers tell their children to ignore bullies, and even the Bible instructs us to turn the other cheek. However, when certain issues are not dealt with, they can fester until they become something far more serious than they were originally; racism is one such issue. As the passage suggests, colorblindness and neutrality are not equalizers; they are merely blinders that allow people to continue as though nothing is out of balance. By adopting a "neutral stand" and by failing to recognize the innate differences between racial groups, one not only perpetuates racism, but also promotes the homogenization of cultures and races, in itself a form of racism.

Sooner or later, the issues one faces must be dealt with. Ignorance, in this case, is not bliss; the longer a problem is put aside, the harder it is to conquer when one finally decides to face it. In the United States, the quintessential example of such a problem is racism. The 1950s and 1960s were a demonstration of just what can happen when an entire nation pretends that nothing is wrong or unequal. Race riots all over the country were the culmination of a race's mounting frustrations. The passage states that "identifying problems and actively promoting solutions are necessary to effect useful change." In fact change, in the form of various civil rights legislatures, only took place when racism was recognized and dealt with by the federal government. Only strong action, like the integration of the Central High School in Little Rock, Arkansas, could ever hope to remedy the situation. By bringing the problem into the spotlight and making everyone consider it and its implications, the government steps toward change, progress, and equality.

The only successful neutral stance ever taken in history was by Switzerland, during all the wars that raged around the country's borders. However, a neutral stance requires more effort to maintain than a stance that is evidently one-sided, because neutrality involves denying the "social and historical context for every situation...[and]...ignoring personal contexts." When this occurs, it would seem that one is assenting that we are all the same equal people, yet that very assertion is flawed, since it eliminates the "differences that exist." If one does not take a side or a stance, one is, in effect, resigning oneself to the current state of affairs, the status quo. As the author of the passage points out, ignoring inequalities and differences allows "the inequalities to continue to exist, given that [one] wouldn't do anything to help change them." Until the public began noticing and sympathizing with the victims of racism, it took no collective action to change the status quo. Finally recognizing the inequality which was the status quo, the public could no longer remain neutral—it split into those who wanted to maintain the status quo and those who wanted to change it and improve the situation.

In essence, neutrality is supposed to be an equalizer because it declares that there are no differences between human beings. However, that denial takes away that which makes us inherently human. Without our cultures and races, we would have nothing to separate one person from another. Thus neutrality states that it is better for a group of people to lack differences than to embrace those differences. Racism is looking down on and rejecting the differences between two people. In much the same way, neutrality turns a blind eye to differences, lending validity to ignorance. Without action and discussion, societies become stale. It is only with a firm stance that one can hope to incite progress and reform; there must be recognition and a definite lack of neutrality if racism is to be prevented. "Being neutral is consenting to the status quo," a status quo which is unequal, unfair, and socially unbalanced.

HOW TO SCORE PRACTICE TEST 1

Section I: Multiple-Choice

_____ × 1.2500 = _____
Number of Correct   Weighted
(out of 54)   Section I Score
                          (Do not round)

Section II: Free Response

(See if you can find a teacher or classmate to score your essays using the guidelines in Chapter 4.)

Question 1   _____ × 3.0556 = _____
             (out of 9)   (Do not round)

Question 2   _____ × 3.0556 = _____
             (out of 9)   (Do not round)

Question 3   _____ × 3.0556 = _____
             (out of 9)   (Do not round)

Sum = _____
Weighted Section II
Score (Do not round)

AP Score Conversion Chart English Language and Composition	
Composite Score Range	AP Score
112-150	5
98-111	4
80-97	3
55-79	2
0-54	1

Composite Score

_____ + _____ = _____
Weighted   Weighted   Composite Score
Section I Score Section II Score (Round to nearest
                                  whole number)

Part III
About the
AP English
Language and
Composition
Exam

- The Structure of the AP English Language and Composition Exam
- How the AP English Language and Composition Exam is Scored
- Overview of Review Topics
- How Colleges Use AP Scores
- Other Resources
- Designing Your Study Plan

THE STRUCTURE OF THE AP ENGLISH LANGUAGE AND COMPOSITION EXAM

Below is a helpful outline that describes the basic format for the exam. The total time allotted for the completion of this exam is 3 hours and 15 minutes, or 195 minutes.

Section I: Multiple Choice (60 minutes)—counts for 45 percent of your grade

Total number of questions: 55

Section II: Free Response (135 minutes)—counts for 55 percent of your grade

Composed of three essays, which the College Board describes in the following way:

1. Fifteen-minute reading period
2. Synthesis essay (40-minute essay that integrates information from a variety of sources that ETS provides)
3. Rhetorical analysis essay (40-minute essay on a passage that ETS provides)
4. Argumentative essay (40-minute essay that supports, refutes, or qualifies a statement provided by ETS)

HOW THE AP ENGLISH LANGUAGE AND COMPOSITION EXAM IS SCORED

Your Multiple-Choice Score

In the multiple-choice section of the test, you are awarded one point for each question that you answer correctly, and you receive no points for each question that you leave blank or answer incorrectly. That is, the famous "guessing penalty" on the SAT and SAT Subject Tests does not apply to this test. So, even if you are completely unsure, guess. In Part III, we'll show you how to narrow down your choices and make educated guesses.

Your Free-Response Score

Each AP essay is scored on a scale from 0 to 9, with 9 being the best score. Essay readers (who are high school or university English instructors) will grade your three essays, and the scores for your three essays will be added together. The resulting total (which ranges from 0 to 27) constitutes your free-response score.

We will go into the details of essay scoring in Part III, but in general an essay that receives a "9" answers all facets of the question completely, making good use of specific examples to support its points, and is "well-written," which is a catch-all phrase that means its sentences are complete, properly punctuated, clear in meaning, and varied (that is, they exhibit a variety of structure and use a large academic vocabulary). Lower-scoring essays are considered to be deficient in these qualities to a greater or lesser degree, and students who receive a "0" have basically written gibberish. If you write an essay that is not on the topic, you will receive a blank ("—"). This is equivalent to a zero.

The essay readers do not award points according to a standardized, predetermined checklist. The essays are scored individually by individual readers, each of whom scores essays for only one prompt. Thus, you will have three different readers, and each reader will be able to see only the single essay that he or she reads. The readers do not know how you did on the other essays or what score you received on the multiple-choice section.

Your Final Score

Your final score of 1 to 5 is a combination of your scores from the two sections. Remember that the multiple-choice section counts for 45 percent of the total and the essay section counts for 55 percent. This makes them almost equal, and you must concentrate on doing your best on both parts. If you can get a score of 36 (number correct) on a multiple-choice section with 54 questions, you have exactly a 99 percent chance of getting at least a score of 3 on the exam.

You will have the opportunity to calculate your final score for each Practice Test in this book. Both Answers and Explanations chapters include a worksheet to guide you through ETS's formula step by step.

What Your Final Score Will Mean

After taking the test in early May, you will receive your scores sometime around the first week of July, which is probably when you'll have just started to forget about the entire harrowing experience. Your score will be, simply enough, a single number that will either be a 1, 2, 3, 4, or 5. Here is what those numbers mean.

Score Meaning	Approximate percentage of all test takers receiving this score	Roughly equivalent first-year college course grade	Will a student with this score receive credit?
5—Extremely qualified	9.5%	A	Usually
4—Well qualified	18%	A–, B+, B	Usually
3—Qualified	28.5%	B–, C+, C	Maybe
2—Possibly qualified	30%	N/A	Very Rarely
1—Not qualified	14%	N/A	No

OVERVIEW OF REVIEW TOPICS

The AP English Language and Composition Exam tests your abilities to understand how authors use rhetoric and language to convey their purpose. Students are also expected to apply these techniques to their own writing and research projects. Some of the major skills tested include the ability to

- identify an author's purpose and intended audience

- recognize rhetorical devices and strategies in an author's work

- demonstrate understanding of citations in research papers

- apply these skills and techniques to their own writing

- create and organize an argument defended with evidence and reasoning

- plan, write, and revise cogent, well-written essays

More Great Books
Check out The Princeton Review's college guide books, including *The Best 380 Colleges, The Complete Book of Colleges, Paying for College Without Going Broke*, and many more!

HOW COLLEGES USE AP SCORES

Colleges make their own decisions about the minimum AP score required to earn credit (points that count toward your college degree), the amount of credit hours awarded and whether advanced placement (the opportunity to skip introductory courses and enter higher-level courses) is offered.

Policies differ widely. Some colleges require a score of 3, while others require a 4, for instance. Some offer both credit and placement; some offer only credit, and some only placement.

The AP exam administrators have created a helpful tool that lets you check the AP credit policy for most colleges. Go to **https://apstudent.collegeboard.org/ creditandplacement/search-credit-policies** and enter the names of the colleges that interest you. The tool will give you the minimum score required for credit and/or placement. It will also give you a link to the college's website so you can check the most up-to-date policy information.

OTHER RESOURCES

There are many resources available to help you improve your score on the AP English Language and Composition Exam, not the least of which are your **teachers**. If you are taking an AP class, you may be able to get extra attention from your teacher, such as obtaining feedback on your essays. If you are not in an AP course, reach out to an English teacher and ask if he or she will review your essays or otherwise help you review.

Another wonderful resource is **AP Central**, the official site of the AP exams. The scope of the information at this site is quite broad and includes

- A Course Description, which provides details on what is covered and sample questions

- The 2001 and 2007 AP English Language and Composition Released Exams, available for purchase at the College Board Store

- Essay prompts from previous years

- Frequently Asked Questions (FAQ's)

- Practice material for grammar, including a quiz and grammar guide

- Tips for succeeding on the essays

The AP Central home page address is: **http://apcentral.collegeboard.com/home**

The AP English Language and Composition Course home page address is: **http://apcentral.collegeboard.com/apc/public/courses/teachers_corner/2123.html**

Finally, **The Princeton Review** offers tutoring and small group instruction for the AP English Language and Composition Exam. Our expert instructors can help you refine your strategic approach and add to your content knowledge. For more information, call 1-800-2REVIEW.

Break up your review into manageable portions. Download our helpful study guide for this book, once you register online.

DESIGNING YOUR STUDY PLAN

In Part I, you identified some areas of potential improvement. Now let's delve further into your performance on Practice Test 1, with the goal of developing a study plan appropriate to your needs and time commitment.

Read the answers and explanations associated with the multiple-choice questions (starting on page 35). After you have done so, respond to the following questions:

- Review the Overview of Review Topics on page 50 and, next to each skill listed, indicate your rank as follows: "1" means "I need a lot of work on this," "2" means "I need some review of this," and "3" means "I have sufficiently mastered this."

- How many days/weeks/months away is your AP English Language and Composition Exam?

- What time of day is your best, most focused study time?

- How much time per day/week/month will you devote to preparing for your AP English Language and Composition Exam?

- When will you do this preparation? (Be as specific as possible: Mondays & Wednesdays from 3:00 to 4:00 P.M., for example.)

- Based on the answers above, will you focus on strategy (Part IV) or the terms and modes review (Part V) or both?

- What are your overall goals in using this book?

Part IV
Test-Taking Strategies for the AP English Language and Composition Exam

PREVIEW

Review your responses to the questions on page 3 of Part I and then answer these:

- How many multiple-choice questions did you miss even though you knew the answer?

- On how many multiple-choice questions did you guess blindly?

- How many multiple-choice questions did you miss after eliminating some answers and guessing based on the remaining answers?

- Did you create an outline before you wrote each essay?

- Did you find any of the essays easier or harder than the others—and, if so, why?

Those answers will give you an idea of what you're doing now and where you could improve your performance on the multiple choice section and the three essays.

- Did you miss too many multiple-choice questions when you knew (or think you should have known) the answer? Perhaps you're not working carefully enough, or you're letting test anxiety get the better of you.

- Did you guess blindly at more than a few questions? Maybe you didn't make your guesses in the most successful way, using the "Letter of the Day"?

- Did you use POE (Process of Elimination) to get rid of the obviously wrong answers, and still miss the correct response when you took a guess from the remaining answers? The "Letter of the Day" approach probably would have helped there, too.

- Did you simply start writing your essay without planning what you were going to say and organizing your points? A few minutes spent on an outline will save you from getting half an hour into your essay time and realizing you're seriously off track.

- If you found one essay more difficult than the others (typically it's the rhetorical analysis essay that gives students the most grief), you know where to focus your efforts. The techniques and practice you'll find in the essay chapters will help you gain confidence in tackling all three of the essays on the exam.

HOW TO USE THE CHAPTERS IN THIS PART

Before you read the following strategy chapters, think about what you are doing now. As you read and work through the directed practice, you'll start to recognize ways you can change your current approach in order to be more successful on each section of the exam. At the end of Part IV, you'll have the opportunity to reflect on the changes you plan to make.

Chapter 1
How to
Approach
Multiple-Choice
Questions

WHAT TO EXPECT IN THE MULTIPLE-CHOICE SECTION

The multiple-choice section counts for 45 percent of your total score, but you're only given 31 percent (one hour) of the total exam time to earn that large chunk of points. So how you spend that hour is extremely important.

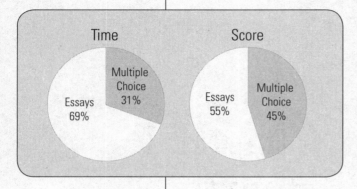

The exam presents you with five passages, all nonfiction. Some are from the twentieth and twenty-first centuries, and some are pre-twentieth century. Our practice tests include passages from earlier works just like the real exam does, so that type will be familiar by the time you get to the test.

"Nonfiction" is a very broad term, so you could find passages taken from all sorts of works—essays, biographies, diary entries, speeches, letters, literary criticism, science and nature writing, and writings about politics or history. The passages will also run the gamut as far as types of diction (word choice), syntax (how words are combined into phrases and sentences), imagery, tone, style, point of view and purpose. You have an hour to read them and answer 55 questions, divided roughly equally among the five passages. Your responses are then scored by computer.

The questions emphasize not just *what* the author is saying, but especially *how* the author says it. The idea is to get you to focus on rhetorical devices, figures of speech and intended purposes, under rigid time constraints and with material you haven't seen before. You'll need to identify rhetorical devices and structures in a passage, and understand why and how the author used them. (Review Chapters 8–11 to learn more about rhetorical strategies. You'll find this helpful for the rhetorical analysis essay, too.) The multiple choice section is a challenging opportunity to demonstrate your ability to analyze how writers use language to achieve their purposes.

So where do you start preparing to get that much done in such a short time? In this chapter you'll find techniques for reading the passages and answering multiple-choice questions under the conditions that will confront you in the exam.

Active Reading

These passages are often heavy reading, particularly the older nonfiction, with the long sentences and sometimes obscure words that were common at the time. You need to read quickly but with understanding. If you just skim through the passage, you will have wasted much of your precious two or three minutes of reading time and will likely have to keep rereading parts just to gain a sense of what the author is talking about.

The solution? Active reading. That means you take control of the passage instead of simply letting it pour sentences and paragraphs into your head. Engage with it.

As you read each paragraph, ask yourself these questions:

- What is the author's main point in this paragraph?

- How does it connect to the paragraph that came before it?

- Where is it likely to lead in the next paragraph?

At the end of the passage, ask yourself:

- What is the author's "big picture" purpose and main point in this passage as a whole?

- Did the author convince me? Interest me? Lead me to disagree strongly? How did the author achieve that effect on me as a reader?

- What impact would this passage likely have had on readers who lived when it was written? What techniques did the author use to achieve that effect?

You can practice this type of active reading with any written material—textbooks, printed ads or product descriptions, for example. Once you get into the habit, you'll find that your reading comprehension increases considerably, along with your critical thinking skills. With enough practice, active reading will be second nature to you by the time you encounter the AP English Language and Composition Exam passages, where it's a necessity if you're to wade through most, if not all, of the questions and answer them successfully.

Active Reading
Look for the main point of the passage, the author's purpose and the rhetorical strategies used to achieve that purpose.

Words in Context

With these nonfiction passages, especially the older ones, chances are you'll encounter some words that aren't familiar to you. Another active reading technique can take you over that hurdle, too: guessing the meaning of a word from its context.

For example, let's say the passage is describing a politician who is trying to sell an unpopular new law to the voters in his constituency.

Guess the meaning of an unfamiliar word from its context.

> The speaker's passion and ebullience began to cut through
> the dour mood of the audience that confronted him.

If you had no idea what "ebullience" and "dour" meant, you could still figure them out from the context. The speaker is passionate about this law he's trying to promote, so—paired with "passion"—"ebullience" must have something to do with enthusiasm and excitement. The voters, on the other hand, don't like it at all, so "dour" must signify something opposite—gloomy, unreceptive. The word even sounds dark and unfriendly.

Again, guessing a word's meaning from its context is something you can practice on material you encounter in your daily life. Then you can check a dictionary or thesaurus to see how your skill is improving.

Attack the Questions and Go Back to the Passage

Each question is setting a specific task for you. Make sure you understand exactly what it's telling you to do. Read the question stem carefully, word for word.

Your memory will fool you. Always go back to the passage.

When a question refers to specific lines in the passage, always go back to the passage and reread them. Read a few lines before and after the lines specified, too; context is often critical in determining the correct answer.

Relying on your memory—particularly in the dense, nonfiction works you'll encounter on the exam—can easily lead you astray. Sometimes a sneaky question will start out partly correct, but then make a U-turn into something that isn't in the passage. Half wrong is all wrong, but if you're relying on your memory and get a glimmer of recognition from the first part of the question, you might pick the wrong answer and miss out on scoring a point.

POE—Process of Elimination

After you understand the question task and have gone back to the passage to review the lines it specifies, look at the answer choices. Your active reading, careful analysis of the question task and rereading of specific lines will most likely show you at least a couple of answer choices that are clearly wrong. Now instead of five possible answers, you have only three or perhaps two, and your chances of choosing—or even guessing at—the correct answer just went up substantially.

> **POE**
>
> First, eliminate the wrong answers.
>
> Then look for the right answer within the remaining choices.

So start there—by quickly getting rid of choices that are obviously wrong – instead of starting by puzzling through five possible answers looking for the one right choice. That's the Process of Elimination approach, and it will increase your success rate on multiple-choice questions significantly.

Guessing and the Letter of the Day

So you've tossed out two clearly wrong answers using POE, and narrowed five possible choices down to three. Suppose you still can't tell *which of* those three is the correct answer, though.

What do you do? Two things: guess and use the Letter of the Day.

Guessing

You get no points for a question that isn't answered at all. The good news with this exam, though, is that you don't lose any points for incorrect answers. So answer every single question, even if your answer is a guess. By using POE, you've raised your chances of guessing correctly within a smaller number of possible answers. There's another technique you can add that will increase your guessing success rate even more.

Letter of the Day

If you make a random guess for each question you can't answer—(A) for one and (D) for another and maybe (E) for this one—you've just made an excellent start at getting every one wrong. The solution? Pick one letter—any letter—and use it for every single guess. That's the Letter of the Day approach.

Let's say there are 10 questions you can't answer. If you pick, for example, (B) as your Letter of the Day and answer (B) on every one of those 10 questions, what are the chances that (B) really is the correct answer to at least one of them, possibly more? Pretty good. On the other hand, if you jump around with a different random letter for each guess, you stand a good chance of missing the correct answer on every one.

The Two-Pass System

With 55 questions and five passages, you have roughly one minute to answer each question, about 12 minutes for each passage and accompanying set of questions. The Two-Pass System will help you use that time most efficiently. Here are the steps to take:

On your first pass through the questions:

- Answer all the easy questions first. If you can answer a question as you come to it, do so.

- Each time you come to a hard question that you can't answer, fill in a "guess" answer using your Letter of the Day and circle the question.

On your second pass through:

- Look at your watch to see how much time you have left for this passage. Go back to the hard questions you circled and tackle as many as you can before the chunk of time available for that passage runs out.

This system works well since all the questions are worth the same number of points, regardless of whether you think they're easy or hard, and since the order in which you answer the questions doesn't matter.

Now let's examine a sample passage.

Proven Techniques

Use POE, Letter of the Day, and the Two-Pass System to help boost your score.

> ### The Two-Pass System
> Pass one: Answer the easy questions and guess at the hard ones, using the Letter of the Day.
>
> Pass two: Tackle as many of the hard ones as you can during the time left for that passage.

SAMPLE PASSAGE—HERE'S HOW IT'S DONE

(The following passage is excerpted from Henry David Thoreau's Walden.*)*

One day when I went out to my wood-pile, or rather
my pile of stumps, I observed two large ants, the one red,
the other much larger, nearly half an inch long, and black,
Line fiercely contending with one another. Having once got
5 hold they never let go, but struggled and wrestled and
rolled on the chips incessantly. Looking farther, I was
surprised to find that the chips were covered with such
combatants, that it was not a *duellum*, but a *bellum*, a war
between two races of ants, the red always pitted against
10 the black, and frequently two red ones to one black. The
legions of the Myrmidons covered all the hills and vales
in my wood-yard, and the ground was already strewn with
the dead and dying, both red and black. It was the only
battle which I have ever witnessed, the only battle-field I
15 ever trod while the battle was raging; internecine war; the
red republicans on the one hand, and the black imperi-
alists on the other. On every side they were engaged in
deadly combat, yet without any noise that I could hear,
and human soldiers never fought so resolutely. I watched
20 a couple that were fast locked in each other's embraces, in
a little sunny valley amid the chips, now at noonday prepared to fight till the sun went down, or life went out. The
smaller red champion had fastened himself like a vice to
his adversary's front, and through all the tumblings on
25 that field never for an instant ceased to gnaw at one of
his feelers near the root, having already caused the other
to go by the board; while the stronger black one dashed
him from side to side, and, as I saw on looking nearer,
had already divested him of several of his members.
30 They fought with more pertinacity than bulldogs. Neither
manifested the least disposition to retreat. It was evident
that their battle-cry was "Conquer or die." In the meanwhile there came along a single red ant on the hillside of
the valley, evidently full of excitement, who either had
35 dispatched his foe, or had not yet taken part in the battle;
probably the latter, for he had lost none of his limbs;
whose mother had charged him to return with his shield
or upon it. Or perchance he was some Achilles, who had
nourished his wrath apart, and had now come to avenge
40 or rescue his Patroclus. He saw this unequal combat from
afar—for the blacks were nearly twice the size of the
red—he drew near with rapid pace till he stood on his
guard within half an inch of the combatants; then, watching his opportunity, he sprang upon the black warrior, and
45 commenced his operations near the root of his right fore
leg, leaving the foe to select among his own members;
and so there were three united for life, as if a new kind
of attraction had been invented which put all other locks

and cements to shame. I should not have wondered by
50 this time to find that they had their respective musical
bands stationed on some eminent chip, and playing their
national airs the while, to excite the slow and cheer the
dying combatants. I was myself excited somewhat even
as if they had been men. The more you think of it, the less
55 the difference.

Analyzing the Passage

Since this is all one paragraph, you might have difficulty with the active reading technique of determining the main point of each paragraph before moving on to the next. You can tell when the author makes a major shift in his narrative, though, dividing this passage into chunks that would function as paragraphs. He first describes the battlefield as a whole, then narrows his lens to describe two particular fighters and the injuries they inflict on each other (line 19), turns his attention to the arrival of one new red ant (line 32), and finally steps back to his elevated position far above the carnage (line 49) where he began his narrative.

The dominant rhetorical strategy Thoreau employs is the analogy that compares the behavior of the ants with that of human beings. He dwells on details about the struggling ants and the injuries they inflict on each other in order to lead his readers to a revelation about human beings. His references to epic battles in Greek mythology (the Myrmidons may not be familiar to you, but Achilles and the Trojan war likely are) draw a sharp contrast between how immensely important this contest is to the ants, and how insignificant it is to the human far above. Thoreau is commenting on how foolish it is to associate warfare with romance and great significance. He is basically asking, "What difference do the struggles of the ants make, when we examine them from far above?" Likewise, what difference does human warfare make, when seen from far above or even from a divine perspective?

This is the overall main point of the passage. As you read it, you need to keep in mind the author's purpose for taking this strong interest in ants. The last lines of the passage should help you make the important conceptual leap from the behavior of the ants to the behavior of men. Thoreau comes right out and says, "I was myself excited somewhat even as if they had been men. The more you think of it, the less the difference."

Some types of big-picture questions will ask you to characterize the speaker's tone, style or attitude in the passage. Another type will ask you to describe how a particular detail fits into the big picture—what a particular word means in context or how the reader is meant to interpret a word based on the tone, style or attitude of the passage as a whole.

Let's look at a typical big-picture question.

1. The author's tone in this passage can best be described as one of

   (A) suspicion and confusion
   (B) horror and shock
   (C) detachment and criticism
   (D) condescension and bemusement
   (E) admiration and empathy

Apply Strategy

Use POE to crack this question.

The correct answer is (D). The narrator gives no evidence of the two emotions in choice (B), so you can get rid of that one right away as you work through the Process of Elimination. "Detachment" is plausible, as is some hint of "admiration" for the heroic ant warriors and "confusion" about the reason for their fierce battle, but the narrator gives no sign of "criticism" or "empathy" or "suspicion." Half wrong is all wrong, so choices (C), (E) and (A) can be eliminated, too. That leaves (D). When you consider the overall main point and purpose of the passage, Thoreau's intention is to show that the observer is to the ants as some higher being would be to humans, leaving the tone of superiority (condescension) and bewilderment (bemusement) as the main one.

Here is another typical big-picture question that gets at pretty much the same issues as the previous one.

2. In this passage, the author exaggerates the greatness of the ants' struggle to

   (A) exaggerate the greatness of nature
   (B) show the true greatness of nature
   (C) demonstrate the importance of war
   (D) illustrate the fierceness of ants
   (E) suggest the exaggerated greatness of humans

The answer is (E). When you have identified the author's main point and purpose, it's obvious that the other four answers are incorrect and can be eliminated. From his superior human position, the narrator sees the ants' fierce struggle as insignificant.

Now, let's take a look at some questions that show what types of details will be tested—and how.

3. In lines 1-2, Thoreau changes "wood-pile" to "pile of stumps" because he wants to

   (A) enhance the sense of realism in the passage
   (B) trivialize the setting of the action
   (C) be thoroughly truthful in his depiction
   (D) create a sense of drama
   (E) make the setting more natural

Using POE, you can immediately eliminate choices (A), (C), and (E). You know from understanding Thoreau's main point that he probably wouldn't be trying to "enhance the sense of realism," or "be thoroughly truthful." Nor is he trying to "make the setting more natural." The setting is just about as natural as it can get.

Even if you thought that (D) reinforced your view that the battle of the ants was a serious epic drama and chose that answer, you may have been saved at the last minute if you noticed that (B) lined up nicely with the answer choices from the first two questions. If you got those two questions right, then (B) would have been a choice that reinforced the purpose and main point you have already identified.

Take a look at the next question on this passage.

4. All of the following humorously aggrandize the battle EXCEPT

(A) it was not a *duellum*, but a *bellum* (line 8)

(B) the hills and vales of my wood-yard (lines 11-12)

(C) human soldiers never fought so resolutely (line 19)

(D) whose mother had charged him to return with his shield or upon it (lines 37-39)

(E) Or perchance he was some Achilles (line 38)

In case you missed the big picture, the question writer goes so far as to *say* that the battle is humorously aggrandized. If "aggrandize" is new to you, here's a fairly easy way to guess at its meaning. The root of the word is "grand"—as in "great" or "magnificent." The "ag-" and "-ize" around that root suggest "make grand." So, the question stem is asking which answer choice does NOT (the "EXCEPT") make the ants' battle look great and epic in a humorous way.

This question also demonstrates the importance of reading the question stem carefully, word for word, to identify the task it is setting for you. If you missed the "EXCEPT," you would immediately be headed for a wrong answer.

Now let's look through the answer choices, starting with (A). Even if your Latin is weak or nonexistent, you can probably see the word "duel" (a fight between two people) in *duellum*. *Bellum* is presented as a contrast to *duellum*, so it must mean a fight involving many people (a war). The "hills and vales" (B) are, of course, only minuscule piles of wood chips or sawdust. The humor in the personifications in (D) and (E) should also be apparent, since these references to epic mythological battles are applied to insignificant ants.

The correct answer is (C). While it does "aggrandize" the ants' struggle, it is almost the only line in the passage that could be considered not tinged with humor.

As you come to questions that refer you back to specific lines in the passage, always go back to those places and read more closely instead of relying on your memory.

Remember to read a line or two above and below the lines specified, too, so you won't miss any important information from the context. Reread only as much as you need to, though. If you can't answer a question without spending too much time rereading, then guess at the answer (using your Letter of the Day) and, if you have time, return to it on your second pass through the questions for that passage.

Here are a couple of examples of questions that send you back to specific parts of the passage.

5. In context, "pertinacity" (line 30) most nearly means
    (A) pertinence
    (B) loyalty
    (C) perspicacity
    (D) obstinacy
    (E) attentiveness

On this type of question, the instruction that you are to find the meaning "in context" almost guarantees that the answer won't be the first definition that pops into your head, even when you do know the usual meaning of the word. It will probably have a unique meaning in virtue of the context that surrounds it.

For this question, if you go back and look at the context—especially the word "bulldogs"—you should be able to eliminate all the answers except (D). Another clue is the adverb "resolutely" that appears slightly earlier in the passage. The ants are fighting resolutely and obstinately—like bulldogs.

Let's look at one more.

6. The phrase "who had nourished his wrath apart" (lines 38-39) serves mainly to
    (A) create the impression of an epic tone
    (B) sustain the seriousness of the author's point of view
    (C) highlight the extent of the hatred between the enemies
    (D) underscore the loneliness of the combatants
    (E) emphasize the cannibalistic nature of the combatants

We have already determined that there is a playful humor in the humanization of the insects in combat, and this allows us to eliminate choices (B), (C) and (D), which are there just to trick students who missed the author's tone. Choice (E) can also be tossed out quickly; the ants are depriving their enemies of limbs, not eating them.

The correct answer is (A). There is "the impression" of an epic tone (rather than a true epic tone) because Thoreau's aim is to have us understand the futility and insignificance of the ants' (and humans') struggles in the grand scheme of things.

TO SUM UP

- Use active reading to identify the main point of each paragraph (or chunk) of the passage, then see how they connect to form the main point of the passage as a whole.

- Concentrate on the author's purpose, tone and point of view.

- Look for the rhetorical strategies the author uses to achieve that purpose.

- Always go back to the passage when multiple choice questions refer you to specific lines. Relying on your memory can easily lead you to select a close—but incorrect—answer.

- Read a couple of lines above and below the lines specified in the question. The context of the lines is almost always critical in determining the correct answer.

- Pace yourself. Divide the multiple choice section into 12-minute chunks for each passage.

- Use the Two-Pass System. On your first pass, answer the questions you can and guess at the rest, using your Letter of the Day. Circle the questions you guessed at, and go back to them later if time remains in your 12-minute chunk.

- Use POE to eliminate wrong answers instead of looking for the right answer among five alternatives.

You'll have the opportunity to practice what you've learned on the drills in Chapter 3. First, let's look a bit more closely at some approaches to two essential aspects of doing well on the multiple-choice questions: timing and pacing.

Chapter 2
Using Time Effectively to Maximize Points

STUDYING ISN'T EVERYTHING

Very few students stop to think about how to improve their test-taking skills. Most assume that if they study hard, they will get a high score, and if they do not study, they will do poorly.

Have you ever studied really hard for an exam, then blown it on test day, though? Have you ever aced an exam for which you thought you probably hadn't studied enough? Most students have had one, if not both, of these experiences. The lesson should be clear: factors other than how much you've studied influence your final test score, particularly on a test such as the AP English Language and Composition Exam, where timing and pacing are important aspects of thorough preparation.

This chapter will provide you with some insights that will help you perform better on the multiple-choice section of the AP English Language and Composition Exam, and on other exams as well.

Pacing and Timing

A big part of scoring well on an exam is sharpening your awareness of time. Another other big part is working at a consistent pace.

If you can't answer a question, guess and move on.

The worst mistake made by inexperienced test takers is that when they come to a question that stumps them, rather than just skipping it, they panic and stall. Time stands still when you're working on a question you can't answer, and it is not unusual for students to waste five minutes on a single multiple-choice question (especially a question involving a long selection from the passage or the word EXCEPT) instead of cutting their losses and moving on to questions they *can* answer.

Every question is worth the same one point, whether it's a hard question or an easy one. The computer that scores your responses doesn't know whether you agonized for three minutes over a hard question or breezed through an easy one in a few seconds; it only knows whether your answer is right or wrong.

It is important to be aware of how much time you have spent on a given question or section. There are several ways to improve your pacing and timing for the test.

- **Know your average pace.** While you prepare for your test, gauge how long you take on a passage with 11 or so questions. Knowing how long you spend on average per passage (and per question) will help you identify how many passages you can read (and questions you can answer) effectively in 55 minutes, and how best to pace yourself for the test.

- **Have a watch or clock nearby.** You are permitted to have a watch or clock nearby to help you keep track of time. However, constantly checking the clock is in itself a waste of time and can be distracting and stressful. Devise a plan. Try checking the clock after every passage or two to see if you are keeping the correct pace or whether you need to speed up. This will ensure that you're managing your time but won't permit you to fall into the trap of dwelling on it.

- **Know when to move on.** Because all of the multiple-choice questions are scored equally, and you are not penalized for wrong answers, investing long stretches of time on a single question is inefficient and can potentially deprive you of the chance to answer easier questions later on. If you can eliminate answer choices with POE, do so, but on your first pass through the questions, just guess from among the remaining choices (using your Letter of the Day) and move on if you can't find the correct answer. Remember, tests are like marathons: you do best when you work through them at a steady pace.

- **Be selective.** You don't have to do the multiple-choice questions in order. If you are stumped by a question, guess, skip it and choose a different one. You might not have to answer every question correctly to achieve the score you need for your first choice of college. Select the questions you can answer and work on them first. This will boost your confidence, make you more efficient and give you the greatest chance of getting the most questions correct.

- **Use Process of Elimination on Every Question.** Every answer choice that can be eliminated increases the odds that you will answer the question correctly.

Remember, when all the questions on a test are of equal value, and you don't lose any points for incorrect answers, no one question is that important. Your overall goal for pacing is to get the most questions correct.

You don't lose any points for wrong answers in the multiple-choice section.

Getting the Score You Need

Depending on the score you need, it may be in your best interest *not* to try to work through every multiple-choice question. Check with the schools to which you are applying. If you're aiming for credit hours and need to score a 5, it's best to find out as early in your preparation as possible. On the other hand, if you're simply aiming for placement and you find out your first choice of college sets the cut-off point at a score of 3, some of the pressure is off and you can prepare without feeling crushed by anxiety.

More Great Books
Check out The Princeton Review's test prep titles for ACT and SAT:
Cracking the ACT Premium, Cracking the New SAT Premium, ACT Elite, SAT Elite, and many more!

Getting the Score You Want

On the most recently released official exam, out of 150 points total for the three essays and multiple-choice questions, students needed at least 112 points to get a score of 5, 98 points for a 4, 80 points for a 3, and 55 points for a 2. Because the College Board has not recently released its grading statistics, the following is an approximation of how to pace yourself on the multiple-choice section:

If you want to get a:	Work on this many:
2	28
3	36
4	45
5	54

Below is a table to give you an idea of how many questions you must get right and how you must do on the essays to get the score you need. Realize that these numbers are approximations and will vary from year to year depending upon test performance. From these data, it becomes readily apparent that you must attempt and perform well on the essays to have a chance to score a 4 or 5. As you take practice tests, you can use this information to evaluate how best to get the score you want and what areas of the exam are hindering your progress. You can calculate your own score on the practice tests in this book using the worksheets in the Answers and Explanations chapters. It is important to remember that there are multiple ways to achieve your desired score.

How to Get the Score You Want		
Total AP Score Desired	Multiple-choice Correct (out of 54)	Average Score Needed on Essays (out of 9)
5	54	5
	50	6
	45	6
	40	7
4	50	4
	45	5
	40	5
	35	6
3	40	4
	30	5
	25	6
	20	6
2	35	1
	25	3
	20	4
	10	5

Reducing Test Anxiety

No matter what score you need, everybody experiences anxiety before and during an exam. To a certain extent, test anxiety *can* be helpful. Some people find that they perform more quickly and efficiently under stress. If you have ever pulled an all-nighter to write a paper and ended up doing good work, you know the feeling.

However, too much stress is definitely a bad thing. If you find that your stress level prevents you from doing your best work during exams, here are a few actions you can take to stop excessive stress in its tracks.

- **Take a reality check.** Evaluate your situation before the test begins. If you have understood and practiced all of the techniques we give for success on the exam, remind yourself that you are well prepared. Remember that many others taking the test are not as well prepared as you are, and you're being graded against them, so you have an advantage.

  Don't fixate on how much you don't know. Your job is to score as high as you can by maximizing the benefits of what you do know. Think of a test as a game. How can you get the most points in the time allotted?

- **Try to relax.** Slow, deep breathing works for almost everyone. Close your eyes, take a few slow, deep breaths, and concentrate on nothing but your inhalation and exhalation for a few seconds. This is a basic form of meditation, and it should help clear your mind of stress and, as a result, concentrate better on the test. If you have ever taken yoga classes, you probably know some other good relaxation techniques you could use in the test setting.

- **Visualize.** Imagine your favorite park or beach or hiking trail or indoor room, and visualize yourself sitting there taking the exam, all alone, calm and relaxed and enjoying your surroundings. You're still writing the test, but in a pleasant place instead of in a stress-filled atmosphere. Most likely you'll need to practice this technique in advance in order to be able to slip into another place mentally while you're writing the test. Try it while you're having breakfast, or riding the bus, or walking down a noisy, chaotic street.

- **Eliminate as many surprises as you can.** Make sure you know where the test is being given, how long it will take you to get there, where to park if you're driving. Take a "dry run" trip to the test center before the day of the exam. Know when the exam room will open, when the actual exam starts, what type of questions you are going to be asked, and how long each section of the test will take. You don't want to be worrying about any of these things on the test day.

- **Plan to reward yourself.** After all, you deserve a reward for all of your hard work. Make a plan for doing something enjoyable right after the test is over. While you're preparing, keep thinking of the reward you've promised yourself.

The best way to avoid stress is to become familiar with the test material and practice doing exam questions under actual time constraints. (By buying or reading this book, you are taking a major step toward a stress-free AP English Language and Composition Exam.)

In the next chapter, you'll have an opportunity to practice the strategies you've learned.

Chapter 3
Pacing Drills

DRILL 1

Questions 1-8. Read the following passage carefully before you choose your answers.

(The following passage is excerpted from the British Prime Minister's 1846 speech about the repeal of the Corn Laws.)

Sir, believe me, to conduct the Government of this country is a most arduous duty; I may say it without irreverence, that these ancient institutions, like our physical
Line frames, are "fearfully and wonderfully made." It is no easy
5 task to ensure the united action of an ancient monarchy, a proud aristocracy, and a reformed constituency. I have done everything I could do, and have thought it consistent with true Conservative policy to reconcile these three branches of the State. I have thought it consistent with true
10 Conservative policy to promote so much of happiness and contentment among the people that the voice of disaffection should be no longer heard, and that thoughts of the dissolution of our institutions should be forgotten in the midst of physical enjoyment. These were my attempts,
15 and I thought them not inconsistent with true and enlarged Conservative policy. These were my objects in accepting office—it is a burden too great for my physical, and far beyond my intellectual structure; and to be relieved from it with perfect honour would be the greatest favour that
20 could be conferred on me. But as a feeling of honour and strong sense of duty require me to undertake those responsible functions, I declare, Sir, that I am ready to incur these risks, to bear these burdens, and to front all these honourable dangers. But, Sir, I will not take the step with
25 mutilated power and shackled authority. I will not stand at the helm during, such tempestuous nights as I have seen, if the vessel be not allowed fairly to pursue the course which I think she ought to take. I will not, Sir, undertake to direct the course of the vessel by the observations which have
30 been taken in 1842. I will reserve to myself the marking out of that course; and I must, for the public interest, claim for myself the unfettered power of judging of those measures which I conceive will be better for the country to propose.
35 Sir, I do not wish to be the Minister of England; but while I have the high honour of holding that Office, I am determined to hold it by no servile tenure. I will only hold that office upon the condition of being unshackled by any other obligations than those of consulting the public inter-
40 ests, and of providing for the public safety.

1. The opening sentence of the passage contains
   (A) an expression of fear
   (B) an appeal to authority
   (C) a humorous simile
   (D) an irreverent attack
   (E) equivocation

2. The speaker is addressing
   (A) a friend
   (B) a group of his peers
   (C) a king
   (D) a crowd of voters
   (E) his political adversaries

3. The most significant transition takes place in
   (A) line 9 ("I have thought it consistent…")
   (B) line 16 ("These were my objects…")
   (C) line 20 ("But as a feeling of honour…")
   (D) line 24 ("But, Sir, I will not…")
   (E) lines 28-29 ("I will not, Sir, undertake…")

4. All of the following are part of the same extended metaphor EXCEPT
   (A) "helm" (line 26)
   (B) "vessel" (line 27)
   (C) "fairly" (line 27)
   (D) "course" (line 29)
   (E) "unshackled" (line 38)

5. Which term in the first paragraph serves to prepare the dominant point of the final paragraph?
   (A) "disaffection" (lines 11-12)
   (B) "enjoyment" (line 14)
   (C) "dangers" (line 24)
   (D) "tempestuous" (line 26)
   (E) "unfettered" (line 32)

6. Based on the passage, the speaker's motivation to serve as Prime Minister is dictated mostly by

(A) greed
(B) political ambition
(C) sense of honor
(D) political power
(E) youthful exuberance

7. The tone of the entire passage

(A) remains consistently cynical
(B) shifts according to the speaker's mood
(C) shifts from light to serious
(D) becomes more frivolous in the final paragraph
(E) remains consistently lighthearted

8. Which of the following best describes the rhetorical function of lines 17-20 ("it is a burden too great… the greatest favor that could be conferred upon me.")?

(A) It makes an appeal to emotion.
(B) It states the overall thesis of the passage.
(C) It expresses a causal relationship between events in the past and events in the present.
(D) It provides a specific example for the preceding argument.
(E) It reinforces the author's claim of responsibility in the following sentence.

DRILL 2

Questions 9-16. Read the following passage carefully before you choose your answers.

(The following passage is excerpted from an influential work published in 1839.)

This archipelago consists of ten principal islands, of which five exceed the others in size. They are situated under the Equator, and between five and six hundred miles
Line westward of the coast of America. They are all formed
5 of volcanic rocks; a few fragments of granite curiously glazed and altered by the heat, can hardly be considered as an exception. Some of the craters, surmounting the larger islands, are of immense size, and they rise to a height of between three and four thousand feet. Their flanks are
10 studded by innumerable smaller orifices. I scarcely hesitate to affirm, that there must be in the whole archipelago at least two thousand craters. These consist either of lava or scoriae, or of finely-stratified, sandstone-like tuff. Most of the latter are beautifully symmetrical; they owe their
15 origin to eruptions of volcanic mud without any lava: it is a remarkable circumstance that every one of the twenty-eight tuff-craters which were examined had their southern sides either much lower than the other sides, or quite broken down and removed. As all these craters apparently have
20 been formed when standing in the sea, and as the waves from the trade wind and the swell from the open Pacific here unite their forces on the southern coasts of all the islands, this singular uniformity in the broken state of the craters, composed of the soft and yielding tuff, is easily
25 explained.

The Beagle sailed round Chatham Island, and anchored in several bays. One night I slept on shore on a part of the island, where black truncated cones were extraordinarily numerous: from one small eminence I counted sixty of
30 them, all surmounted by craters more or less perfect. The greater number consisted merely of a ring of red scoriae or slags, cemented together: and their height above the plain of lava was not more than from fifty to a hundred feet; none had been very lately active. The entire surface of this
35 part of the island seems to have been permeated, like a sieve, by the subterranean vapours: here and there the lava, whilst soft, has been blown into great bubbles; and in other parts, the tops of caverns similarly formed have fallen in, leaving circular pits with steep sides. From the regular
40 form of the many craters, they gave to the country an artifi-cial appearance, which vividly reminded me of those parts of Staffordshire, where the great iron-foundries are most numerous. The day was glowing hot, and the scrambling over the rough surface and through the intricate thickets,

45 was very fatiguing; but I was well repaid by the strange Cyclopean scene. As I was walking along I met two large tortoises, each of which must have weighed at least two hundred pounds: one was eating a piece of cactus, and as I approached, it stared at me and slowly walked away; the
50 other gave a deep hiss, and drew in its head. These huge reptiles, surrounded by the black lava, the leafless shrubs, and large cacti, seemed to my fancy like some antediluvian animals. The few dull-coloured birds cared no more for me than they did for the great tortoises.

9. This passage is most notable for its

    (A) meticulous classification
    (B) unusual point of view
    (C) precise description
    (D) resourceful analogies
    (E) lyrical prose

10. The speaker in the passage can best be described as

    (A) a scientist making entries in a nature journal
    (B) a professional sailor touring a remote island
    (C) a fiction writer on holiday
    (D) a surveyor measuring land for future development
    (E) a volcanologist studying the site of a recent eruption

11. In context, one can infer that "tuff" is

    (A) an alternate spelling for "tough"
    (B) a kind of sand
    (C) made up principally of grass
    (D) volcanic rock
    (E) dense and resistant

12. In this passage, the speaker is most notably impressed by

    (A) the flora on the islands
    (B) the force of the Pacific Ocean
    (C) the fragments of granite
    (D) the symmetrical craters on the islands
    (E) the topography of the smaller islands

13. Which of the following phrases represents a literary allusion?

    (A) "parts of Staffordshire" (lines 41-42)
    (B) "the strange Cyclopean scene" (lines 45-46)
    (C) "situated under the Equator (lines 2-3)
    (D) "the coast of America" (line 4)
    (E) "the swell from the open Pacific" (line 21)

14. Which of the following landscape features are described throughout the entire passage?

    (A) craters and lava
    (B) craters and tortoises
    (C) tortoises and birds
    (D) islands and bays
    (E) tuff and volcanic mud

15. In line 52, "antediluvian" most nearly means

    (A) artificial
    (B) lifeless
    (C) prehistoric
    (D) volcanic
    (E) enormous

16. Which of the following are virtually synonymous as presented in the author's description?

    (A) "ten principal islands" (line 1) and "two thousand craters" (line 12)
    (B) "tuff" (line 13) and "volcanic mud" (line 15)
    (C) "iron-foundries" (line 42) and "intricate thickets" (line 44)
    (D) "craters" (line 40) and "caverns" (line 38)
    (E) "tortoises" (line 47) and "birds" (line 53)

DRILL 3

Questions 17-25. Read the following passage carefully before you choose your answers.

(The following passage is excerpted from an essay by a nineteenth-century British writer.)

Art begins with abstract decoration, with purely imaginative and pleasurable work dealing with what is unreal and non-existent. This is the first stage. Then Life
Line becomes fascinated with this new wonder, and asks to
5 be admitted into the charmed circle. Art takes Life as part of her rough material, re-creates it, and refashions it in fresh forms, is absolutely indifferent to fact, invents, imagines, dreams, and keeps between herself and reality the impenetrable barrier of beautiful style, of decorative
10 or ideal treatment. The third stage is when Life gets the upper hand, and drives Art out into the wilderness. That is the true decadence, and it is from this that we are now suffering.

Take the case of the English drama. At first in the hands
15 of the monks Dramatic Art was abstract, decorative and mythological. Then she enlisted Life in her service, and using some of life's external forms, she created an entirely new race of beings, whose sorrows were more terrible than any sorrow man has ever felt, whose joys were keener
20 than lover's joys, who had the rage of the Titans and the calm of the gods, who had monstrous and marvelous sins, monstrous and marvelous virtues. To them she gave a language different from that of actual use, a language full of resonant music and sweet rhythm, made stately
25 by solemn cadence, or made delicate by fanciful rhyme, jeweled with wonderful words, and enriched with lofty diction. She clothed her children in strange raiment and gave them masks, and at her bidding the antique world rose from its marble tomb. A new Caesar stalked through
30 the streets of risen Rome, and with purple sail and flute-led oars another Cleopatra passed up the river to Antioch. Old myth and legend and dream took shape and substance. History was entirely rewritten, and there was hardly one of the dramatists who did not recognize that the object of Art
35 is not simple truth but complex beauty. In this they were perfectly right. Art itself is really a form of exaggeration; and selection, which is the very spirit of art, is nothing more than an intensified mode of over-emphasis.

But Life soon shattered the perfection of the form. Even
40 in Shakespeare we can see the beginning of the end. It shows itself by the gradual breaking-up of the blank-verse in the later plays, by the predominance given to prose, and by the overimportance assigned to characterization. The passages in Shakespeare—and they are many—where

45 the language is uncouth, vulgar, exaggerated, fantastic, obscene even, are entirely due to Life calling for an echo of her own voice, and rejecting the intervention of beautiful style, through which alone should life be suffered to find expression. Shakespeare is not by any means a
50 flawless artist. He is too fond of going directly to Life, and borrowing Life's natural utterance. He forgets that when Art surrenders her imaginative medium she surrenders everything.

17. The author of this passage is most likely

    (A) a poet
    (B) a novelist
    (C) an art critic
    (D) a journalist
    (E) an actor

18. The author relies principally on which of the following to substantiate his thesis?

    (A) a faulty analogy
    (B) process analysis
    (C) deductive reasoning
    (D) an accumulation of facts
    (E) illustration by example

19. "…when Art surrenders her imaginative medium she surrenders everything" (lines 51-53) is in the form of

    (A) a maxim
    (B) a chiasmus
    (C) an antithesis
    (D) an understatement
    (E) an analogy

20. Above all else, the author reveres

    (A) beauty
    (B) life
    (C) Shakespeare
    (D) Caesar
    (E) English drama

21. In the context of the entire passage, "Life gets the upper hand" (lines 10-11) is best interpreted as having which of the following meanings?

    (A) Art is favored over Life in English drama.
    (B) Life re-writes history.
    (C) Life drives Art out of English drama.
    (D) Life is uncouth, vulgar, and unsophisticated.
    (E) Life dominates Art in English drama.

22. The quality discussed in lines 23-28 is most directly the antithesis of which of the following?

    (A) "marble tomb" (line 29)
    (B) "The passages in Shakespeare" (line 44)
    (C) "to find expression" (line 49)
    (D) "her imaginative medium (line 52)
    (E) "a flawless artist" (line 50)

23. The author's observation in the first three sentences (lines 1-5) is best described as an example of which of the following?

    (A) Personification
    (B) Linguistic paradox
    (C) First-person narrative
    (D) Dramatic irony
    (E) Authorial intrusion

24. In line 28, "She" refers to which of the following?

    I.   "Dramatic Art" (line 15)
    II. "English drama" (line 14)
    III. "Life" (line 16)

    (A) I only
    (B) II only
    (C) I and III only
    (D) II and III only
    (E) I, II, and III

25. The author's tone in the passage as a whole is best described as

    (A) harsh and strident
    (B) informal and analytical
    (C) rueful and expository
    (D) superficial and capricious
    (E) enthusiastic and optimistic

EXPLANATIONS FOR DRILL 1

1. **C**   The simile in this first sentence compares the great and ancient parliamentary institutions with the august, but somewhat ancient bodies of the members of Parliament. The speaker is warming up his audience with a bit of humor before launching into what amounts to a very serious ultimatum: that the speaker will continue to serve as Prime Minister, but only if they concede to him much greater authority than before (1842).

2. **B**   The speaker is addressing a group of his peers, who are the other members of Parliament. The tricky part here is, of course, the repetition of "Sir," a political convention in Great Britain—it is as if the Prime Minister were addressing each member of Parliament as an individual. We know that he is the Minister of England because of the final sentences; and these sentences also reveal definitively that he is speaking to peers: "Sir, I do not wish to be the Minister of England; but while I have the high honour of holding that Office, I am determined to hold it by no servile tenure. I will only hold that office upon the condition of being unshackled by any other obligations than those of consulting the public interests, and of providing for the public safety."

3. **D**   Everything before this line is an introduction to the Minister's real message; until this point, he has joked, given a general review of his former motivations and actions as the leader of the Conservative party, and explained his reasons for accepting to serve again as prime minister ("feeling of honour") in spite of his failing health and aged mind ("a burden too great for my physical, and far beyond my intellectual structure"). The transition comes with "But, Sir, I will not take the step with mutilated power and shackled authority." He will do the country and his peers a favor, but only if he is granted much more authority to rule.

4. **E**   Eliminate (A), (B), and (D), so you're left with (C) and (E), which do not fit neatly into the nautical terminology. Answer (C) is the one to eliminate. All the other terms fit neatly into the nautical terminology. However, one could stretch a point and claim that "fairly" is related to fair weather; whereas "unshackled" is clearly unrelated to this metaphor.

5. **E**   Naturally, the first step is to determine the "dominant point" of the final paragraph. Thankfully, the second paragraph is short—it is the rhetorical summation of his ultimatum. The key phrases are "servile tenure" and "unshackled by any other obligations." Of course, "unfettered" and "unshackled" are synonyms, so the best answer is (E), "unfettered."

6. **C**   The minister states unequivocally that honor is his motivation, in the following passage in particular: "and to be relieved from it [the position] with perfect honour would be the greatest favour that could be conferred on me. But as a feeling of honour and strong sense of duty require me to undertake those responsible functions, I declare, Sir, that I am ready to incur these risks, to bear these burdens, and to front all these honourable dangers." The word honor comes up numerous times in this excerpt.

7. **C**   You should be able to narrow your options to (B) and (C). But be careful! Do you think that the speaker, the most powerful man in Great Britain, allowed his mood to shift or to affect his tone? The speech was carefully constructed, and the tone was coolly calculated when William Gladstone wrote it. The Prime Minister began with a light tone because he was looking to set up his audience, not because he started his speech in a good mood. In fact, his real mood never shifts: He manipulates tone for maximum effect.

8. **E** In lines 17-20, the author describes his time in office as a "burden" and how he wishes to be "relieved of it." But in the following sentence, lines 21-24, the author states that "a strong sense of duty" requires him to "incur these risks, bear these burdens, and to front all these honourable dangers." So the author is burdened, but feels a sense of responsibility. This aligns with (E). Although we may feel sympathy with the author, an appeal to emotion is not the primary goal (A). The overall thesis of the passage has more to do with duty than burden, so not (B). The author's sense of burden did not cause anything to happen, so not (C), and there is no specific example, so rule out (D).

EXPLANATIONS FOR DRILL 2

9. **C** This is a scientifically precise description of the Galapagos Islands. Choice (A) is incorrect since nothing is being classified in this passage. Choice (B) is also wrong—no point of view is presented here—just facts. The passage is not dominated by analogies, so (D) can't be right. Finally, you know that (E) is incorrect, since "lyrical" pertains to personal sentiment, and there are practically no personal feelings expressed at all; the closest we get to personal sentiment is the statement that some of the craters are "beautifully symmetrical."

10. **A** You can use POE to answer this question. Choice (B) is the easiest to eliminate; the passage is factual, not fictional. The passage is about the islands themselves, not about volcanoes as (E) suggests, and, according to the second paragraph, "none had very lately been active." Choices (B) and (D) are somewhat plausible; however, we have no evidence that the author is a "professional" sailor, nor that he has done any formal "surveying." The passage contains a detailed description of nature, so (A) is the best match.

11. **D** In this case, the answer is made clear from the passage; the craters have a border of soft stone (tuff) that has worn away on the southern side. The specific line from the passage that allows you to answer this question is: "These consist either of lava or scoriae, or of finely stratified, sandstone-like tuff." Sandstone is a type of rock. The definition of "tuff" is actually "a rock composed of compacted volcanic ash varying in size from fine sand to coarse gravel."

12. **D** The author doesn't address (A) or (E), so you can eliminate those and look more closely at the middle three choices. While it is true that the speaker mentions the Pacific Ocean and the fragments of granite, he incorporates these elements in his overarching discussion of the symmetrical craters.

13. **B** A literary allusion is a reference, usually to a character from art, literature, or mythology, which requires the reader to have some outside knowledge of the topic. Staffordshire (A) is a place, but is not a feature of literature or mythology. The Cyclops (B) is a character from Greek mythology, so this is the best match. Choices (C), (D), and (E) are geographical references, but are not literary or mythological.

14. **A** Check BOTH paragraphs. Tortoises are only mentioned toward the end of the passage, so eliminate (B) and (C). Tuff is only mentioned in the first paragraph, so eliminate (E). Bays are only mentioned at the beginning of paragraph two, so eliminate (D). Craters and lava are mentioned through the passage, making (A) the best answer.

15. **C**   If you know the definition of "antediluvian," then you have a distinct advantage here, but, if not, we can get clues from the context of the passage. Since the word is describing animals, they would not be "artificial" or "volcanic," so eliminate (A) and (D). The tortoises are not "lifeless" (B), since one of them hisses at the author. "Enormous" (E) is tempting, since the tortoises are described as "huge," but that would ignore the middle phrase in that sentence and create a redundancy. "Black lava," "leafless shrubs," and "large cacti" are not features of many modern landscapes, and the tortoises are larger than normal, so "old" or "primordial" is meaning we're looking for here. Choice (C) is the closest choice.

16. **D**   Synonymous phrases would represent virtually the same idea. The islands have craters, but they are not, in themselves, actual craters, so eliminate (A). Tuff and volcanic mud (B) may be associated together in the first paragraph, but we don't for sure if they are the same substance. Iron-foundries are more closely aligned to craters, not thickets (C). And the tortoises and birds are in opposition, according to the author, since they react to him in different ways. That leaves us with (D); craters and caverns are both holes in the landscape.

EXPLANATIONS FOR DRILL 3

17. **A**   In reality, the author is both a poet and a novelist, but you are asked to make a judgment based on the passage. To answer this question correctly, you would need to use POE and your best judgment to eliminate all of the least likely answer choices. The passage is an attack against the intrusion of prosaic life into the realm of art. The panegyric (high praise) of classical language is a key to understanding the author's point of view: "a language different from that of actual use, a language full of resonant music and sweet rhythm, made stately by solemn cadence, or made delicate by fanciful rhyme, jeweled with wonderful words, and enriched with lofty diction." In a word, this is poetry.

The writing is far too lyrical for the author of the passage to be a journalist (D) or an actor (E); the latter choice is thrown in for those superficial readers who assume that a passage that purports to deal with English drama should be somehow related to a theatrical term. The same may be said for choice (C). The author capitalizes "art" because he is not discussing painting specifically, but the general realm of artistic creation that encompasses all the arts.

18. **E**   The example is stated rhetorically–"Take the case of the English drama"–and lasts for most of the passage. "Illustration by example" is definitely the defining rhetorical device of this passage.

19. **A**   A maxim is a truism or pithy saying, a gnomic statement similar to a proverb, so choice (A) is the best answer.

POE can help you narrow down your choices. Clearly, the statement does not compare Art to something else, so you can eliminate (E). If anything, the statement is overstatement (hyperbole), and for that reason (D) can be discarded. For the statement to be an antithesis, the author would have needed to put two things or concepts in opposition, but we have only one element (Art); thus, you can eliminate choice (C). At this point, your chances are fifty-fifty, so you could guess and move on.

But let's look at choice (B). A "chiasmus" is a syntactic figure wherein the elements in one clause are reversed in another. The most famous example is President Kennedy's statement: "Ask not what your country can do for you, but what you can do for your country."

20. **A**   The author does not revere life above everything else—for example, he clearly states that he doesn't like life as an intrusion on Art, at the very least or as it appears in certain parts of William Shakespeare's work. He includes these examples of Caesar and English drama for rhetorical reasons, and while he admires English drama, he does not appear to revere it. (By the way, to "revere" something is "to regard it with awe, deference, and devotion.) Beauty is held up as an ideal, and this is clear when the author says, "the object of Art is not simple truth but complex beauty."

21. **E**   The idiom "getting the upper hand" means having an advantage over something or someone. If "Life gets the upper hand," then (A) is clearly wrong. Choice (D) is a trap, since it sounds like a direct quote from line 47 and does not connote having an advantage. Choice (B) is likewise irrelevant to "getting the upper hand." Choices (C) and (E) have very close meanings, but (C) is too extreme, since we can't say for sure that Art is absent from all English drama. Choice (E) is the safest choice.

22. **B**   The quality in lines 23-28 is "a language full of resonant music and sweet rhythm." This is the antithesis (direct opposite) of the author's description on Shakespeare's writing in line 44. Choice (B) is the best answer.

23. **A**   Throughout the first paragraph, the author refers to Life and Art as though they were people: "Life becomes fascinated.." (line 4), "Art takes life as part of her rough material…" (lines 5-6). This is known as personification (A). Although Life and Art are in opposition to each other, there is no inherent confusion or contradiction (B). The passage is not written in first-person narration ("I," "me," etc.), choice (C). And there is no sense that circumstances are the opposite of how one might anticipate (D). Authorial intrusion is an interruption in the narrative, so rule out (E).

24. **A**   Check the beginning of the paragraph. In line 15, "Dramatic Art" is mentioned. In line 16, "she enlisted Life." So the "she" used throughout this paragraph is "Dramatic Art," not "Life," and certainly not "English drama" as a whole.

25. **C**   First of all, eliminate the extreme answers: (A) and (E). "Informal" (B) is not a good match, since the passage is written in a rather lofty style. Choice (D) would make the author seem petty or unpredictable. Overall, the author laments the "takeover" of Art by Life. This is especially obvious in the last line of the passage. Thus, he is "rueful" (C). "Expository" simply means that the author is "exposing" the supposed problem with English drama.

Chapter 4
How to
Approach
the Essays:
Basic Principles

ESSAY SECTION TASKS

Yes, that's right—tasks. You'll need to write three different essays: synthesis, rhetorical analysis and argument.

In the **synthesis essay**, you'll be given a scenario and tasked with writing a response using at least three of six or seven short accompanying sources for support. You'll need to cite the sources you use (in a simple format such as "Source A"), and incorporate them into your own position (instead of simply quoting them). At least one of the sources will be a visual (such as a picture, drawing or graph) rather than text.

The **rhetorical analysis essay** asks you to analyze the techniques (such as choice of language or organization of points) an author uses, and discuss how those techniques contribute to the author's purpose. The passage you'll be asked to analyze is typically about a page long.

The **argumentative essay** presents a claim or assertion in the prompt, then asks you to argue a position based on your own knowledge, experience or reading. You can choose to agree with the claim, disagree with it or give it qualified support (for example, arguing that the claim is true only in certain circumstances).

In Chapters 5–7, you'll learn more about the approach and expectations for each type of essay.

For all three essays, you will be writing cold on a prompt or passage you read just two minutes ago for the first time. You have to come up with good ideas and get them written down efficiently—on the very first try.

Writing a clear, effective, well-organized essay under rigid time constraints is a learned skill; writing three consecutive essays under such conditions requires special techniques and lots of practice. Fortunately, this book provides you with both of those.

Three Rules for Successful Essay Preparation

1. Do plenty of TIMED practice on all three essay types.

2. Hand-write your practice essays; don't use a computer.

3. Ask for feedback on your essays from a trusted source (such as an English teacher or Princeton Review tutor).

Time Crunch

You'll have two hours to write all three essays, which allows about 40 minutes each. Before you even start working on the essays, though, you'll have 15 minutes to read all three prompts and the source documents for the synthesis essay. During this time, you can underline key words and make rough notes in the prompt booklet (which is not collected at the end of the exam), but not in the essay booklet.

This 15-minute period is crucial for building a solid foundation in understanding the prompts and the source documents. You'll need to put your active reading skills in high gear to get the best possible head start from the reading time available.

Why *Three* Essays?

The AP English Language and Composition Exam is designed to predict your ability to perform college-level work on such assignments as research papers and on-demand essay questions on tests. The AP exam's three types of essays essentially give you an opportunity to demonstrate some of the important skills required for those types of college assignments:

- using research sources to support your own position,

- examining sources critically in order to assess credible or faulty support, and

- arguing your own position persuasively.

The three essays simply separate—and highlight—these skills. In college work, you'll often be combining them.

HOW ARE THE ESSAYS SCORED?

The essays are scored separately on a scale of 9–0; then the three scores are combined. Each essay has equal weight in that combined score, which is then amalgamated with the result of the multiple-choice section to yield a final AP score of 1–5.

Together, the essays count for 55 percent of your final score. However, they take up 69 percent of the exam time, so it's easy to lose perspective and feel as if the essay section is more crucial to your success than it actually is. Doing well on the multiple-choice section is almost as important, even though it's only an hour long.

The grading is holistic, meaning that the reader will assess the overall quality of the essay rather than using a point-by-point checklist to arrive at a score. There are only a couple of exceptions, such as using fewer than three sources in the synthesis essay or consistently expressing ideas in such a confused way that the reader has great difficulty following the argument. Such lapses automatically knock an essay down to a lower point on the scoring scale.

Essays are graded holistically, based on the overall impression created by

- your grasp of the prompt.

- your ability to present concrete evidence and link it to your thesis.

- your skilful use of language to develop your argument.

Who Does the Scoring?

The readers are college English professors and AP course teachers who come together in June for an intense week of scoring. Thousands of readers go through thousands of essays in a few short days. A different person will read each of your essays.

Before the scoring starts, though, readers are trained in assessing that particular year's group of essays. Educational Testing Service (ETS), the non-profit organization that develops the exam, combs through the current crop of essays looking for work that represents a top-level 9 synthesis essay, a mediocre 4 rhetorical analysis essay, and so on, from that year's group. These sample essays are used to train the readers so the scoring will be as standardized as possible, given that the readers are still human beings who make subjective decisions.

So what? Well, the readers are your audience—the people you're addressing in your essays—and this scoring process tells you a few important things about them.

- First, they're buried in student essays, most of them mundane and mind-numbingly similar, and are just hoping for that one brilliant piece of writing that breaks the monotony and is a pleasure to read.

- Second, the readers have been trained to score your essays in relation to the work of the other students who took the exam that year. They're not judging your work in relation to some ideal standard of what a "perfect" essay should be.

- Third, these are teachers who guide students through English composition for a living. They know that polished essays require time, draft after draft, revision after revision. They don't expect an essay written in 40 minutes to be polished or perfect—they couldn't produce a flawless essay themselves in 40 minutes.

The essay section is the only place in this exam where your personality—at least to a limited degree—will shine through to test graders. Use it as an opportunity to show off what an exceptional thinker and writer you are.

What Are the Characteristics of Each Score Level?

The 9–0 scale breaks down into four categories: effective, adequate, inadequate and little success.

Effective essays score between 7 and 9. These are the essays with thorough and convincing discussions, perceptive analyses, well-developed positions, smooth organization and sophisticated control of expression. They demonstrate that the writer has understood and thought about the prompt and created an original response.

Adequate essays score 5 or 6. They address the prompt with appropriate explanations and evidence, do an adequate job of organizing and developing points, and express the writer's ideas clearly.

Inadequate work receives a score of 3 or 4. In these essays, the writer may have misunderstood the prompt or (in the case of the synthesis essay) the sources. Evidence and explanations are limited or simplistic, or even flat-out inappropriate. The organization does not flow smoothly, and the writer has less control of English language conventions in expressing ideas.

Essays that demonstrate **little success** receive a score of 0, 1 or 2. Here the writer has oversimplified or completely misunderstood the prompt, and presented evidence that is inappropriate or just plain unrelated. These essays show a consistent weakness in expressing ideas in a clear, organized and grammatically correct way.

Essays fall within one of those four categories based on the general characteristics of that category. The specific score within the two higher bands reflects more or less skill and depth in demonstrating those characteristics. Within the two lower bands, the number score reflects varying degrees of problems.

For the synthesis and argument essays, the 2014 mean score—the mid-point in the range, where half of the essays scored higher and half lower—was just below 5, on the fence between a "low adequate" and a "high inadequate" (if you can imagine such a concept). Students had more difficulty with the rhetorical analysis essay; there the mean score was just below 4, fully in the "inadequate" band.

In Chapters 5–7, you'll learn some more details about how these score levels apply to each type of essay.

WHAT ARE THE KEYS TO REACHING THE "EFFECTIVE" BAND?

Your goal is to rise above the vast middle bulge of essays that score 4 or 5. You're aiming for the "effective" band, or at least for a 6. How do you get there? By familiarizing yourself with the types of essays you'll have to write and by following a few basic tips.

Understand the Prompt

Use your active reading skills to tear the prompt apart.

- What is it *really* asking you to do? Understanding your task and maintaining a laser focus on it will keep you out of the swamp of inappropriate examples and unrelated arguments that populate the lower levels of the scoring scale.

- Does it have broader implications? For example, if a quote in the argumentative essay prompt states that a government has a duty to protect its citizens, could carrying out that duty lead to undesirable limits on people's freedom? And protect citizens from what? Who says that's a government's duty? The key here is to demonstrate some depth of thought instead of simply taking the prompt at face value. Where does it lead you?

- Does the prompt contain any terms that you should define in order to keep your discussion on target? Broad, "fuzzy" concepts such as "justice" or "education" are prime examples. They mean different things to different people. Giving a precise explanation of how you understand the term *as it's used in the prompt* and how you intend to discuss it will help you avoid producing a vague, rambling essay.

Take a Position

No fence-sitting, no ambiguity, no neutral descriptive essays. The highest scoring essays take a definite position on the prompt topic and argue it convincingly. They use strong, relevant evidence to support the position and leave no doubt about where the essay writer stands.

Even in the rhetorical analysis essay you're expected to take a position: "This is the author's purpose, these are the three (or four, or five) most important techniques the author uses to achieve that purpose, and (very important) this is *how* each technique makes the purpose more effective." Another student might see a different purpose or highlight other techniques in the passage, but then that student would be taking a different position.

Manage Your Time

No one is going to tell you that your first 40 minutes are up and it's time to move on to the next essay. That's up to you. Since each essay has equal weight in the combined score, you should devote about the same amount of time to each one. A slightly better score on one essay will not make up for a bad score on another. Aim for the following breakdown within each 40-minute period:

- 3–5 minutes to think through the prompt and plan your essay

- 30–35 minutes to write

- 1–2 minutes to proofread

BC UR 2 GOOD 4 THIS

Even though you're under tremendous time pressure, don't use shorthand symbols such as "&" or "w/" or "tho." Get in the habit of using a relatively high level of discourse on AP exam essays. Email or instant messenger-style writing won't impress the reader who is scoring your essay.

The more you practice writing each type of essay within 40 minutes, the more you'll gain a sense of how that block of time "feels" and the better you'll get at making occasional time checks to stay on track instead of engaging in distracting clock-watching that might only increase your anxiety.

Your school has likely given you sample essay prompts for practice. You can also find example prompts from several previous years on the AP website at **http://apcentral.collegeboard.com/apc/members/exam/exam_information/2001.html**.

Plan Your Response

Just getting into the car and starting to drive could land you anywhere, at a great waste of time and fuel. It's the same with just starting to write—you could easily spend 20 minutes and then realize you're seriously off track.

To make the best use of your 30–35 minutes of writing time, you first need to spend a few minutes planning where you want to end up and how you'll get there.

- Exactly what do you want to conclude about the topic of the synthesis prompt? Which three sources best support the points you want to make? In which order should you incorporate them into your discussion? Does one of the sources present a significant opposing argument that you should mention and then refute?

- In the rhetorical analysis passage, what is the writer's purpose? What techniques make that purpose clear and effective to you? In which order should you explain them?

- What position do you want to take about the topic presented for the argumentative essay? What evidence from your own experiences or reading could you use to support your position? How can you make your argument persuasive?

Organize Your Points

You're likely familiar with the five-paragraph essay model. While it's not the only method of organizing an essay, there's nothing wrong with using it on this exam if it's already a comfortable model for you. It goes like this:

Paragraph 1:

- an introductory sentence or two that captures the reader and announces, "This is going to be a great essay within your pile of boring, mediocre essays."

- the thesis that you intend to argue in your essay. A good thesis is debatable (that is, someone could possibly have a different opinion) and narrow enough to be covered adequately in a short essay.

- a brief list of the three pieces of evidence you'll use in the essay to prove your thesis

- a transition to the body of your essay

Paragraphs 2–4:

- one paragraph for each piece of evidence you listed in the first paragraph, in the same order as you listed them. Each piece of evidence should be linked directly to your thesis, with a clear explanation of *why* it supports your thesis. One of these paragraphs might describe a conflicting view which you then shoot down, or which supports an "only in certain circumstances" position in your thesis.

Paragraph 5:

- a conclusion that doesn't simply restate your thesis. You've developed your argument throughout the body of your essay, so it's now meatier and more convincing. The conclusion should remind the reader of your now-stronger position.

Of course, there's no rule that says you have to stop at three pieces of evidence; you might have four. Just don't take on more complexity and length than you can handle well in 40 minutes. And if you're familiar with another method of organizing an essay and feel more comfortable with it, then use it, as long as it provides a clear organizational framework for your points.

Get Off to a Strong Start

A great first impression goes a long way. Remember your audience of bored readers mired in stacks of mediocre essays? If you can wow them right off the top, you'll create an expectation that the rest of your essay belongs in the "effective" band, too. That initial glow of "finally—*finally*—a good essay!" can diminish the impact of later lapses in greatness.

Suppose the prompt for a rhetorical analysis essay quotes from a speech by Mayor Nellie Smith attributing her election victory to the many volunteers who worked on her campaign. You could clearly announce, "This is going to be a mediocre essay" by starting out with a sentence like, "This essay will describe how Mayor Nellie Smith uses rhetorical strategies to communicate the main point of her speech." Yawn. And do you have any clue what her main point is or what rhetorical strategies she uses? Even if you eventually do get to an insightful point later in the essay, chances are your opening has already caused the reader to tune out and miss it.

On the other hand, you could grab the reader's attention with an opening like, "Dedicated volunteers are the bricks and mortar of successful political campaigns. That's the overriding message of Mayor Nellie Smith's speech thanking them for their passionate support and acknowledging the key role they played. Through the skilful use of parallelism, repetition, and analogy, she makes her listeners feel that the victory is really theirs, likely winning their support after she takes office, too."

That stronger start doesn't take a lot of extra effort or time, but it shows the reader that you understand the mayor's purpose and rhetorical strategies, and can express your ideas with style and sophistication. You've just raised the reader's impression of your abilities, even if your essay tapers off to a more routine effort later on.

Express Your Ideas Clearly, Concisely, Correctly, Persuasively and with Flair

Oh yes, you *can* do that.

Be clear. You should know exactly what you want to say as a result of your initial planning and organizing. Imagine yourself on a clear path instead of stumbling around in the underbrush. If you find you're getting tangled up in long sentences or overlapping ideas, pause for a minute and think of *telling* someone right beside you what you mean to say. This strategy usually helps clarify your thoughts and language in your own mind. Now write down what you just "said."

Be specific. Making a vague statement such as, "The demand for subsidized housing increased a lot during the past few years (Source A)" isn't good enough if Source A actually referred to a study that proved demand grew by 65 percent between 2000 and 2010. Being as specific and concrete as possible will add credibility and impact to your words. Your argument will be clearer and more persuasive.

Be concise. That doesn't mean leaving out details that are essential to your argument. It means leaving out pointless repetition and padding. Say it once, precisely and with punch, then move on.

Say it correctly. Use proper grammar. Essays with so many errors that the reader can't follow the argument are consigned to the bottom of the scoring scale.

Create correct paragraphs, too, Have you ever opened a book and seen nothing but very long paragraphs? Your next thought is probably, "Do I *really* have to read all of this?" That's exactly what readers think when they see an essay without paragraphs.

So create proper paragraphs—one main idea per paragraph, beginning with a topic sentence and ending with a smooth transition to the next paragraph—and make them obvious by leaving a space between or indenting them.

> Create a great first impression before the person scoring your essay even reads a word.
> - Write legibly.
> - Make sure readers can see the paragraphs at first glance.
> - Don't stoke out too many things.
>
> Your work should look neat, organized and clear.

Say it smoothly. Lead the reader through your argument with seamless transitions between your points and paragraphs. Transition words and phrases such as "on the other hand," "in addition," "therefore" and "nevertheless" will do the job.

Say it persuasively. These essays are all evidence-based writing, so you need strong evidence that supports each of your main points. Connect each piece of evidence clearly to the point it supports, and explain exactly how or why the evidence is relevant. Unrelated evidence and vague, weak explanations won't persuade anyone.

The reader expects you to write like someone who is suffering through a tedious, nerve-racking exercise. If you write like someone who enjoys writing, the reader will enjoy reading your essay and reward you.

Say it with flair. Is there a punchier, more descriptive word you could use? Perhaps "shack" or "cabin" or "mansion" instead of "house." Can you make the phrasing of a sentence slicker? For example, instead of "The candidate's appearance was neat, and the boss gave him the job right away," let yourself get carried away and say, "The candidate's Armani suit and sleek silk tie captivated the boss, who slipped a contract across the table without comment or hesitation."

It doesn't take long to think of a more forceful word or a stronger way of saying something if you put your mind in that track, and even a few of these sprinkled throughout your essay can impress the reader with your ability to control the language and use it to achieve your desired effect.

> **Make it Easy for the Reader To Give You a High Score.**
> - Understand the task in the prompt.
> - Think about where the prompt takes you.
> - Stake out a definite position.
> - Plan and organize your points before you start to write.
> - Be clear and specific.
> - Link each piece of evidence directly to your thesis.
> - Use correct grammar and paragraph construction.
> - Vary sentence length and structure.
> - Write legibly.

Proofread

You won't have time to revise, but leaving a couple of minutes to proofread can allow you to fix little errors that you would *never* have made if you weren't writing in such a rush. And that, in turn, might just knock your essay up a notch on the scoring scale. You'll have to write your essay in dark blue or black pen—no pencils allowed on this section of the exam. However, you can stroke out any errors you want the readers to ignore (they will) and then write in (neatly) your correction.

In Chapters 5–7, you'll get a closer look at the types of prompts on the exam, and find additional suggestions for responding to the three different types.

Summary

General Essay Information

- There are three essays: synthesis, rhetorical analysis and argumentative.

- You have a total of 2 hours, 15 minutes—40 minutes for each essay plus 15 minutes to read the prompts and the sources for the synthesis essay.

- The three essays count for 55 percent of your total score. Each essay is worth an equal amount.

Essay Scoring

- Each essay is scored by a different reader on a scale from 0 to 9.

- The essays are scored "holistically" based on the reader's overall impression.

- The reader wants good essays that are easy to score.

- Essays that earn high scores show that the writer has thought deeply about the prompt, taken a clear position, supported that position with appropriate examples, and argued that position persuasively with sophisticated control of the language.

- Boring essays that do only an adequate job of those things earn mid-range scores.

- Students who misunderstand the prompt, use inappropriate examples and can't express their ideas clearly can expect low scores.

Presentation

- Make your essay look neat, clear and well organized with legible writing, obvious breaks between paragraphs and few strike-outs, if any.

Expression

○ Capture the reader and create a great first impression with your opening paragraph.

○ Vary your choice of words and sentence structure. A little extra effort will pay great dividends.

○ Use correct grammar and paragraph construction.

Content

○ Plan and organize your points before you start writing.

○ Address the prompt. If you write a great essay that doesn't address the prompt, you will receive a low score.

○ Develop your argument based on strong, relevant evidence. Connect each piece of evidence directly to the point it supports.

Chapter 5
How to
Approach the
Synthesis Essay

SYNTHESIZE WHAT?

By "synthesis," the AP exam writers mean two things:

1. using sources to develop your position, and

2. citing those sources accurately.

High-scoring synthesis essays draw a clear connection between a source and a particular point in the writer's argument. By the time you get down to a score of 5 (the bottom of the "adequate" band), the link is still apparent but "strained."

Also at the higher score levels, the essay writer cites the specific source being used (with a simple reference such as "Source A"; you're not expected to remember formal citation formats for this exam). Writers who score in the lower bands merely summarize a jumbled collection of points they've read in various sources, without citing a specific source and linking it to a particular point in their argument.

Your performance on the synthesis essay will help the readers (and yourself) predict how well you'll be able to handle college research assignments. In particular, your essay will show whether you can

- judge the best sources to back up your position

- incorporate other writers' claims or explanations into your *own* argument

- draw on sources in the order that develops your argument in the most logical, persuasive way

Steps to Choosing Sources

1. Analyze the prompt.

2. Decide which position you want to take.

3. Select three sources that provide the best support for your position.

How Many Sources?

The prompt will instruct you to use at least three, and in most cases that's a safe choice. Trying to use more than three might lead you into an unnecessarily complicated essay at best, and at worst, a pyramid of similar, superficially treated points piled up on top of each other. Using fewer than three will definitely knock your essay down into the "inadequate" scoring band.

Three sources are enough to show progress in your argument (for example, a more general or older source of support followed by increasingly specific or more recent claims, each one building upon the previous one). If you choose to argue a qualified position, three sources will give you, for instance, two authors who argue against something and one who is in favor of it in particular circumstances, supporting your qualified rejection of the claim.

Having a Conversation with Your Sources

Since your aim is synthesis, you need to weave the three sources into your own discussion of the prompt, using them to support and develop the position you've chosen to take. The exam writers offer a helpful image of how to do that. They call it having a conversation with your sources.

Imagine the creators of your chosen sources are sitting together in a living room discussing the topic of the prompt. Now you walk in and join the conversation. You wouldn't simply record each author's (or artist's) comments. That's the equivalent of just copying and pasting chunks from each source into your essay and stringing them together.

No, you'd respond to each person's comments, build on them, use them to enrich your own views about the topic. You would add something to the discussion your three authors are having, and they would add something to your own understanding of the topic. Then, if you had a conversation with each author individually, you'd try to understand that author's position and add your own ideas to the discussion. That's what the test writers mean.

Direct Quote vs. Paraphrase

When you're drawing a source into your argument, you have a choice of paraphrasing (summarizing in your own words) what the author says, or quoting some of his or her words directly (within quotation marks, of course).

In many cases, paraphrasing makes it easier to incorporate someone else's ideas smoothly into your own. Several quotes, too, could make your essay appear to be more of a copy-and-paste exercise than a synthesis. However, if an author uses a particularly striking phrase or unusual wording that would be difficult to paraphrase accurately, then an occasional direct quote could make your essay more vivid.

SAMPLE ESSAY—HERE'S HOW IT'S DONE

Here's an example of a synthesis essay prompt. As you go through it, use your active reading skills to make sure you understand exactly what it's asking you to do.

The Directions

(Suggested writing time—40 minutes. This question counts for one-third of the total essay section score.)

Directions: The following prompt is based on the accompanying six sources.

This questions requires you to synthesize a variety of source into a coherent, well-written essay. When you synthesize sources you refer to them to develop your position and cite them accurately. *Your argument should be central; the sources should support this argument. Avoid merely summarizing sources.*

Remember to attribute both direct and indirect citations.

Introduction

Throughout history, people have portrayed men and women differently, often requiring of the former masculinity and of the latter femininity. What does it mean to be a man, or masculine, and a woman, or feminine?

Assignment

Read the following sources (including the introductory information) carefully. **Then, in an essay that synthesizes at least three of the sources for support, take a position that defends, challenges, or qualifies the claim that men must be masculine and women must be feminine.**

You may refer to the sources by their titles (Source A, Source B, etc.) or by the descriptions in parentheses.

Source A (Kipling)

Source B (De Beauvoir)

Source C (Shakespeare)

Source D (Wollstonecraft)

Source E (David)

Source F (Angelou)

It's Time to Read

There's quite a lot of reading (not to mention some art interpretation) as you go through the sources for a synthesis essay question. In order to use your reading time effectively, before you start you should already be clear on what the prompt is asking you to do and have some idea which position you want to take.

In this example, the prompt clearly tells you to "defend" (agree with), "challenge" (disagree with) or "qualify" (agree or disagree, but only in certain defined circumstances) the claim that "men must be masculine and women must be feminine." To show the depth of thought that pulls an essay up into the "effective" score band, you also need to consider questions beyond that claim. In other words, use your active reading skills on the prompt. It doesn't take much extra time if you've already put your brain into "active reading" mode. What do "masculine" and "feminine" mean? Who says men and women "must" be something? Why would a society of "masculine" men and "feminine" women be desirable—or not desirable?

After you've examined the prompt's claim, decide which of the three positions (defend, challenge, or qualify) you'd probably like to take. Now you're ready to read through the sources with a fairly clear idea of what you're looking for. You want three sources that will enrich the position you've chosen, and will help you develop your argument in a logical way. If two sources say essentially the same thing, you probably don't need both—which one is stronger? Which sources deal with the "beyond the prompt" questions you asked during your active reading? If you've chosen to take a qualified position, which source presents an opposing viewpoint that will support your "only in these circumstances" argument?

> ### Linear Graffiti
> Underlining, circling, and making notes in the margins of the sources are all good practices, but don't get too carried away! A good rule of thumb is to underline no more than five words at a time. Anything longer should be marked with simple brackets. The purpose of marking the passage is to make information easy to retrieve.

To help you locate supporting points later on while you're writing, underline a few key words and put a stroke through sources you don't want to use. Then plan your essay—jot down a quick outline of the points you want to make, the order in which you'll explain them as you develop your argument, and the source you'll use (and cite) to support each point.

If you can keep your head when all about you
Are losing theirs and blaming it on you;
If you can trust yourself when all men doubt you,
But make allowance for their doubting too;
If you can wait and not be tired by waiting,
Or, being lied about, don't deal in lies,
Or, being hated, don't give way to hating,
And yet don't look too good, nor talk too wise;

If you can dream—and not make dreams your master;
If you can think—and not make thoughts your aim;
If you can meet with triumph and disaster
And treat those two impostors just the same;
If you can bear to hear the truth you've spoken
Twisted by knaves to make a trap for fools,
Or watch the things you gave your life to broken,
And stoop and build 'em up with wornout tools;

If you can make one heap of all your winnings
And risk it on one turn of pitch-and-toss,
And lose, and start again at your beginnings
And never breath a word about your loss;
If you can force your heart and nerve and sinew
To serve your turn long after they are gone,
And so hold on when there is nothing in you
Except the Will which says to them: "Hold on";

If you can talk with crowds and keep your virtue,
Or walk with kings—nor lose the common touch;
If neither foes nor loving friends can hurt you;
If all men count with you, but none too much;
If you can fill the unforgiving minute
With sixty seconds' worth of distance run,
Yours is the Earth and everything that's in it,
And—which is more—you'll be a Man my son!

Source B

De Beauvoir, Simone. <u>The Second Sex</u>. Translated by H. M. Parshley.
New York: Alfred A. Knopf, 1949.

The following passage is excerpted from a work of feminist philosophy.

The fact that I ask [the question, "What is a woman?"] is in itself significant. A man would never set out to write a book on the peculiar situation of the human male. But if I wish to define myself, I must first of all say: 'I am a woman'; on this truth must be based all further discussion. A man never begins by presenting himself as an individual of a certain sex; it goes without saying that he is a man. The terms masculine and feminine are used symmetrically only as a matter of form, as on legal papers. In actuality the relation of the two sexes is not quite like that of two electrical poles, for man represents both the positive and the neutral, as is indicated by the common use of man to designate human beings in general; whereas woman represents only the negative, defined by limiting criteria, without reciprocity. In the midst of an abstract discussion it is vexing to hear a man say: 'You think thus and so because you are a woman'; but I know that my only defense is to reply: 'I think thus and so because it is true,' thereby removing my subjective self from the argument. It would be out of the question to reply: 'And you think the contrary because you are a man', for it is understood that the fact of being a man is no peculiarity. A man is in the right in being a man; it is the woman who is in the wrong. It amounts to this: just as for the ancients there was an absolute vertical with reference to which the oblique was defined, so there is an absolute human type, the masculine. Woman has ovaries, a uterus: these peculiarities imprison her in her subjectivity, circumscribe her within the limits of her own nature. It is often said that she thinks with her glands. Man superbly ignores the fact that his anatomy also includes glands, such as the testicles, and that they secrete hormones. He thinks of his body as a direct and normal connection with the world, which he believes he apprehends objectively, whereas he regards the body of woman as a hindrance, a prison, weighed down by everything peculiar to it.

Source C

Shakespeare, William. <u>Henry V</u>. c. 1599.

In the following dialogue, Henry the Fifth is speaking to one of his nobles, Lord Exeter. Exeter has just seen two of Henry's uncles, the Duke of York and the Earl of Suffolk, die in the tremendous battle with the French.

Exeter: The Duke of York commends him to your Majesty.
King: Lives he, good uncle? Thrice within the hour
I saw him down; thrice up again and fighting,
From helmet to the spur all blood he was.

Exeter: In which array, brave soldier, doth he lie,
Larding the plain; and by his bloody side,
Yoke-fellow to his honor-owing wounds,
The noble Earl of Suffolk also lies.
Suffolk first died; and York, all haggled over,
Comes to him, where in gore he lay insteeped,
And takes him by the beard, kisses the gashes
That bloodily did yawn upon his face.
He cries aloud, "Tarry, my cousin Suffolk!
My soul shall thine keep company to heaven.
Tarry, sweet soul, for mine, then fly abreast;
As in this glorious and well-foughten field
We kept together in our chivalry!"
Upon these words I came, and cheered him up;
He smiled me in the face, raught me his hand,
And, with a feeble gripe, says, "Dear my lord,
Commend my service to my Sovereign."
So did he turn, and over Suffolk's neck
He threw his wounded arm, and kissed his lips;
And so, espoused to death, with blood he sealed
A testament of noble-ending love.
The pretty and sweet manner of it forced
Those waters from me which I would have stopped;
But I had not so much of man in me,
And all my mother came into mine eyes
And gave me up to tears.

Source D

Wollstonecraft, Mary. A Vindication of the Rights of Women. 1792.

The following passage is excerpted from a treatise on women's rights.

To account for, and excuse the tyranny of man, many ingenious arguments have been brought forward to prove, that the two sexes, in the acquirement of virtue, ought to aim at attaining a very different character: or, to speak explicitly, women are not allowed to have sufficient strength of mind to acquire what really deserves the name of virtue. Yet it should seem, allowing them to have souls, that there is but one way appointed by Providence to lead mankind to either virtue or happiness.

If then women are not a swarm of ephemeron triflers, why should they be kept in ignorance under the specious name of innocence? Men complain, and with reason, of the follies and caprices of our sex, when they do not keenly satirize our headstrong passions and groveling vices. Behold, I should answer, the natural effect of ignorance! The mind will ever be unstable that has only prejudices to rest on, and the current will run with destructive fury when there are no barriers to break its force. Women are told from their infancy, and taught by the example of their mothers, that a little knowledge of human weakness, justly termed cunning, softness of temper, outward obedience, and a scrupulous attention to a puerile kind of propriety, will obtain for them the protection of man; and should they be beautiful, every thing else is needless, for, at least, twenty years of their lives.…

How grossly do they insult us who thus advise us only to render ourselves gentle…

The following painting depicts a scene from Roman legend.

Source F

Angelou, Maya. "Phenomenal Woman." <u>And Still I Rise.</u> New York: Random House, 1978.

Pretty women wonder where my secret lies.
I'm not cute or built to suit a fashion
model's size
But when I start to tell them,
They think I'm telling lies.
I say,
It's in the reach of my arms
The span of my hips,
The stride of my step,
The curl of my lips.
I'm a woman
Phenomenally.
Phenomenal woman,
That's me.

I walk into a room
Just as cool as you please,
And to a man,
The fellows stand or
Fall down on their knees.
Then they swarm around me,
A hive of honey bees.
I say,
It's the fire in my eyes,
And the flash of my teeth,
The swing in my waist,
And the joy in my feet.
I'm a woman
Phenomenally.
Phenomenal woman,
That's me.

Men themselves have wondered
What they see in me.
They try so much
But they can't touch
My inner mystery.
When I try to show them
They say they still can't see.
I say,
It's in the arch of my back,
The sun of my smile,
The ride of my breasts,
The grace of my style.
I'm a woman

Phenomenally.
Phenomenal woman,
That's me.

Now you understand
Just why my head's not bowed.
I don't shout or jump about
Or have to talk real loud.
When you see me passing
It ought to make you proud.
I say,
It's in the click of my heels,
The bend of my hair,
The palm of my hand,
The need of my care,
'Cause I'm a woman
Phenomenally.
Phenomenal woman,
That's me.

You Try It

Now you're ready to begin writing. Remember to leave a couple of minutes at the end to proofread your work.

After you're finished writing your essay, take a look at the following page. This is a student essay that was written in the allotted 40 minutes. As you read it, evaluate how well it

- addresses the prompt

- integrates the sources

- develops the writer's argument

- expresses the writer's ideas.

It's Not Me

Your essay will seem more professional and credible if you use third-person narrative instead of first-person ("I think...").

A Student Essay

Every society tries to define what is masculine and what is feminine. In doing so, all societies assign certain traits to men, and others to women. In our own society, manhood is associated with bravery, stoicism, strength, and wisdom; the conventional (and insulting) view is that womanhood is the lack of those virtues. Instead, women are valued primarily because they are pleasing to men—even when they try to show themselves as powerful and strong on their own terms, they still look to male approval to measure their success. While one may wish to challenge these notions, men and women alike seem to agree with them—suggesting an inherent truth about men and women.

Our society's traditional view is that manhood is associated with bravery in battle, strength in the face of suffering, and level-headed rationality. Rudyard Kipling's poem, "If," provides a conclusive summary to manly virtues. For him, a boy becomes a man when he can wait patiently, endure the criticisms of lesser men and the reversals of fortune without complaint, and give his all by seeking success at every moment, neither proud in victory nor broken in defeat. These are admirable qualities in anyone—but Kipling assigns them specifically to men. Men are also stoic in the face of emotion: all the way back to Shakespeare's time, men were supposed to be strong enough to fight their own tears. Losing that battle is a feminine sign of weakness.

This cultural assumption has not gone unnoticed by women. Simone De Beauvoir notices that in discussions between men and women, the man's viewpoint is naturally considered to be "both the positive and the neutral" one. Men are the standard, the "absolute vertical," by which women are judged—and found wanting. An earlier feminist writer, Mary Wollstonecraft, also noticed (and objected to) the difference in social roles for men and women: in her view, men keep women in ignorance by denying them education and responsibility, but then say that women are not worthy of these things because it is their nature to be frivolous and overly emotional. Instead, women are to appeal to men for protection. Men are valuable in themselves; women cannot be, but must only be measured by their relationships with men.

It would be easy to dismiss the complaints of the feminist writers, except that both male and female creators reinforce those same complaints. Consider David's "Oath of the Horatii." The scene shows a father stoically offering swords to his three sons, who are ready to go bravely off to war. Meanwhile, the women helplessly cry in the background, victim of their emotions and their own lack of courage. And in Maya Angelou's "Phenomenal Woman," for all the speaker's efforts to describe herself as a powerful, phenomenal woman, the measure of her quality is in the way "fellows...swarm around" her, wondering "what they see in" her. In the end, rightly or wrongly, both women and men have subconsciously agreed with the judgment: men are brave doers, while women are their accessories.

What did you think? This essay has some strong points:

- The writer shows excellent control of the language, expressing her ideas clearly and concisely.

- Sources are integrated smoothly into the writer's argument, and are cited accurately.

- She develops her argument skilfully, first defining "masculine" and "feminine," then outlining feminist objections, then circling back to the statement that, nevertheless, everyone seems to agree on the traditional definitions.

Did you pick up the weaknesses in this essay, though? They're significant.

- Right answer to the wrong question: The writer misread the prompt. It didn't ask her to define "masculine" and "feminine." It asked her to take a position on the claim that "men must be masculine and women must be feminine." She touches upon the real question when she mentions that in Shakespeare's time, "men were supposed to be strong," but then she drops it immediately and goes back to simple definitions, ignoring the crucial word "must" and not staking out a definite position.

- Too many sources: Instead of choosing the best three sources to support her argument, the writer seems determined to use them all. As a result, her argument functions as glue holding a string of sources together, none of them discussed in much depth, instead of as a case for the writer's own position, made stronger by the source pulled in to support each major point. In this essay, the sources shape her argument, piling up one similar point on top of another, instead of her argument determining her choice of sources.

There are some minor weaknesses, too. The opening isn't a strong one that would grab the reader and make him want to keep reading, and the conclusion seems tacked on. The most serious problem, though, is the writer's misreading of the prompt, which takes her whole essay off track and pushes it down the scoring scale. The "sources over argument" quality, the oversimplification and misreading of the prompt would put this essay into the "inadequate" band at a 4. However, the writer's strong control of expression and flowing organization would likely elevate it to a 5.

By following our strategies and using the essays that you've seen as models, you can aim for—and achieve—higher scores.

Next, let's take a look at how to tackle the rhetorical analysis essay.

Chapter 6
How to Approach the Rhetorical Analysis Essay

FIRST THING'S FIRST: WHAT'S A RHETORICAL STRATEGY?

Authors use certain techniques, in both the language and the structure of the piece they're writing, to convey their messages effectively and to achieve the intended effect(s) on their audiences. Speakers use these techniques, too. Often they're trying to persuade their audiences to do something or to agree with their points of view.

In Chapters 8–11, you'll find explanations and examples of rhetorical strategies, plus questions so you can practice using them. Once you become familiar with rhetorical strategies and the effects they can have, you'll probably start spotting them in your day-to-day life, too—in ads, in interviews given by politicians or in instructions from your teachers, for instance.

YOUR TASKS IN THE RHETORICAL ANALYSIS ESSAY

The AP readers are looking for three main things in the rhetorical analysis essay:

- an understanding of the author's intended purpose

- the ability to identify the chief rhetorical strategies used to achieve that purpose effectively

- an analysis of *how* those strategies contribute to the development and effectiveness of the writer's argument, *supported by references to the text*

Of course, they readers are also assessing the usual skilful control of the language, clear expression and smooth organization that they want to see in all three essays.

In the rhetorical analysis essay, the AP readers don't want a summary of the entire passage, or an argument for or against the author's main point. Your focus is strictly on what the author's purpose is, and what rhetorical strategies the author uses to achieve it effectively. Students typically find this essay the most challenging of the three, and straying from that focus is often where they go wrong.

Another common problem that lands essays in the lower score bands is being too general. An essay might describe the author's purpose right up front, in the first paragraph (a good idea, incidentally), and identify the three or four most important rhetorical strategies, but then fail to link each one to the author's purpose with a specific, thorough explanation of exactly how that strategy makes the message more effective. Direct references to the passage are a must, too, or the explanation runs the risk of being too general and oversimplified.

So your first task is to identify the author's purpose, which your active reading skills will enable you to do. After that, your task is to detect the main rhetorical strategies and build a convincing case for why and how each one of them advances the author's purpose.

The Rhetorical Diamond

While you're reading the prompt and the passage, imagine—and try to flesh out—a baseball diamond with the following four points:

- author

- purpose

- audience

- context

The passage represents an interaction among those points. Understanding them will help you recognize rhetorical strategies that a particular type of author might use to achieve a definite purpose with a specific type of audience within a distinct context.

For example, you would expect a politician trying to win support from a mass audience at a rally to use different rhetorical techniques than a heart disease specialist writing the findings from a research study for publication in a professional, peer-reviewed journal. The politician, because of the verbal delivery and the diversity of the mass audience, would use simpler language, emotional appeals (pathos) and techniques such as repetition. The heart disease specialist, on the other hand, would use technical language and techniques to inspire respect for her qualifications and the thoroughness of her work (ethos).

The prompt will give you some of the information you need to describe the four points of the rhetorical baseball diamond. With a solid understanding of those points, you'll be able to predict at least some of the rhetorical strategies you can expect to find as you apply your active reading skills to the passage.

More Tips for Spotting Rhetorical Strategies

The author's main point will give you some clues about the rhetorical strategies you might find in the passage. Does it deal with a controversial topic, or with a "motherhood and apple pie" position that would create almost no opposition from anyone? Is it promoting a new, "fuzzy" concept that the audience would find hard to understand, or a topic that would be familiar to most people?

Trying to put yourself in the audience's shoes can also help you uncover rhetorical strategies. If you were part of that audience, at that time and in that context, would this piece of writing influence you? Why? Did it help you understand something through the use of examples, for instance? Did it make you feel the author sympathized with your concerns, perhaps through the use of anecdotes that echoed your own experiences? Did it keep bringing you back to one central idea through the skilful use of repetition?

Now that you know your tasks and where you need to focus, let's look at a couple of rhetorical analysis prompts and passages.

A PERSUASIVE SPEECH EXAMPLE

Below is a sample rhetorical analysis prompt. Start by squeezing as much information as you can from the instructions

The Directions

Question 2

(Suggested time—40 minutes. This question counts for one-third of the total
essay score.)

The passage below is extracted from Booker T. Washington's most famous speech,
known as "The Atlanta Compromise Address." Washington presented the address
to the Cotton States and International Exposition in 1895. Read the entire passage
carefully. Then write an essay analyzing the rhetorical strategies that Washington
uses to convey his point of view.

As you're reading the prompt, look for how much it tells you about the four points
on the rhetorical diamond.

- **Author**—You'll need to draw on your own knowledge about Booker T.
  Washington. You may already know that he was a famous African American
  leader and scholar of the nineteenth century. Even if you're not familiar with
  him, though, the prompt does give you some clues that he was influential
  ("most famous speech" and "International Exposition").

- **Purpose**—Sometimes the prompt will outline the author's purpose; sometimes it won't. In this case, the prompt isn't too helpful. However, you can
  guess that with the opportunity to speak at such a major event, Washington's
  purpose probably involves persuading his listeners about something.

- **Audience**—At a southern ("Cotton States") trade gathering ("Exposition")
  casting a broader geographical net ("International") back in 1895 (just
  30 years after the end of the Civil War), you can guess that the listeners
  Washington is addressing are primarily white business, industrial and political leaders from both the south and the north.

- **Context**—Washington is giving a speech to a large, important audience, so
  you can be looking for rhetorical strategies that you would expect to find in
  verbal delivery (such as repetition).

Armed with the information you've gained from the prompt, you can now put your
active reading skills into gear looking for Washington's purpose and his rhetorical
strategies in the passage. As you identify each rhetorical strategy, keep asking yourself, "Why did Washington use this? How does it help him achieve his purpose?"
because you'll need to answer those questions in your essay.

First try writing your own essay in 40 minutes, then read the sample student essay
and assessment that follow the passage.

The Passage

One-third of the population of the South is of the Negro race. No enterprise seeking the material, civil, or moral welfare of this section can disregard this element of our

Line population and reach the highest success. I but convey
5 to you, Mr. President and Directors, the sentiment of the masses of my race when I say that in no way have the value and manhood of the American Negro been more fittingly and generously recognized than by the managers of this magnificent Exposition at every stage of its progress. It is
10 a recognition that will do more to cement the friendship of the two races than any occurrence since the dawn of our freedom.

Not only this, but the opportunity here afforded will awaken among us a new era of industrial progress. Ignorant
15 and inexperienced, it is not strange that in the first years of our new life we began at the top instead of at the bottom; that a seat in Congress or the state legislature was more sought than real estate or industrial skill; that the political convention or stump speaking had more attractions than
20 starting a dairy farm or truck garden.

A ship lost at sea for many days suddenly sighted a friendly vessel. From the mast of the unfortunate vessel was seen a signal, "Water, water; we die of thirst!" The answer from the friendly vessel at once came back, "Cast
25 down your bucket where you are." A second time the signal, "Water, water; send us water!" ran up from the distressed vessel, and was answered, "Cast down your bucket where you are." And a third and fourth signal for water was answered, "Cast down your bucket where you are." The
30 captain of the distressed vessel, at last heeding the injunction, cast down his bucket, and it came up full of fresh, sparkling water from the mouth of the Amazon River. To those of my race who depend on bettering their condition in a foreign land or who underestimate the importance
35 of cultivating friendly relations with the Southern white man, who is their next-door neighbor, I would say: "Cast down your bucket where you are"—cast it down in making friends in every manly way of the people of all races by whom we are surrounded.
40 Cast it down in agriculture, mechanics, in commerce, in domestic service, and in the professions. And in this connection it is well to bear in mind that whatever other sins the South may be called to bear, when it comes to business, pure and simple, it is in the South that the Negro
45 is given a man's chance in the commercial world, and in nothing is this Exposition more eloquent than in emphasizing this chance. Our greatest danger is that in the great leap from slavery to freedom we may overlook the fact that the masses of us are to live by the productions of our hands,
50 and fail to keep in mind that we shall prosper in proportion as we learn to dignify and glorify common labor, and put brains and skill into the common occupations of life; shall prosper in proportion as we learn to draw the line between

the superficial and the substantial, the ornamental gewgaws
55 of life and the useful. No race can prosper till it learns
that there is as much dignity in tilling a field as in writing
a poem. It is at the bottom of life we must begin, and not
at the top. Nor should we permit our grievances to over-
shadow our opportunities.
60   To those of the white race who look to the incoming of
those of foreign birth and strange tongue and habits for the
prosperity of the South, were I permitted I would repeat
what I say to my own race, "Cast down your bucket where
you are." Cast it down among the eight millions of Negroes
65 whose habits you know, whose fidelity and love you have
tested in days when to have proved treacherous meant the
ruin of your firesides. Cast down your bucket among these
people who have, without strikes and labour wars, tilled
your fields, cleared your forests, built your railroads and
70 cities, and brought forth treasures from the bowels of the
earth, and helped make possible this magnificent repre-
sentation of the progress of the South. Casting down your
bucket among my people, helping and encouraging them
as you are doing on these grounds, and to education of
75 head, hand, and heart, you will find that they will buy your
surplus land, make blossom the waste places in your fields,
and run your factories. While doing this, you can be sure
in the future, as in the past, that you and your families will
be surrounded by the most patient, faithful, law-abiding,
80 and unresentful people that the world has seen. As we have
proved our loyalty to you in the past, in nursing your children, watching by the sick-bed of your mothers and fathers,
and often following them with tear-dimmed eyes to their
graves, so in the future, in our humble way, we shall stand
85 by you with a devotion that no foreigner can approach,
ready to lay down our lives, if need be, in defense of yours,
interlacing our industrial, commercial, civil, and religious
life with yours in a way that shall make the interests of
both races one. In all things that are purely social we can be
90 as separate as the fingers, yet one as the hand in all things
essential to mutual progress.

The Analysis

What is Washington's purpose? Is he an angry man demanding change? Is he an
outraged man warning of rebellion? Is he a timid man begging indulgence? No,
he is none of these. Booker T. Washington's persona is that of the inspirational
Southern preacher who urges blacks and whites to rally round the same economic
flag. He employs three principal rhetorical strategies in this part of his speech.

1. Throughout, there is an appeal to ethos.

2. Next, there is the central image of the bucket, which could be considered
   part of either an extended metaphor or an allegory; this is first addressed to
   the black population, then to white people.

**Give 'Em What They
Want**

When you're analyzing
an author's rhetorical
strategies, the AP reader
wants to see direct
references to the passage.

3. Finally, to support the imagery, Washington uses analogy (e.g., "there is as much dignity in tilling a field as in writing a poem"), scare tactics (e.g., the references to people of foreign birth), and interesting deductive reasoning. Washington contends that the continual loyalty and hard work of blacks in the past proves that they will be loyal, hardworking collaborators in the future. While the claim is reasonable, the logic is not; in the past that Washington is talking about, the blacks were slaves. For the most part, they had no choice but to be hardworking and loyal.

Now, keep all the above information in mind as you read the following sample essay, which was written in 40 minutes under actual test conditions.

A Student Essay

Born into slavery and liberated by the Emancipation Proclamation, Booker T. Washington is widely regarded as one of the most influential African American figures in the history of the United States. In 1881, he started the Tuskegee Normal and Industrial Institute, and soon became recognized, admired, and respected for his wisdom. Because a number of well-placed business leaders and political figures turned to him for advice, he delivered his most famous speech "The Atlanta Compromise Address" in 1895. It is an explication of his beliefs that his fellow African Americans and other former slaves should make the best of what they have and strive to excel in the positions and jobs they already occupy rather than continually fighting for something. Furthermore, he argues that the people of the white race also do not see what they have around them. A moving speech, the impact of the "Atlanta Compromise" was so powerful partially because of Washington's skill as an orator and partially because of his strong rhetorical strategies of appeal to ethos, allegory, and repetition, and style and tone.

One of the most memorable quotes from the "Atlanta Compromise" is "cast down your buckets where you are." In this short allegory about a lost ship without drinking water being found by another ship and saved by using what was around them, Washington conveys his central idea that African Americans can help themselves and save themselves by using what resources they already have. The lost ship, in thinking that it is surrounded by salty water, does not even attempt to try the water before the second ship suggests the idea. Similarly, Washington implies that simply because they do not think they have anything to work with, the African Americans who were once slaves do not try to see what can be done with what they have. The impact of the allegory of the two ships is strengthened by Washington's repetition of the phrase "cast down your bucket where you are." However, in repeating it, he applies it to not only the African Americans, but also to "those of the white race." In that context, he states that the white Americans could look to the African Americans for

Simon Says

Try to use more varied verbs in your essay. Instead of constantly writing, "The author says," how about "The author… claims, suggests, implies, states…"?

help with the "prosperity of the South" instead of looking to "those of foreign birth and strange tongue and habits." Again, he implores both sides to look around and make use of what is already present.

The idea of the speech is set up in the introductory paragraph, wherein Washington states that the recognition of the race of the "American Negro" at the Exposition will do much to "cement the friendship of the two races." It is in this paragraph and these phrases that Washington turns to the strategy of an appeal to ethos. By asserting that the Exposition will help further the friendship between the white Americans and the African Americans, he subtly suggests that this end, this friendship, is what the organizers of the exposition should want (a moral want). This appeal is utilized again in the final paragraph of the passage. In asking the white Americans to cast down their buckets, Washington also asks them to remember that the African Americans "have proved [their] loyalty to [the white Americans] in the past." Thus, he seems to be saying it would be immoral for the white Americans to turn away from proved loyalty when they are in search of help and employees.

However, the most compelling element of Washington's speech is his tone and style. When reading the passage, one can almost imagine Washington delivering his oration. His tone and style are uplifting, optimistic, and emphatic, much like the tone of a passionate Southern preacher. His own emotions seem to be invested in every word. With phrases like "it is at the bottom of life that we must begin, and not at the top," or "there is as much dignity in tilling a field as in writing a poem," Washington lends nobility and a right to pride to the common labor that most African Americans performed at the time. When he speaks of casting down the bucket "in agriculture, in mechanics, in commerce, in domestic service, and in the professions," he assures both the African Americans and the white Americans that hard labor is not something to be looked down on. Neither, he implies, is the struggle to rise above your station a condemnable action. Nevertheless, he always comes back to the point that one must first make use of what is already present and readily available before searching for something else.

A wise and powerful man and speaker, Booker T. Washington often knew just what to say to convey his ideas and opinions. Even more important, he knew how to phrase and present what was important. In "The Atlanta Compromise Address," Washington successfully utilizes the strategies of appeal to ethos, repetition, allegory, style, and tone to impart his message of using what one had to improve oneself. In simplified terms, "The Atlanta Compromise" is a speech based on carpe diem, the idea of seizing what one has and using it to one's advantage.

How would you rate that essay? It's obvious from the outset that the student knows about Booker T. Washington and understands the historical context of the speech. Both the introduction and the conclusion demonstrate an attempt to go beyond the bare-bones information given in the prompt and to flesh out those two points of the rhetorical diamond.

The essay zeroes in clearly on Washington's purpose, too—urging both races in his audience to recognize and make the best of what they already have. He wants them to unite and rally around the same economic flag.

Then the student lays out a roadmap for the rest of the essay with an identification of the chief rhetorical strategies Washington employs: "appeal to ethos, allegory, and repetition, and style and tone." The order changes somewhat in the essay's conclusion, and the body paragraphs discuss the rhetorical strategies in a different order again. A consistent order would have been preferable to avoid confusing the reader. In 40 minutes, however, such shifts are understandable.

The essay does a thorough job of explaining how allegory and repetition advance Washington's purpose. The explanation of ethos is much less successful. The student does attempt to connect this strategy to Washington's purpose, but shows confusion about what the term "ethos" means, and seems to equate it with some sort of moral imperative rather than with building credibility and identifying with the audience.

Tone and style are linked (as you'll see in Chapter 8). In this essay, the student treats them as one rhetorical strategy and again does a thorough, vivid job of explaining how they contribute to Washington's purpose and grounding the explanation with direct references to the passage.

Overall this is a very successful rhetorical analysis which would likely earn a score of 8. Ideas are clearly expressed and well organized (with the exception of the changes in the order of the rhetorical strategies discussed), and made concrete and specific with frequent references to the passage. Only the rather confused interpretation of "ethos" would keep this essay from reaching the top level of 9.

Let's look at another example of an analytical/expository essay, to get more practice.

HERE'S A LETTER EXAMPLE

Now let's look at a very different type of passage. When you read the prompt, squeeze out as much information as you can about the points on the rhetorical diamond.

The Directions

Question 2

(Suggested time—40 minutes. This question counts for one-third of the total essay score.)

In 1676, Madame de Sévigné wrote the letter below. Read it carefully; then write an essay in which you identify the writer's purpose and analyze how she uses language to achieve that purpose. Pay particular attention to organization, point of view, and diction.

Analyzing the Prompt

The author's name and the fact that she could write a letter in 1676 reveal that she was a member of the privileged class. The prompt tells us nothing about her audience. It's likely safe to assume, however, that the letter's intended recipient is from the same social class and is probably another woman or perhaps a relative. The recipient lives somewhere else, or it wouldn't be necessary to describe an event that has captivated Paris.

The prompt also isn't helpful in understanding the context (other than the fact that this is a letter). We don't know what inspired Madame de Sévigné to write it, or what purpose she had in describing the de Brinvilliers affair in the way she did.

This prompt does convey an unusual amount of information about the rhetorical strategies to look for. Most of the time, the prompt will leave the discovery of rhetorical strategies up to you.

With that much knowledge taken from the prompt, you're ready to tackle the passage. As you're reading it, keep asking yourself, "What is the author's purpose? How do I know? What effect is this having on me? What rhetorical strategies is the author using to achieve that effect?" Keep watching, too, for the three strategies the prompt specifically highlights: organization, point of view and use of language (diction).

First, write your own rhetorical analysis essay in response to this prompt. Then read the student essay that follows the passage.

The Passage

The Brinvilliers Affair is still the only thing talked about in Paris. The Marquise confessed to having poisoned her father, her brothers, and one of her children. The Chevalier *Line* Duget had been one of those who had partaken of a poi-
5   soned dish of pigeon pie, and when the Brinvilliers woman was told three years later that he was still alive, her only remark was: "That man surely has an excellent constitution." It seems she fell deeply in love with Sainte Croix, an officer in the regiment of her husband, the Marquis, who
10 lived in their house. Believing that Sainte Croix would marry her if she were free, she attempted to poison her husband. Sainte Croix, not reciprocating her desire, administered an antidote and, thus, saved the poor Marquis' life.

And now, all is over. The Brinvilliers woman is no more. Judgment was given yesterday, and this morning her sen-
15 tence was read to her; she was to make a public confession in front of Notre Dame, after which she was to be executed, her body burned, and her ashes scattered to the winds. She was threatened with torture, but she said that it was unnecessary and that she would tell all. Accordingly, she
20 recounted the history of her whole life, which was even more horrible than anyone had imagined, and I could not hear of it without shuddering.

At six in the morning she was led out, barefoot, and clad only in a loose garment, with a halter round her neck. From
25 Notre Dame she was taken away in a wagon, in which I saw her lying on straw, with the doctor on one side of her and the executioner on the other; the sight of her struck me with horror. I am told that she mounted the scaffold with a firm step and died as she had lived, resolutely, and without
30 fear or emotion.

She asked her confessor to place the executioner so that she need not gaze on Degrais, who, you will remember, tracked her to England and ultimately arrested her at Liège. After she had mounted the ladder to the scaffold, she
35 was exposed to the public for a quarter of an hour, while the executioner prepared her for execution. This raised a murmur of disapproval among the people, and it was a great cruelty. It seems that some say she was a saint, and after her body had been burned, the people crowded near to
40 search for bones as relics, but little was to be found, as her ashes were thrown into the fire. And, it may be supposed, that we now inhale what remains of her. It is to be hoped that we shall not inhale her murderous instincts also.

A Student Essay

In the 1600s, life was by no means easy for women. They were expected to cater to any whim their husband might have, and they were treated like property. Whenever a woman outstepped the boundaries society had established for her, and her crime was serious enough, she was humiliated and punished publicly. In her 1676 letter, Madame de Sévigné writes of the Brinvilliers affair and incites questions regarding the treatment of women in her time.

Society of the seventeenth century, especially the upper echelons of France, was mostly occupied with the scandalous doings of others in their class. Each affair was picked apart, discussed, and passed from ear to eager ear. Naturally, details tended to be embellished and exaggerated, and each individual's opinions and emotions wormed their way into the retelling. In her description of the Brinvilliers affair, Madame de Sévigné includes many of her own feelings upon witnessing and hearing of the fiasco. Watching the Marquise de Brinvilliers' be taken from Notre Dame to the scaffold, Sévigné declares that "the sight of [the Marquise] struck [her] with horror." Expressing her condemnation of the criminal, Sévigné writes that "it seems that some say [the Marquise] was a saint," implying that Sévigné herself does not share in that opinion. The Marquise's life story affected Madame de Sévigné in such a way that she shuddered. Further evidence of Sévigné disdain is evident in her hope that the Marquise's "murderous instincts" will not be inhaled by the people along with her ashes. Nevertheless, a certain reluctant admiration is evident in Sévigné's declaration that the Marquise "died as she had lived, resolutely, and without fear or emotion." Despite the Marquise's transgressions, one must respect a woman who displayed such strength in the face of the poor treatment they received from men, society, and even other women.

Though she has included some personal sentiments and observations, the majority of Sévigné's letter is dedicated to a fairly objective account of the proceedings of the Brinvilliers affair. She begins by explaining how the entire affair began— "The Marquis...poisoned her father, brothers...one of her children," and her husband because she believed that "Sainte Croix would marry her if she were free." Tracked to England by Degrais and arrested in Liege, the Marquise was brought back to France and sentenced. Her punishment included a public confession, an execution, and a cremation. Sévigné's narrative continues with details of the public punishment and humiliation of the Marquise. In a matter-of-fact manner, Sévigné relates the unfortunate end that the Marquise de Brinvilliers met with after her crimes against her family.

In the most obvious manner, Madame de Sévigné paints the Brinvilliers affair as a shocking event—she simply states that "the Brinvilliers affair is still the only thing talked about in Paris." The fact that the Marquise's proper first name is never mentioned lends the air and quality of an unmentionable scandal to the whole affair. One can imagine this straightforward letter being read in a shocked tone of voice, an underlying excitement and eagerness evident in the speaker's voice due to the very "deliciously scandalous" nature of the event. Her crime was so abominable that her persecutors even threatened her with torture to procure her confession. Sévigné's diction, quite candid, underscores the shocking quality of the Brinvilliers affair.

Madame de Sévigné effectively portrays society's treatment of women who have overstepped their limits in the seventeenth century. Her hinted-at emotions relay Sévigné's condemning opinion of the Marquise, while simultaneously they convey reluctant admiration. Both her narrative and her diction underline the fact that the Brinvilliers affair was a major scandal. However, overall, one is imparted with the sense that this treatment is ultimately unjust.

How well do you think this student met the requirements in the prompt? Not very perceptively or thoroughly, although ideas are expressed clearly and the mechanics of the language are correct.

The first task was to identify the letter writer's purpose, described in the essay as a portrayal of "society's treatment of women who have overstepped their limits." No evidence from the passage is brought in to support that claim, though. Would a man who poisoned several relatives have been treated any differently? Is it society's treatment of a criminal from the aristocracy (female or male) that's being described? Wouldn't poisoning a bunch of family members be considered "overstepping" boundaries by just about any society for either sex? Was the Marquise even really guilty? This essay doesn't present a convincing, well-grounded case for Madame de Sévigné's purpose in narrating the crime and punishment. Perhaps she was simply trying to inform or entertain the letter's recipient.

The prompt also highlights point of view. For the most part, Madame de Sévigné uses a third person narrator. The only event she actually witnesses, and for which she switches to a first person narration, is the condemned being taken to the scaffold in a wagon. This choice of narrator again conveys the air of a news story intended to inform or entertain someone who doesn't live in Paris. However, the essay doesn't deal with the type of narrator at all. It does treat the letter writer's less-than-objective position, pointing to feelings of condemnation and "reluctant admiration," backed by references to the passage. It never links those feelings to purpose or to narrative stance, however.

The student describes the narrative's organization, as instructed, but doesn't explain how the primarily chronological progression helps Madame de Sévigné achieve her purpose. Diction (the third specific requirement in the prompt) is mentioned once at the end, tossed in as an afterthought. The student doesn't seem to understand the meaning of the term, and doesn't connect the letter writer's word choices (such as her vivid descriptions and her refusal to use the Marquise's first name) to her purpose.

Overall, the essay is superficial in treating the prompt's instructions, even for a 40-minute effort, and devotes too much space to the student's descriptions of the social context instead of focusing on the passage. Its organization is rambling—a more effective essay would have stated the letter writer's purpose in the first paragraph, explained each of the three points from the prompt in the next three paragraphs, then concluded. The student has grabbed a purpose out of thin air, without support from the passage, and the analysis of the rhetorical strategies specified in the prompt is inadequate. This essay probably wouldn't score above a 4.

In the next chapter, we move on to the argumentative essay.

Chapter 7
How to Approach the Argumentative Essay

WHERE YOUR OPINION COUNTS

At last—a chance to make your own argument, without being limited by the source documents you're given and without having to focus on rhetorical strategies instead of the merits of what an author says. Here you get to take a stand and present your point of view on the topic in the prompt. This should be an essay you look forward to!

Even better, there is no "right" or "wrong" answer. All that matters is how effectively you argue and back up your position. If you like to debate, this is the part of the free-response section where you can really shine.

The argumentative essay isn't a license to ramble on about your own personal views, though. To get a high score, you need to do three things:

- Take a definite position, so no one would question where you stand on the topic of the prompt.

- Develop an argument that builds and moves forward instead of simply repeating the same point several times in different ways.

- Support the points in your argument with evidence drawn from your own knowledge, reading, experiences and observations.

Lower-scoring essays tend to simply summarize what the author says in the passage, or wander aimlessly through an impassioned list of the student's own beliefs without giving any evidence to support them. As in the synthesis essay, the concept of a conversation with the author is helpful. If you were talking with this author and either agreeing, disagreeing or giving a "yes...but" (qualifying) opinion, how would you argue your position? What evidence would you offer to back it up?

Let's look at an example. We'll work through an analysis of the prompt and passage before you try writing your own essay in 40 minutes. Then read the student essay and evaluation that follow.

SAMPLE ESSAY #1—HERE'S HOW IT'S DONE

Here's a sample argumentative essay prompt. The passage that follows this prompt is typical of argumentative essays you'll see on the test—they're much shorter than the analytical essays.

The Directions

Question 3

(Suggested time—40 minutes. This question counts for one-third of the total essay section score.)

Read and think carefully about the following quotation, taken from *Utilitarianism*, by John Stuart Mill. Then write an essay in which you refute, support, or qualify the author's claim. Make sure to use appropriate evidence from literary, historical, or personal sources to develop your argument.

The Passage

The creed which accepts as the foundation of morals, Utility, or the Greatest Happiness Principle, holds that actions are right in proportion as they tend to promote happiness, wrong as they tend to produce the reverse of happiness. By happiness is intended pleasure, and the absence of pain; by unhappiness, pain, and the privation of pleasure. To give a clear view of the moral standard set up by the theory, much more requires to be said; in particular, what things it includes in the ideas of pain and pleasure; and to what extent this is left an open question. But these supplementary explanations do not affect the theory of life on which this theory of morality is grounded—namely, that pleasure, and freedom from pain, are the only things desirable as ends; and that all desirable things (which are as numerous in the utilitarian as in any other scheme) are desirable either for the pleasure inherent in themselves, or as means to the promotion of pleasure and the prevention of pain.

Analyzing The Prompt

If you've taken a lot of history courses, then you may have studied John Stuart Mill, and this would give you some information about context. If not, then the prompt still gives you rich material for a thoughtful argumentative essay.

Your first task is to identify the author's main point, so you can decide what position you want to argue. In this case, the author's main point is clearly stated: "… actions are right in proportion as they tend to promote happiness, wrong as they tend to produce the reverse of happiness." In the next sentence, Mill defines happiness ("pleasure") and unhappiness ("pain or the privation of pleasure").

You still have terms to define when you write your own essay, though. Happiness may equal pleasure, but one person's pleasure may be a matter of complete indifference to another person. What does Mill mean by "pleasure"? How will you define it?

You can see why this particular example is tailor-made to take you beyond the prompt. Here you can really demonstrate that you've thought deeply about the topic. Is "pleasure" the same thing for everyone? What are the consequences of individuals pursuing a "pleasure" that doesn't mean the same thing to all of them?

Whatever you decide to argue, make your position perfectly clear in the first paragraph of your essay.

If everyone pursued pleasure, what consequences might result for society? Does one person pursuing pleasure mean someone else has to experience pain?

As you think through those questions, what kind of evidence from your own experiences or reading pops into your mind? Which would be the strongest and the easiest to develop? That evidence should determine what stand you take on the argument. Remember that no reader knows or cares what you really think about an issue. You'll want to take the stand that's easiest for you to defend at that particular moment, based on the ideas that come to you. The most important things are that you have clearly decided how you feel about the issue and that you have the examples to back up your position.

> **I remember when...**
> If you're describing your own experience or observation in the argumentative essay, you can use first-person narration.

Let's look at an essay that was written by a student under actual testing conditions.

A Student Essay

In John Stuart Mill's work Utilitarianism, the author advances a theory of morality that associates "the promotion of pleasure and the prevention of pain" with ethical correctness. While the pursuit of happiness can sometimes lead to a path of moral righteousness, Mill's claim is flawed in that it assumes hedonism will inherently bring positive results. By championing any action that produces pleasure, Mill condones humanity's greed, lust, and selfishness; three traits that are clearly immoral. As history and literature have demonstrated, pursuing goals motivated purely by self-interest does not lead to ethically responsible outcomes. Furthermore, the greatest achievements often arise when people readily eschew pleasure to attain a nobler end.

During the second half of the nineteenth century, a number of technological advances made the American economy blossom and helped to make the nation a world power. Eager to enjoy the pleasures made possible by great wealth, entrepreneurs and businessmen sought to increase profits and lower costs in any possible way. Workers were paid abysmally low wages, conditions were highly unsafe, and monopolies were commonplace. Though the heads of "Big Business" clearly adhered to Mill's "Greatest Happiness Principle," their actions were highly unethical. Their pleasure came at the expense of the poor and created a polarized society. In contrast, patriots seeking independence from England a century before, gladly relinquished the "absence of pain" afforded by accepting the status quo. Despite the great "privation of pleasure" brought about by the Revolutionary War, the patriots achieved their lofty goal of freedom, a morally desirable outcome. Evidently, seeking happiness does not necessarily entail finding "what is right and good."

F. Scott Fitzgerald's portrait of the Roaring Twenties, <u>The Great Gatsby</u>, examines hedonism and reaches a conclusion much different than Mill's. Jay Gatsby pursues pleasure in the form of rekindling a relationship with a former love, Daisy. Following utilitarian principles, seeking the desirable outcome should be an ethically sound choice. However, it instead leads Gatsby to engage in questionable business and to court a married woman, two clear violations of ethical standards. Clearly, morality based on pleasure is an unsound principle.

This essay is rather short. An additional example—perhaps from the student's own experience—would have made it stronger. However, it does the job quite well, and would likely earn a score of 7, at the bottom of the "effective" band.

The introduction is slightly long, but notice how well this student addresses the two tasks set forth. Right away, the student states the author's claim ("... the author advances a theory of morality that associates the 'promotion of pleasure and the prevention of pain' with ethical correctness....") and takes a firm stand against it: "As history and literature have demonstrated, pursuing goals motivated by mere self-interest does not lead to ethically responsible outcomes." The student's clear definition of pleasure ("...humanity's greed, lust, and selfishness...") both explains and reinforces this stand.

> ## Write in the Present Tense
> This student does an excellent job of handling verb tenses. Particularly important is the use of the present tense when addressing the author, text and claim: "the author advances," "it assumes," "achievements often arise," and so on. The student uses the past tense only when presenting historical facts in the second paragraph.
>
> One of the most common grammatical errors that students make in AP essays is using improper verb-tense shifts.

The student gives the reader a road map for the rest of the essay by first mentioning history, then literature, and follows that roadmap in the same order.

The conclusion is weak and seems tacked on. It would have been stronger if it reminded the reader of the evidence brought in to support the student's stand against Mill's claim.

What keeps this essay from scoring an 8 or 9 is the student's failure to follow the prompt where it leads. This essay simply takes the prompt at face value and doesn't examine the broader ethical questions it raises.

SAMPLE ESSAY #2—GIVING IT ANOTHER TRY

Let's try another one. Again, now that you're comfortable with the process for writing the argumentative essay, try writing this one on your own before you look at the student's essay.

The Directions

Question 3

(Suggested time—40 minutes. This question counts for one-third of the total essay section score.)

The former slave and abolitionist Frederick Douglass (1818-1895) wrote, "Once you learn to read, you will be forever free." In a well-written essay, examine the relationship between literacy and freedom in the world today, supporting your position with appropriate evidence.

A Student Essay

Frederick Douglass once wrote, "Once you learn to read, you will be forever free" and this is true of the modern world. Though everyone in America can read, alot of people in the world can't read today and that's a serious problem for them. There are too many people in places like India and China who can't read and this iliteracy is holding them back. If we would have more programs to teach literacy to people in these Third World countries, then we we would have more literacy and therefore more freedom for all.

One reason I think there should be more literacy is that you need to educate children early on in their educational experience, otherwise, they will not learn what they need to succeed. Once the children in a given country achieve literacy, then the country can also improve the quality of life and the children can teach there parents how to read when they return home from school. This would help the parents to find better jobs and allow for more financial freedom for the family. Also, if the people in China and India learned English, they could get jobs using their new skills in English.

Another reason why I think literacy increases freedom is because literacy is the key concept to the development of political freedom. When Frederick Douglass was a slave in America, black people were enslaved and deprived of literacy. When the slave owners didn't teach their slaves to read, they were holding them back from the freedoms they deserved; including the right to read. If the slaves learned to read, though, they would have been more free and this would have threatened the slave masters. So with slaves having been deprived of literacy, the owners could keep control of them.

In conclusion, literacy is the key to freedom around the world. As the examples of India and slavery have demonstrated, freedom is possible for people who have a chance to read the way we do.

Short, But Not Sweet

Shorter essays usually indicate a less successful effort. It's difficult to examine a prompt thoroughly and present enough strong evidence to support your position if the essay is too short.

This essay has significant flaws in both content and style and would not score above a 5. The most serious problem is the absence of a strong connection between literacy and freedom. This is not an easy concept and many students would struggle to find good, specific examples to bridge a connection between these ideas. While literacy in the Third World and in American slavery could be excellent examples, they are not made specific or relevant in this essay. In the discussion of slavery, for example, the student wrote

> If the slaves learned to read, though, they would have been more free and this would have threatened the slave masters. So with the slaves having been deprived of literacy, the owners could keep control of them.

What does this mean? How would literacy have made slaves "more free"? How did illiteracy help slave owners "keep control of them"? Good essays on the AP English exam develop specific examples and then carefully connect them to the issue at hand. They also demonstrate a depth of thought and complexity that is mostly absent in this essay. As you write your own essays, be sure to have a clear, stable definition of the essential terms (in this case, "literacy" and "freedom") in mind and don't be afraid to talk about how complex the terms can be.

The style of this essay did not help. It is not necessary, for example, to repeat the quote verbatim in the first sentence: the grader already knows what Frederick Douglass said. Also, the first paragraph does not really contain a thesis or any clear statement about how literacy allows people to be more free. Throughout, the student makes some awkward errors in style and diction, which detract from the overall effect.

But, in spite of these flaws, the essay does provide some examples and at least attempted to address the relationship between literacy and freedom, so it would receive a score of 3 or 4.

Now let's take a look at a more successful essay, which was also written by a student under time constraints.

A Student Essay

Literacy is something we take for granted in America. Most children learn to read at an early age and receive formal education until they are eighteen years old. During this time, they develop a deep understanding of their own language, both in its written and spoken forms. I remember when I first learned to read and how it made me feel so empowered over my younger sister, who hadn't learned yet. As my teachers encouraged me in elementary school, I grew to enjoy reading adventure stories and then much harder books. In my AP English class this year, my teacher Mrs. Lasko assigned extremely challenging books, such as Paradise Lost, Gulliver's Travels, and Lord of the Flies. In all these cases, literacy empowered me to feel more and more intellectually free and to explore new ideas through reading.

But literacy does more that just free our minds: it is the key to bringing about political and economic freedom for ordinary people. There are many times in history when increasing literacy allowed people to experience a new kind of political freedom. For example, during the Protestant Reformation, ordinary people began to read because the printing press allowed books to be printed quickly rather than copied by hand. As the people began to read the Bible for themselves, they developed their own interpretations about theology and they challenged the teachings of the Catholic Church. People also read political pamphlets and were empowered to overthrow the leaders in power during that time. These kinds of political pamphlets, which only work when the majority of the population can read, have formed the basis of many political movements in the modern era.

In women's history, too, increasing literacy has brought about an increase in political freedoms. For centuries, few women could read or write and thus they were denied freedoms we now consider basic: the freedom to vote, the freedom to hold political office, the freedom to represent oneself in court. When we think of the movement for women's suffrage a century ago, how could the suffragettes have succeeded if they did not have a largely literate population of women to support them. As women learned to read in large numbers, they began to develop the political tools necessary to fight for their own freedom. In this way, literacy was a prerequisite to real political freedom for millions of women around the world.

When Frederick Douglass wrote of literacy and freedom, he was speaking of real freedom from the bondage of slavery. For him, the power to read and write played a role in his abolitionist activities. But as I have discussed in this essay, literacy can bring about more than just freedom from slavery: it can free us to think for ourselves, determine our own theologies, and fight for real political freedom. And whether it is African Americans, children, the poor, or just ordinary people, reading can transform the lives of those with less power. Literacy is thus a direct cause of freedom, both in the distant historical past and in the future of our constantly evolving world.

This essay is an obvious success and would score very highly (probably an 8) on the real AP. Not only did the student specifically answer the question at hand, she offered a nuanced assessment of the relationship between literacy and freedom. In fact, she took pains to define multiple senses of the word freedom (intellectual, political, etc.) throughout the paper. The examples were specific, detailed, and relevant to the topic at hand.

The student begins by briefly recounting her own history of literacy and how it empowered her as she developed her reading skills. The first body paragraph then explicitly connects increasing literacy with newfound political and religious freedom during the Protestant Reformation. Notice how the student takes her time in introducing each example and then adds as much relevant, specific information as possible. The next body paragraph is equally effective and shows yet another dimension of the complex link between literacy and freedom.

The student also helped her score by creating fluid prose and elegant transitions from one paragraph to the next. The range of vocabulary was good, but not exceptional—it never needs to be to get a high score on this test. Offer the readers as wide a range of vocabulary as you can, but focus on writing a good essay as you design, develop, and execute your response.

COMING UP...

In this and the two preceding chapters, you've seen a range of examples of essays. In the next part of this book, you'll learn (or review) the important aspects of formal training in rhetoric and composition that will prepare you to craft essays that equal—or exceed—the ones that you've examined so far.

REFLECT

Think about what you've learned in Part IV, and respond to the following questions:

- How long will you spend on multiple-choice questions?

- How will you change your approach to multiple-choice questions?

- What is your multiple-choice guessing strategy?

- How much time will you spend on the first essay? The second? The third?

- What will you do before you begin writing an essay?

- How will you change your approach to the essays?

- Will you seek further help, outside of this book (such as a teacher, tutor, or AP Central), on how to approach multiple-choice questions, the essay, or a pacing strategy?

Part V
Terms and Modes Review for the AP English Language and Composition Exam

HOW TO USE THE CHAPTERS IN THIS PART

You may need to come back to the following chapters more than once. Your goal is to obtain mastery of the content, and a single read of a chapter may not be sufficient. At the end of each chapter, you will have an opportunity to reflect on whether you truly have mastered the content of that chapter.

Chapter 8: Words and Their Use

This chapter introduces you to the most important terminology that appears on the AP English Language Exam. If you have heard the words "diction," "syntax," and "rhetoric," but you're not really sure what they mean, this chapter will finally help you figure them out. In addition, it covers the entire vocabulary of rhetorical and literary devices that appear most commonly on the exam.

Chapter 9: Rhetorical Fallacies

This brief chapter introduces you to the kinds of faulty reasoning that commonly appear in student writing. The errors may even be lurking in the background of the passages you have to analyze on the AP English Language and Composition Exam.

Chapter 10: Basic Rhetorical Modes

"Rhetorical modes" refers to the ways that writers organize their arguments. What is the difference between an illustration and a classification? Why do some authors structure their essays around comparisons and contrasts? This brief chapter will help you identify these structures quickly on the multiple-choice passages.

Chapter 11: Complex Rhetorical Modes

This chapter expands on the content of the previous chapter and goes much deeper into analyzing how authors conceptualize their evidence and arguments. If you are running low on time, you could skim through this chapter and jump right to the practice exam questions.

Chapter 8
Words and Their Use

THE GOOD NEWS AND THE BAD NEWS ABOUT THE AP ENGLISH LANGUAGE AND COMPOSITION EXAM

The Good News

While the title of this exam allows people to differentiate between this test and the AP English *Literature* Exam, it's still somewhat misleading. The AP English *Language* Exam is not a language exam—at least not in the sense that you may think. For example, it is possible not to know the difference between a gerund and a present participle—or even a gerund and a giraffe—and still score a 5 on this exam.

In the multiple-choice section of the exam, test writers will attempt to evaluate your ability to analyze how writers use language to explain or to argue; in the free-response, or essay, section they will expect *you* to use language to explain or to argue. Naturally, you'll want to avoid making egregious errors in grammar or usage on the test, but as you study don't get hung up on the rules of language. If you're considering taking the AP exam, your language skills are probably sufficient for the task. Now, you may be wondering what *is* tested on the exam. The answer is *composition,* and we'll spend Chapters 9 through 11 of this book reviewing all you need to know about composition to be fully prepared for the test.

The Bad News

Now for the bad news. Despite the test's lack of emphasis on the rules of language, there are some aspects of language that we must examine here to make sure you're ready for test day. We'll start by discussing diction, style, tone, and point of view. We'll move on to circumlocution and euphemism, and discuss irony and satire. Finally, we will review the many types of figurative language and go through some drills that will prepare you for the types of questions you'll see on all of these topics. Let's begin!

DICTION

The basic definition of diction is "word choice." Generally, the diction questions you'll see on the test will ask you to evaluate why an author's choice of words is particularly effective, apt, or clear. However, as we explained in the multiple-choice section, more often than not it is the test writer's diction that you have to creak. While knowledge of grammar and usage is almost irrelevant for this exam, a broad vocabulary is a necessity.

> Vocabulary is important for both the multiple-choice section AND the essays. Start a vocabulary journal: Write down any unfamiliar words from this book and look up their definitions. There is a good chance you will see many of these words on your test!

1. The style of the first paragraph on the previous page can best be described as

   (A) pedantic
   (B) lyrical
   (C) terse
   (D) ludic
   (E) edifying

While it's possible that none of the answers stands out to you as the correct choice, you could rule out *pedantic* if you knew that it meant "narrowly, stodgily, and often ostentatiously learned,"—it isn't possible that you could think that of the writing in this book! Likewise, an AP test and lyricism (intense, intimate display of emotion) make for an unlikely pair, so you can use Process of Elimination and get rid of that choice too. The test writers slipped *ludic* (pertaining to game, playful) in there in case you wanted to misremember some Latin (*ludus*); and finally *terse* (concise, without superfluous detail) shows up regularly on this exam but probably doesn't describe the writing in this book very well. Given that the last choice can mean both enlightening and informative, (E) is the best answer.

But as you can see, if you knew none of these words, the question may as well have read as follows:

2. The style of the paragraph above can best be described as

   (A) pompom
   (B) banana
   (C) dog
   (D) tire iron
   (E) Susan

And then which would seem like the correct answer? Obviously, vocabulary is important, so start that vocabulary journal.

Tactics for Syntax

Syntax is simply another way of talking about grammar and sentence structure.

Syntax

Another language term that you should be familiar with for the AP English Language Exam is *syntax*. **Syntax** is the ordering of words in a sentence; it describes sentence structure. Syntax is not a topic that excites many high school students—or teachers—and therefore is not discussed very much. However, *syntax* is a word that finds it way onto AP English Language Exams on a regular basis. Don't worry: You don't need to be an expert on this subject, but you should know how manipulating syntax can enhance an author's meaning, tone, or point of view. Let's look at an example from *Candide,* taken from the famous opening of Chapter 3.

> Example: Never was anything so gallant, so well outfitted, so brilliant, and so finely disposed as the two armies. The trumpets, fifes, reeds, drums, and cannon made such harmony as never was heard in Hell.

The first sentence poses as a fairly simple sketch of a glorious battle scene. The second begins in the same fashion, but its words are arranged in a way that maximizes the effect of surprise that comes at the end of the sentence. The cannons are slipped in as the final member of a list of military musical instruments; the formation of the list creates an expectation that the final element will fit nicely into the set. It doesn't, but we don't have time to register our surprise because we're immediately distracted by a new setup with the phrase "such harmony as never was heard…." We expect harmony to be something beautiful, and we already begin to supply the final word (Earth? Heaven?) when—surprise—we are jolted by the word that Voltaire chose instead: hell. The syntax in this sentence is brilliant.

Here's another slightly different example. In the following example, Candide through his servant and sidekick, Cacambo, is asking about the proper etiquette for greeting the King of Eldorado.

> Example: When they drew near to the royal chamber, Cacambo asked one of the officers in what manner they were to pay their respects to His Majesty; whether it was the custom to fall upon their knees, or to prostrate themselves upon the ground; whether they were to put their hands upon their heads, or behind their backs; whether they were to lick the dust off the floor; in short, what was the usual ceremony for such occasions.

The syntax of this long sentence is very carefully constructed; Voltaire uses all of the parallel clauses that begin with "whether" to achieve great comic effect. At first, the text is fairly straightforward—after all, going down on one's knees before a king would have been fairly standard for a European reader of the eighteenth century; however, with each clause, the groveling etiquette becomes more extreme, and the final image—of licking the dust off the floor—pushes the concept beyond the believable. The syntax of this sentence is structured in a way that allows us to see the absurdity of *all* forms of ceremonial deference. In fact, in this story the enlightened King of Eldorado simply embraces both Cacambo and Candide.

Related to syntax are style, tone, and point of view. As you will read in the next section, these elements work together with syntax to create a "profile" of the speaker that tells us how the speaker or author feels about the subject at hand.

Style, Tone, and Point of View

You can count on seeing some combination of the terms *style, tone,* and *point of view* in both multiple-choice and essay questions on this exam, so let's make sure you're familiar with their definitions.

Style is the manner of expression. It describes how the author uses language to get his or her point across (e.g., pedantic, scientific, and emotive).

Tone is the attitude, mood, or sentiments revealed by the style. Tone describes how the author seems to be feeling (e.g., optimistic, ironic, and playful).

Point of view is the stance revealed by the style and the tone of the writing. The author's point of view expresses his or her position on the topic discussed. Point of view can be tricky—sometimes, especially in works of fiction, it is difficult to determine point of view, and, thus, you may be left with nothing more to say than "first-person narrator" or "third-person omniscient narrator."

Consider this excerpt.

> Example: Our left fielder couldn't hit the floor if he fell out of bed! After striking out twice (once with the bases loaded!), he grounded into a double-play. My grandmother runs faster than he does! In the eighth inning, he misjudged a routine fly ball, which brought in the winning run. What a jerk! Why didn't the club trade him last week when it was still possible? What's wrong with you guys?

The *style* is simple, direct, unsophisticated, truculent, and even crass. The style helps evoke a simple sentiment: anger. The *tone* is angry, brash, emotional, and even virulent.

The *point of view* is clear; the author appears to be a disgruntled spectator who doesn't like the player at all and wants the team to get rid of him.

Now let's try a sample question with an excerpt from Fyodor Dostoyevsky's *Notes from Underground.*

> The long and the short of it is, gentlemen, that it is better to do nothing! Better conscious inertia!

4. The tone of the speaker is best characterized as
   (A) ironic
   (B) nihilistic
   (C) reflective
   (D) optimistic
   (E) accusatory

You probably immediately eliminated (C) and (D) because the passage did not sound particularly reflective or optimistic. The author is not accusatory (E) either. Choice (B) may have confused you a bit; nihilism refers to a belief in nothing. (Again notice the importance of vocabulary!) The speaker's tone can indeed by described as "nihilistic," so the correct choice is (B).

RHETORIC AND FIGURATIVE LANGUAGE

Rhetoric is the art of speaking or writing effectively. **Figurative language** is strictly defined as speech or writing that departs from literal meaning to achieve a special effect or meaning. The terms covered later in this section are terms you should know cold before taking the exam. Multiple-choice questions may use them in answer choices, and you are certainly expected to use them in your free-response essays.

Rhetoric

First of all, what *is* rhetoric? It is often referred to as the stylistic devices an author uses to appeal successfully to a specific audience and is usually persuasive in nature. Before we get into the nitty gritty of figurative language and how it's used, let's review the three classical rhetorical appeals—methods of persuasion—you should know for the exam.

Classical Appeals

Aristotle identified three methods of appealing to an audience in order to persuade them to your point of view: *logos*, *pathos*, and *ethos*.

Logos is an appeal to reason and logic. An argument that uses logos to persuade needs to provide things like objective evidence, hard facts, statistics, or logical strategies such as "cause and effect" to back up its claim. (*Logos* is the root of our word "logic," which is a good way to remember which of the appeals this is!)

Ethos is an appeal to the speaker's credibility—whether he or she is to be believed on the basis of his or her character and expertise. For example, the prosecution in a murder trial might put a renowned psychiatrist on the stand to testify that the defendant is able to identify right and wrong and is thus capable of standing trial. Their argument would be using an appeal to *ethos* to persuade the jury (their audience) that the testimony of this expert is to be trusted. (*Ethos* is related to our word "ethics"—the principles of conduct that govern people and organizations and give them the authority to speak on certain topics.)

Pathos is an appeal to the emotions, values, or desires of the audience. Aristotle felt that, although ideally people would be persuaded by appeals to logic (*logos*, remember?), they would probably most often be persuaded by their emotions and beliefs instead. This is why, in that same murder trial, a defense attorney might tell the jury about the lonely childhood and difficult life of the defendant—he would be appealing to the *pathos* of the audience to convince them that his client should not be convicted. (*Pathos* is also the root of "pathetic," a word we use to describe something that is, shall we say, *suffering* from inferiority.)

Figurative Language

As we stated at the beginning of this chapter, you don't need to be an expert in rhetoric to ace the AP English Language and Composition Exam; however, you do need to have some understanding of how language works. With the exception of technical manuals (like the one that helped you assemble your entertainment center), few texts are written such that all of their language is meant to be taken literally. Take, for example, the end of one of Abraham Lincoln's inaugural speeches.

> Example: With malice toward none, with charity for all, with firmness in the right as God gives us to see the right, let us strive on to finish the work we are in, to bind up the nation's wounds, to care for him who shall have borne the battle and for his widow and his orphan, to do all which may achieve and cherish a just and lasting peace among ourselves and with all nations.

Are we supposed to take "to bind up the nation's wounds" literally? Of course not. Lincoln has personified our country to make the suffering of particular individuals relatable to all the people of the nation. And what about "him who shall have borne the battle"? Clearly, Lincoln is using the singular (a man) to represent the collective mass of soldiers, and when he adds "his widow and his orphan," we understand that "shall have borne the battle" really means "shall have died in battle." Lincoln personalizes the suffering of this group of people by instead speaking of individual sacrifice, which he knows is far more likely to strike a profound emotional chord in his listeners.

Despite the effectiveness of Lincoln's speech, you should keep in mind that many other perfectly convincing arguments and explanations are conveyed primarily through literal language. On this exam, there's no need for you to strain yourself attempting to use figurative language in the free-response section. But it will be very helpful for you to review the common terms associated with figurative language that we've listed below because you will be obliged to analyze texts that contain figurative language on this test.

With all this in mind, here is a list of some common terms related to figurative language; we've put them in order of their decreasing relevance to the test.

Imagery

For the purposes of this exam, you may consider **imagery** to be synonymous with figurative language. However, in a more restricted sense, imagery is figurative language that is used to convey a sensory perception (visual, auditory, olfactory, tactile, or gustatory).

Hyperbole

Hyperbole is overstatement or exaggeration; it is the use of figurative language that significantly exaggerates the facts for effect. In many instances, but certainly not all, hyperbole is employed for comic effect.

Example: If you use too much figurative language in your free-response essays, the AP readers will crucify you!

Clearly, this statement is a gross exaggeration; while the readers may give you a poor grade if you use figurative language that doesn't suit the purposes of your essay, they will not kill you.

Understatement

Understatement is figurative language that presents the facts in a way that makes them appear much less significant than they really are. Understatement is almost always used for comic effect.

Example: After dinner, they came and took into custody Doctor Pangloss and his pupil Candide, the one for speaking his mind and the other for appearing to approve what he heard. They were conducted to separate apartments, which were extremely cool and where they were never bothered by the sun.

Taking the last sentence literally would lead you astray. The understatement in this case ("They were conducted to separate apartments, which were extremely cool and where they were never bothered by the sun") should be taken to mean that the poor men were thrown into horribly dark, dank, and cold prison cells.

Simile

A **simile** is a comparison between two unlike objects, in which the two parts are connected with a term such as *like* or *as*.

Example: The birds are like black arrows flying across the sky.

You can easily identify a simile—and distinguish it from a metaphor—because of the use of *like* or *as*.

Metaphor

A **metaphor** is a simile without a connecting term such as *like* or *as*. Here's an example of a metaphor.

Example: The birds are black arrows flying across the sky.

Birds are not arrows, but the commonalities (both are long and sleek, and they travel swiftly through the air—and both have feathers) allow us to easily grasp the image.

Extended Metaphor

An **extended metaphor** is precisely what it sounds like—it is a metaphor that lasts for longer than just one phrase or sentence. A word of caution for the exam, however; do not use extended metaphors in your own AP essays, for many scholars (and many AP graders) believe that the extended metaphor is a poor expository or argumentative technique.

> Example: During the time I have voyaged on this ship, I have avoided the cabin; rather, I have remained on deck, battered by wind and rain, but able to see moonlight on the water. I do not wish to go below decks now.

As surprising as this may seem, this passage is not about nautical navigation. The ship's voyage is the central metaphor (representing the course of life); the writer extends the metaphor by relating elements of figurative language: cabin, deck, wind and rain, moonlight, water, and decks. The cabin is a safe place, but it's a place where you can't experience much; on deck, you're exposed to the elements, but you can experience beauteous sights. Having made the difficult, dangerous, but rewarding choice of staying on deck, it would be a personal defeat, a kind of surrender to wish for the safety, comfort, and limited horizons of the cabin later in life.

> **Metaphors vs. Symbols**
> Sometimes, it is difficult to distinguish between metaphor and symbol. Remember that a metaphor always contains an implied comparison between two elements. Recall the metaphorical image of the birds and the arrows: The birds remain birds, and the arrows remain arrows—and the metaphor serves to give us an image of the flight of the birds by suggesting a visualization of arrows. However, in the case of a symbol, the named object really doesn't count. There is no lamb; *lamb* is merely an object that's meant to conjure up another object or element.

Symbol

A **symbol** is a word that represents something other than itself.

> Example: The Christian soldiers paused to remember the lamb.

In this case, the rough, tough soldiers did not stop to think about the actual animal; the lamb is a traditional Christian symbol for Jesus Christ.

Denotation and Connotation

Denotation refers to a word's primary or literal significance, while **connotation** refers to the vast range of other meanings that a word suggests. Context (and at times, author's intent) determines which connotations may be appropriate for a word. An author will carefully pick a particular word for its connotations, knowing or hoping a reader will make an additional inference as a result. Some literary critics argue that it is impossible to distinguish between denotation and connotation. Who, they ask, is to determine which meaning to assign as a primary significance? Let's move on and look at an example.

> Example: I am looking at the sky.

The denotation of the underlined word should be as clear as a cloudless sky (the space, often blue, above the earth's surface). However, there can be connotations associated with the word. The sky is often associated with heaven; it can also evoke the idea of freedom or vast openness. Because of connotation, one can't help but believe that the sky evokes in the writer a sense of longing for freedom from work, the computer, or the AP English Language and Composition Exam.

Oxymoron

An **oxymoron** is an apparent contradiction of terms.

Example: I advise you to make haste slowly.

What would you do if someone said this to you? At first, you might think that this is simply a foolish, contradictory statement, and you might ignore the advice. However, it is possible to make sense of the apparent contradiction, which is in fact an oxymoron. In essence, the sentence advises you to go as fast as you can, while going slowly enough to do things right.

Don't Be a "Moron"!

Oxymorons and paradoxes both involve contradictions. Oxymorons, however, almost always involve only brief phrases ("jumbo shrimp"), whereas paradoxes involve situations, usually longer.

Paradox

The **paradox** is an apparent contradiction of ideas or statements and, therefore, is closely related to the oxymoron. Think of a paradox as an oxymoron on a larger scale.

Example: The only way to overcome death is to die.

This paradox pops up in various contexts; it is not a contradiction, for some would say that only after death is it possible to pass on to eternal life (in heaven, for instance), and *eternal* life precludes (another) death. Thus, one dies (physically) but then lives (spiritually) forever.

It is possible to have a paradox that offers no real hope of resolution. For instance, the Liar Paradox, dating from the fourth century B.C.E., arrives at a contradiction by reasoning that if "this sentence is false" is true, then the sentence is false, but if "this sentence is false" is false, then the sentence is true.

Personification

Personification is the figurative device in which inanimate objects or concepts are given human qualities. It can enhance our emotional response because we usually attribute more emotional significance to other humans than to things or concepts.

Example: He had been wrestling with lethargy for days, and every time that he thought that he was close to victory, his adversary escaped his hold.

This figurative wrestling match, in which lethargy is personified as the opponent to the author of this sentence, brings the struggle to life—human life. If you don't believe this, think about the literal alternative: He tried to stop being lethargic, but he was not successful. This doesn't sound very lively.

> **Anthropomorphism** is a specific type of personification wherein animals are given human qualities, i.e., the Fox in Aesop's fables.

Rhetorical Question

A **rhetorical question** is a question whose answer is obvious; these types of questions do not need to be answered—and usually aren't. Rhetorical questions attempt to prove something without actually presenting an argument; sometimes they're used as a form of irony, in which something is stated, but its opposite is meant.

> Example (no irony): With all the violence on TV today, is it any wonder kids bring guns to school?

Since it has already been determined that you agree (even if you don't), the writer need not substantiate this remark.

> Example (with irony): Aren't AP exams great fun?

Here, there is an assumption that you would answer in the negative, although there is no way for you to respond—unless you write a letter. Rhetorical questions allow a writer to make a point without further support, whether it's a straightforward remark or one with a touch of irony.

Bombast

Bombast (adjective = bombastic) is language that is overly rhetorical (pompous), especially when considered in context. Generally speaking, graduation speeches contain bombast; pedantic people (those who use their learning ostentatiously) tend to use bombast. Occasionally, a passage on the AP English Language and Composition Exam will contain bombast.

> We are here in these hallowed halls, accompanied by
> genial kin and erudite mentors, surrounded by Corinthian
> columns and the three wisdoms of the ages, to celebrate
> *Line* the conjunction of fare thee well and many happy returns
> 5 and to proffer advice worthy of Athena to these prodigal
> sons and daughters as they depart our august institution.
> You happy survivors are not graduates, but champions who
> have been assailed on all sides by demons of mathematics,
> dragons of science, and inhuman beasts of humanities, but
> 10 who have emerged victorious from each and every battle.
> In this respect, one is reminded of Thucydides, who writes:
> "So long as a vessel was coming up to charge another boat,
> the men on the decks rained darts, arrows, and stones upon
> her, but once alongside, the heavy infantry tried to board
> 15 each other's vessel, fighting hand to hand. In many quarters
> it happened, because of the restricted space, that a vessel
> was charging an enemy on one side and being charged
> herself on another, and that two or even more ships were
> entangled all around one, obliging the helmsmen to attend
> 20 to defense here, offense there, not to one thing at a time,
> but to many things on all sides, while the huge commotion
> caused by the number of ships crashing together not only
> spread terror, but also made the orders of the boatswains
> inaudible." I urge you to remember Attica, and to remem-
> 25 ber the Spartan way, for.

The passage above is marked by pretentious and inflated speech; it is a perfect example of bombast.

Pun

A **pun** is a play on words. In general, a pun either plays on the multiple meanings of a word or replaces one word with another that is similar in sound but very different in meaning. Puns are almost always used for comic effect.

> Example: In *Star Wars,* why did the Evil Empire leave the Catholic nuns alone? Force of habit.

If you know anything about the significance of "the Force" in *Star Wars* and about the double meaning of "habit," you'll get the play on words here.

Metonymy and Synecdoche

Meto-WHAT?

Don't worry! Metonymy and synecdoche are tested very rarely on the AP Language exam.

Both *metonymy* and *synecdoche* are terms that mean the use of figurative language in which characteristics are substituted for the things with which they are associated.

In **metonymy,** one term is substituted for another term with which it is closely associated.

> Example: The sailors drank a glass of hearty red.

Red is a color; sailors cannot drink it. However, metonymically, the color represents wine (red wine), which sailors over the age of twenty-one may drink.

Synecdoche is a form of metonymy that's restricted to cases where a part is used to signify the whole.

> Example: All hands on deck!

The hands (part of each sailor) represent the sailors (the whole).

If you have an aversion for learning rhetorical terms, then for the purposes of this exam you can feel free to forget the definition of synecdoche; you can get away with using the term *metonymy* for any situation in which a characteristic of a certain thing is used to represent the thing.

Theme

A **theme** is a general idea contained in a text; the theme may be stated explicitly or only suggested. A theme is not just an idea; it is *an idea that is developed,* often over the course of a chapter or an entire book. Usually, one can identify a central theme and several minor ones. Sometimes both are overtly stated, as in the example that follows:

> Example: Many scholars agree that the central theme in *Huckleberry Finn* is the conflict between nature and civilization. But clearly, the book contains other themes, such as the worth of honor and the voyage of self-discovery.

Read the following passage, and see if you can identify a central theme.

> We now touch on civilization's most sensitive spot; it is an unpleasant task to raise one's voice against the folly of the day, against chimeras that have caused a downright epidemic.
>
> *Line*
> 5   To speak against the absurdities of trade today means to expose oneself to anathemas, just as much as if one had spoken against the tyranny of the popes and the barons in the twelfth century. If it were a matter of choosing between two dangerous roles, I think it would be less dangerous
> 10 to offend a sovereign with bitter truths than to offend the mercantile spirit that now rules like a despot over civiliza- tion—and even over sovereigns!
>   And yet a superficial analysis will prove that our com- mercial systems defile and disorganize civilization and that
> 15 in trade, as in all other things, we are being led further and further astray.
>   The controversy on trade is barely half a century old and has already produced thousands of books, and yet the participants in the controversy have not seen that the trade
> 20 mechanism is organized in such a way that it is a slap in the face to all common sense. It has subordinated the whole of society to one class of parasitic and unproductive persons: the merchants. All the essential classes of society—the proprietor, the farmer, the manufacturer, and even the gov-
> 25 ernment—find themselves dominated by a non-essential, contingent class, the merchant, who should be their subor- dinate, their employed agent, removable and accountable, and who, nevertheless, directs and obstructs at will all the avenues of circulation.

It should not surprise you that the title of the essay that this passage is excerpted from is "On Trade." In his essay, the French socialist Charles Fourier develops a central theme: Merchants, through trade, have both corrupted society and become its tyrant.

Many of the passages in the multiple-choice and free-response sections of the AP exam are long enough to permit you to identify at least one central theme, and you will almost certainly be asked to do so.

Aphorism

An **aphorism** is a concise, pithy statement of an opinion or a general truth.

> Example: Life is short, the art [of medicine] is long, opportunity fleeting, experimentation dangerous, reasoning difficult.

That aphorism is attributed to Hippocrates, the "Father of Medicine." Note that his statement is more sophisticated than the "commonplace wisdom" of a saying like "Haste makes waste."

There are several literary terms that have similar meanings. The AP will not test you on the minute differences among the terms but rather on your familiarity with them.

Aphorism: "Power tends to corrupt, and absolute power corrupts absolutely." (Lord Acton)

Adage/Proverb: "Nothing ventured, nothing gained."

Maxim: "Where there's life, there's hope."

Motto: "All the news that's fit to print." *(New York Times)*

Malapropism

Malapropism is the unintentional use of a word that resembles the word intended but that has a very different meaning.

> Example: He was a man of great statue.

The AP English Language and Composition readers often collect malapropisms to share with friends and colleagues as they read through the free-response essays; it isn't in your best interest to provide them with any good laughs, so try to avoid them.

Circumlocution and Euphemism

Circumlocution has two meanings, and you should be familiar with both of them. For the purposes of this exam, we'll say that one meaning of circumlocution is "talking around a subject" and that the other is "talking around a word." Now let's take a closer look at some examples of circumlocution.

It is entirely possible that you have used circumlocution when addressing your parents. For instance, instead of simply asking them straight out if you may borrow the car, have you ever said something such as, "I understand that you guys are going to stay in tonight and watch a DVD, right? If so, since I've already seen that movie, I was thinking about maybe going downtown. It's a nice summer evening and all that, but it's still too far to walk, and I'll be with Nina, anyway, and she'd never agree to walk downtown. We were thinking that she could drive, but, unfortunately, Nina's parents are going out, so she can't take their car. I know that I forgot to put gas in your car the last time that I drove to the mountains, but I learned my lesson. That won't happen again." You may even have gone on speaking for longer. You might never have gotten to the point where you actually asked to borrow the car, but your parents understood what you wanted and put you out of your misery by saying something such as, "We already told your sister that she could use the car tonight."

That kind of circumlocution is an example of the first meaning of circumlocution—"talking around the subject."

On the AP English Language and Composition Exam, you're more likely to encounter the second type of circumlocution—"talking around a word"—that is, using several words or a phrase in place of a specific word (or specific words). You may have noticed that sometimes it is more effective to be wordy than to be precise. For example, some people consider their automobiles cars, and, not surprisingly, they refer to these objects just as cars. Other people, however, use evocative circumlocutions when referring to their heap of metal—one of which is "cruisin' machine" (and the other of which is "heap of metal"). The point is that circumlocution is often an effective means for communicating points of view. Take a look at the following sentence.

> Example: Candide was court-martialed, and he was asked which he liked
> better, to run the gauntlet six and thirty times through the whole regiment,
> or to have his brains blown out with a dozen musket-balls.

In this sentence, we read that in a spirit of compassion and justice, the military court is giving Candide a choice: He may choose to be either beaten to death or executed by firing squad. The wording of the second choice, in particular, provides a wonderful example of the evocative power of well-used circumlocution. While using the phrase "execution by firing squad" would have allowed both the author and the reader to remain distant from the event and dispassionate, the circumlocution that the author employed with "to have his brains blown out with a dozen musket-balls" vividly describes the horror and brutality of the event. In this sentence, Voltaire succeeds in relating his feelings about the court-martial without commenting on it.

A **euphemism** is a word or words that are used to avoid employing an unpleasant or offensive term. Again, you probably (hopefully) use euphemisms all the time. In both fiction and nonfiction, the most common euphemisms have to do with sex. In these cases, the author knows what he or she means, you know what he or she means, and the author knows that you know what he or she means. Let's look at another example from Voltaire's *Candide*. In this passage, Voltaire uses euphemism for comic effect.

> Example: One day when Mademoiselle Cunégonde went to take a walk
> in a little neighboring wood that was called a park, she saw—through the
> bushes—the sage Doctor Pangloss giving a lecture in experimental philosophy
> to her mother's chambermaid, a little brown wench, very pretty and very
> accommodating.

Voltaire knows that his readers know what is really going on here. This particular example of euphemism is used for comic effect rather than direct avoidance of the word *sex*. One may expect Pangloss to limit his sagacity to philosophical matters, but clearly his "lecture in experimental philosophy" is most prosaic.

IRONY AND SATIRE

When reading the passages on the AP English Language Exam, you cannot always take what you see at face value; in fact, when reading you must always be on the lookout for slightly or very veiled meanings behind the words.

Isn't It Ironic?

Irony: Most people use the term without really knowing its definition. Alanis Morissette's 1996 song about irony didn't help the situation. If you don't believe this, ask one of your friends to define irony and see what kind of answer you receive. The two basic types of irony that you'll need to be familiar with for this test are verbal irony and situational irony.

Verbal Irony

Verbal irony refers to the process of stating something but *meaning* the opposite of what is stated. Verbal irony can refer to irony that's used in spoken language as well as in print. In spoken language, intonation is often a clue to ironic intent; however, in writing, it is not possible to imply things through intonation, so there's always a danger that the irony may be missed; in essence, the writer who employs irony risks communicating the exact opposite of what is intended. For example, let's say that you write, "This Princeton Review book is really interesting." Unless your listener or reader hears your remark in context, he or she won't know if this is high praise for this book, or if you're bored silly and have chosen to express your sentiment more forcefully by using verbal irony.

Consider the following passage. The philosopher Pangloss has just given a rather personalized history of venereal disease, a veritable uncontrollable—and uncontrolled—plague in eighteenth-century Europe.

> "O sage Pangloss," cried Candide, "what a strange genealogy is this! Is not the devil at the root of it all?"

> "Not at all," replied the great man, "it was unavoidable, a necessary ingredient in the best of worlds."

The student Candide shows sincere respect for Pangloss when he addresses him as "sage Pangloss;" Candide has no ironic intent. However, the same cannot be said of the narrator—who for all intents and purposes is Voltaire. In *Candide,* one of Voltaire's principal aims is to excoriate (to censure scathingly) the "philosophers of optimism," of whom Pangloss is a caricature. He does this through the frequent use of verbal irony; in the passage above, his use of "great man" is ironic—even though Candide's tone is not. After all, neither the narrator nor the careful reader views Pangloss as a great man—he is just the opposite.

Rain on Your Wedding Day

Irony is not mere misfortune. It is a set of circumstances that wind up the opposite of how the reader would expect them to turn out or how the characters had planned.

In essence, to fully appreciate the passage, we must read in stereo, simultaneously picking up on Candide's serious tone and the narrator's ironic tone. This is a pretty complicated case of verbal irony.

Sarcasm is simply verbal irony used with the intent to injure. It's often impossible to discern between irony and sarcasm, and, more often than not, sarcasm is in the mind of the beholder. Let's say that your close friend and soccer teammate missed a wide-open goal from ten feet away, and you smiled and shouted, "Nice shot!" Presumably your friend, used to your jests, would interpret your quip as playful irony. If the opposing team's goalie said the same words, however, it is far more likely that your friend would take the remark as sarcasm—and reply with a not-so-kind word or two. In written form, irony and sarcasm can be considered to be fairly synonymous—but just think of sarcasm as malicious. Here is an example from Heinrich Ibsen's *Hedda Gabbler*.

> Brack: There's a possibility that the appointment may be decided by competition—
>
> Tesman: Competition! By Jove, Hedda, fancy that!
>
> Hedda: [*motionless in her chair*] How exciting, Tesman.

Of course, it is easier to see the sarcasm when you are familiar with the play, but it is sufficient for you to know that Tesman is the rather boring, plodding husband and that Hedda is an unfulfilled wife. The stage direction ("motionless in her chair") helps us see that her words are at least full of irony; if you add the bitter, malignant intent, which the husband misses but we do not, then you have sarcasm.

Situational Irony

Situational irony refers to a situation that runs contrary to what was expected.

Suppose you live in Seattle during the rainy season and plan a vacation to sunny Phoenix. While you are in Phoenix, it rains every day there, but is sunny the entire week in Seattle. This is situational irony.

Situational Irony

A simple example of situational irony can be found in the classic tale "The Gift of the Magi." Jim and Delia are a poor couple who have no money to buy each other gifts for Christmas. Jim sells his watch to buy Delia a comb for her hair. Delia sells her hair to buy Jim a watch-chain. Both gifts wind up useless to their respective recipients—the ultimate in irony.

Satire

In **satire,** something is portrayed in a way that's deliberately distorted to achieve comic effect. Implicit in most satire is the author's desire to critique what is being mocked. Voltaire's *Candide* is principally a satire of optimism, the philosophy that, given that the first "cause" was perfect (God's creation of the world), all causes and effects must naturally be part of this original perfect plan. The French satirist takes on many other causes, however, and one of his favorite targets is the part of religion that he considers no more than fanatical superstition. Here is what happens after

Candide and Pangloss are caught in the infamous earthquake of Lisbon, Portugal.

> After the earthquake, which had destroyed three-fourths
> of the city of Lisbon, the sages of that country could think
> of no better manner to preserve the kingdom from complete
> *Line* ruin than to entertain the people with an *auto-da-fe,* it hav-
> 5 ing been decided by the University of Coimbra that burning
> a few people alive over low heat and with great ceremony
> is an infallible way to prevent earthquakes.
> In consequence, they had seized a Biscayan for marrying
> his godmother and two Portuguese for taking out the bacon
> 10 of a larded chicken they were eating; after dinner, they
> came and took into custody Doctor Pangloss and his pupil
> Candide, the one for speaking his mind and the other for
> appearing to approve what he heard. They were conducted
> to separate apartments, which were extremely cool and
> 15 where they were never bothered by the sun. Eight days
> later, they were each dressed in a *sanbenito* and their heads
> were adorned with paper *mitres.* The *mitre* and *sanbenito*
> worn by Candide were painted with upside down flames
> and with devils that had neither tails nor claws, but Doctor
> 20 Pangloss's devils had both tails and claws, and his flames
> were right side up. In these clothes they marched in the
> procession and heard a very pathetic sermon, which was
> followed by an anthem accompanied by bagpipes. Candide
> was flogged to the beat of the music while the anthem was
> 25 being sung; the Biscayan and the two men who would not
> eat bacon were burned, and Pangloss was hanged, which
> is not a common custom at these solemnities. The same
> day there was another earthquake, which created the most
> dreadful havoc.

After the real earthquake of 1755, there were real *auto-da-fes* ("acts of faith"), where "evil" inhabitants of Lisbon were sacrificed to appease God, who, ostensibly (to all outward appearances), had provoked the earthquake to punish the city. The "evils" that are being punished say more about the ridiculous prejudices of the persecutors than they do about the so-called evil victims. The two Portuguese who refrained from eating the bacon are guilty of nothing—but they are taken for Jews; the man who married his godmother, who, presumably, is not tied to him by blood, is guilty of no more than infringing on a technicality of the religious code (Catholicism, in this case).

Note that the satire is heightened by Voltaire's use of verbal irony ("the sages"), situational irony (right after the ceremony there is a second earthquake), and a comical circumlocution ("burning a few people alive over low heat and with great ceremony" is a circumlocution for *auto-da-fe*). Satire can be effective in both fiction and nonfiction, and *Candide,* a philosophical story that combines both, is thought to be one of the most brilliant satires of all.

The following terms are similar, but not identical. Know the differences.

Satire: A social or political criticism that relies heavily on irony, sarcasm, and often humor

Parody: Imitation for comic effect

Lampoon: Sharp ridicule of the behavior or character of a person or institution

Caricature: A ludicrous exaggeration of the defects of persons or things

Most critics, however, relegate satire—and satirists—to a secondary sphere in the universe of writing; satire makes for good entertainment, but mocking others does not measure up to the conviction of cogent writing. Had Voltaire been nothing more than a satirist, he would not have been remembered as a brilliant *philosophe,* but as a clever joker—if he were remembered at all. Although Voltaire's satire in *Candide* is quite brilliant, some other examples of satire are a little easier to figure out. Let's look at a sample question based on a passage from Jonathan Swift's *Gulliver's Travels.*

> For about seventy moons past there have been two
> struggling parties in this empire, under the names of
> *Tramecksan* and *Slamecksan,* from the high and low heels
> *Line* of their shoes, by which they distinguish themselves. It is
> 5 alleged, indeed, that the high heels are most agreeable to
> our ancient constitution; but, however this be, his majesty
> has determined to make use only of low heels in the admin-
> istration of the government, and all offices in the gift of the
> crown, as you cannot but observe; and particularly that his
> 10 majesty's imperial heels are lower at least by a *drurr* than
> any of his court (*drurr* is a measure about the fourteenth
> part of an inch). The animosities between these two parties
> run so high, that they will neither eat, nor drink, nor talk
> with each other. We compute the *Tramecksan,* or high
> 15 heels, to exceed us in number; but the power is wholly on
> our side. We apprehend his imperial highness, the heir to
> the crown, to have some tendency towards the high heels;
> at least we can plainly discover that one of his heels is
> higher than the other, which gives him a hobble in his gait.

5. The above passage is an example of

   (A) an analysis of court customs
   (B) a satire of British footwear
   (C) a study of British eccentricities
   (D) a satire of the British court
   (E) a nonsensical account of life at court

Well, the correct answer must be either (B) or (D) because this section is all about satire. The correct answer is (D). The passage serves to satirize the Whig-Tory discord (the Whigs dominated politics during much of the eighteenth century) and the relationship of the "parties" (the Whigs and Tories were not really political parties as we know them today) and the king. Unless you recognize that the passage is satirical, you will not have a good grasp of what is going on—which will lead to major problems with all of the multiple-choice questions on that passage.

REFLECT

Respond to the following questions:

- For which topics discussed in this chapter do you feel you have achieved sufficient mastery to answer multiple-choice questions correctly?

- For which topics discussed in this chapter do you feel you have achieved sufficient mastery to discuss effectively in an essay?

- For which topics discussed in this chapter do you feel you need more work before you can answer multiple-choice questions correctly?

- For which topics discussed in this chapter do you feel you need more work before you can discuss effectively in an essay?

- What parts of this chapter are you going to re-review?

- Will you seek further help, outside of this book (such as a teacher, tutor, or AP Central), on any of the topics in this chapter—and, if so, on which ones?

Chapter 9
Rhetorical Fallacies

AVOIDING THE FATAL FALLACY

A **fallacy** is strictly defined as guile or trickery or a false or mistaken idea. Fallacies have the appearance of truth but are erroneous. Let's say that you really want to attend a famous university in Cambridge, Massachusetts, and you've heard that the acceptance rate for the institution is 25 percent higher for early decision applicants than for regular applicants. However, it is a fallacy that applying early would increase your chances of being accepted. But why? Because if you have a 2.8 GPA, then that university isn't going to accept you regardless of when you apply.

Does this sound more like logic and rhetoric than language to you? What is it doing on the AP English Language and Composition Exam? Well, as we mentioned earlier, although "language" is contained in the title of this exam, the exam primarily tests rhetoric and composition. In other words, this exam tests how language works.

In this chapter we provide you with an overview of some common rhetorical fallacies. You should be familiar with *all* of these for the exam.

> Rhetorical fallacies may appear as answers on the multiple-choice sections. In addition, they may be relevant to your essays in the free-response questions.

COMMON RHETORICAL FALLACIES

Oftentimes, when writers have trouble making convincing "honest" arguments with the facts that they have in hand, they resort to using rhetorical fallacies. As you may expect, when you begin to write your essays in the free-response section of the exam, you shouldn't resort to these tactics. However, you should be able to recognize the use of these common fallacies in the reasoning of others; this will help you substantially on test day.

Ad Hominem Argument

An *ad hominem* (in Latin, "to the man") **argument** is any kind of fallacious argument that criticizes an idea by pointing something out about the person who holds the idea, rather than directly addressing the actual merit of the idea. There are people who learn this form of rhetorical fallacy at a very tender age and may argue thusly: "You're wrong because you're a jerk." But there are plenty of mature examples of *ad hominem* arguments, too.

> Example: Of course the writer supports tax cuts; She's rich!

The attack shifts from the issue (tax cuts) to the wealth of the writer.

Argument from Authority (or Argument from False Authority)

An **argument from authority** tempts us to agree with the writer's assumptions based on the authority of a famous person or entity or on his or her own character (when the writers are well-known).

> Example: It is absurd to believe that professional baseball players have used steroids because the most famous slugger of our time has repeatedly asserted that such a claim is false.

You see how it works? Or how about this: If The Princeton Review put the following quotation on the back cover of a book, how impressed would you be?

> "This is absolutely awesome—it's the best review book ever written."—John Schiff

Would that convince you? Probably not. How about this quote?

> "This is absolutely awesome—it's the best review book ever written."—Shakira

Even though the pop star didn't have to take AP exams in her native Colombia, her fame may give her the authority necessary to get some students to buy the book.

You're My Hero

"Argument from authority" is really *"ad hominum"* turned upside down.

Appeal to Ignorance

Appeal to ignorance is based on the assumption that whatever has not been proven false must be true (or, similarly, whatever has not been proven true must be false).

> Example #1: No one can prove that the Loch Ness monster does not exist; therefore the Loch Ness monster exists.

> Example #2: No one can prove that the Loch Ness monster exists; therefore the Loch Ness monster does not exist.

This is a fairly common form of rhetorical fallacy.

You Can't Prove I'm Not Right

"Appeal to Ignorance" is also known as an "Absence of Evidence" flaw, because the absence of evidence to the contrary does not, in fact, prove anything.

Begging the Question

Begging the question is a fallacious form of argument in which someone assumes that parts (or all) of what the person claims to be proving are proven facts. (Keep in mind that this does not refer to incomplete or illogical statements that actually would prompt someone to ask a question.) This circular form of reasoning is easier to grasp by example than explanation.

> Example #1: The Loch Ness monster spoke to me in my dreams, so it must exist.

Well, wouldn't you want me to prove to you *first* that the Loch Ness monster really did speak to me in my dreams before you would accept my conclusion? I hope so. It may have been the pepperoni pizza that was speaking to me in my dreams.

> Example #2: Examine the following scenario.
>
> Interviewer: Your resume looks impressive, but I need another reference.
>
> Brendan: Heidi can give me a good reference.
>
> Interviewer: Good, but how do I know that Heidi is trustworthy?
>
> Brendan: I can vouch for her.

Hasty Generalization

Sometimes a writer will deliberately lead you to a conclusion by providing insufficient, selective evidence. This is called a **hasty generalization.**

Make Haste

Hasty generalization is also known as a sampling error.

> Example: Ping-pong is an extremely dangerous sport; last year, my friend got hit in the eye with a ping-pong ball and almost lost his vision in that eye.

This rhetorical fallacy can be used very effectively. In the case of hasty generalization, often statistics that are "good"—meaning empirically true—are used to "prove" things that aren't true.

Non Sequitur

In Latin, **non sequitur** means "It doesn't follow." In English, a *non sequitur* is a statement that does not logically relate to what comes before it.

> Example: If you really wanted to earn a 5 on the AP English Language and Composition Exam, you wouldn't spend so much time reading Isabel Allende's novels.

Wait a second. First of all, reading novels may help you prepare for the exam. Second, who says that you don't have plenty of time for preparing for the exam and reading—especially now that you've stopped wasting time in front of the computer? In a *non sequitur,* there is no logical connection between the initial phrase and the one that follows it, so you shouldn't try to make one.

False Dichotomy

False dichotomy consists of a consideration of only the two extremes when there are one or more intermediate possibilities.

Example: AP Calculus BC class is impossible; either you get it or you don't.

This statement sounds like a great way to explain to your parents why you just earned a less-than-stellar grade on your last calculus test, but it sets up a false dichotomy. In fact, there are various levels of understanding and thus various degrees of success in AP Calculus, and as is the case in many fields, success is a direct result of effort.

Slippery Slope

Slippery slope arguments suggest dire consequences from relatively minor causes.

Example: If we stop requiring men to wear coats and ties in the dining room, pretty soon they'll start coming in dressed in beachwear.

Another way that the slippery slope fallacy can be expressed is by the phrase "give 'em an inch, and they'll take a mile."

Faulty Causality

Faulty causality refers to the (sometimes unintentional) setting up of a cause-and-effect relationship when none exists. In faulty causality, one event can happen after another without the first necessarily being the direct cause of the second.

Example: Violent crime among adolescents has risen in the past decade, and that is the result of increased sales of violent video games.

As is the case with all examples of faulty causality, there is no proof for the video game argument, and it is possible to think of a dozen other convincing reasons for the rise of violent crime—a trend that we just made up.

Straw Man Argument

The **straw man argument** consists of an oversimplification of an opponent's argument to make it easier to attack.

Here's an example of how this works.

Example: Students who want to eliminate the school uniform are exhibitionists who want to show off bare midriffs.

Reverse Causation

Causal arguments are often flawed because the reverse causation is equally plausible. For example: "Eating too much chocolate can make you depressed." Well, it's just as likely that depressed people might feel the urge to eat chocolate. If the author says "A caused B," ask yourself, "Is it possible that B caused A"? (Now pass the Dove miniatures!)

In fact, students who are arguing against having to wear a school uniform may be interested only in expressing their individuality; it's even possible that they would be happy in conservative clothing. However, if the author of this sentence attributes a simplistic argument to the students, who had, in reality, a more substantive motivation (individuality), it is easier to attack their position.

Sentimental Appeals

A **sentimental appeal** is a tactic that attempts to appeal to the *hearts* of readers (or, of course, listeners) so that they forget to use their *minds*.

Flashback

Remember pathos?

> Example: "The assignment that I gave you last night was much too long, but just think how pleased your parents and I will be when you score a 5 on the AP exam. Think about the pride you'll feel when tears of joy stream down our faces!"

Here, the teacher knew that arguing that the assignment was an important intellectual exercise wouldn't convince his or her students, even though that may have been a more valid argument. So in this case, he or she decided to use a sentimental appeal. Sentimental appeals are generally not valid arguments, but they work sometimes!

Red Herring

A **red herring** attempts to shift attention away from an important issue by introducing an issue that has no logical connection to the discussion at hand.

> Example: "My opponent talks about the poor quality of military intelligence, but this is a time for decisiveness, not for weakness. We must stick together and present a common front as the other nations look on. If we do not, we could jeopardize our position as a global leader."

As you can see, this is very similar to a sentimental appeal, although the political speaker is (apparently) still appealing to minds, rather than sentiments. In this case, the speaker shifts the discussion from the topic under debate (military intelligence) to a different issue (our role as a super power).

Scare Tactics

The aptly named **scare tactic** is used to frighten readers or listeners into agreeing with the speaker; often, when scare tactics are used, the speaker has no logical argument on which to fall back.

> Example: "My opponent talks about the need to explore stem cell research, but this would bring about an end to ethical uses of technology, and, before long, scientists will be creating superraces—the Nazi dream of an Aryan Nation will ensue!"

Here the speaker mentions Nazis to frighten the listeners; there is no logical (or at least, logically presented) link between exploring stem cell research and the creation of an Aryan Nation. The example may seem to you like a combination of scare tactics and slippery slope; this combination is sometimes seen when a slippery slope argument is used to scare readers or listeners.

Bandwagon Appeals

Bandwagon appeals have a different name in school settings; there, they are known as "peer pressure." A bandwagon appeal encourages the listener to agree with a position because everyone else does. The logic goes something like this: If everybody else is doing it, it must be all right.

> Example: It's time for our county to repeal the ban on strip mining—every other county in the state has already done so!

Notice that the speaker (or writer) avoids having to explain the merits of the issue and explain why the ban is inappropriate.

Dogmatism

Dogmatism does not allow for discussion because the speaker presumes that his or her beliefs are beyond question; essentially, the "logic" runs thusly: I'm correct because I'm correct.

> Example: We are members of the Wombat Party and, as such, know that we are right when we assert that Wombats are the best!

There is no way to rebut the claim.

Your Karma Ran Over My Dogma

A dogma is simply a deeply held belief.

Equivocation

Equivocation is telling part of the truth, while deliberately hiding the entire truth; typically, this is similar to lying by omission.

> Example: There is a Pink Panther movie in which Inspector Clouseau enters a quaint European hotel and, upon spying a cute little dog, asks the owner, "Does your dog bite?" The manager responds, "No," and Clouseau attempts to pet the dog, which growls and bites him. "You told me that your dog does not bite!" exclaims Clouseau. "That's not my dog," responds the owner.

Setting the comedy aside for a moment, the owner of the chalet gave an equivocal answer. Presumably, he was telling the truth when he responded that his dog does not bite, but that truth hid the more relevant truth—the dog he was with at the time does, in fact, bite. It is possible that you have indulged in equivocation. Let's say that you're about to leave the house, but your mom stops you and says, "You're not going to Marina's party tonight, are you? I heard that her parents are out of town and there's not going to be any supervision." "No, Mom, I'm not going there." Your mom smiles in relief and lets you go. You're relieved too because you are going to Dave's party, where there will be no supervision because his parents are out of town. You did not exactly lie because you truly are not going to Marina's party; however, you did lie because you are going to the same kind of party somewhere else, and it is the *kind* of party that your mom objects to, not its specific location.

Faulty Analogy

A **faulty analogy** is an illogical, misleading comparison between two things.

> Example: Why should we invade that country? Let me explain it to you like this. What if you looked out the window and saw a $20 bill in the street? Wouldn't you go outside and take it?

This analogy is *really* faulty! A better analogy would be: What if you saw a person in the street with a $20 bill? Wouldn't you go outside and try to steal it from the person? Analogy is always a weak form of argumentation; a faulty analogy exploits this weakness to mislead listeners (or readers), when true logic may not convince them.

As we mentioned earlier, make sure you have memorized all of these rhetorical fallacies before test day. After you've studied them carefully (make flashcards if you need to, using the examples we gave you), try the following questions.

SAMPLE QUESTIONS

In each question, choose the most fitting rhetorical fallacy.

1. If such actions were not illegal, then they would not be prohibited by law.

   (A) faulty causality
   (B) begging the question
   (C) appeal to ignorance
   (D) argument from authority
   (E) *ad hominem*

2. We all knew he would think abortion is wrong! He's a priest!

   (A) faulty causality
   (B) hasty generalization
   (C) *ad hominem*
   (D) false dichotomy
   (E) dogmatism

3. "Recently, I've been thinking that there is some merit in the Republicans' tax-cut plan. I suggest that we come up with something like it because if we Democrats are going to survive as a party, we have got to show the people that we are as tough-minded as the Republicans, because that is what the public wants."

   (A) red herring
   (B) straw man argument
   (C) slippery slope
   (D) equivocation
   (E) *non sequitur*

4. "We should have a car wash to raise money for Senior Prom. The three classes before us have all done it!"

   (A) begging the question
   (B) bandwagon appeal
   (C) red herring
   (D) scare tactics
   (E) dogmatism

5. The mill must be polluting the river because there has been a recent increase in bird deaths around there.

   (A) straw man argument
   (B) appeal to ignorance
   (C) faulty analogy
   (D) *non sequitur*
   (E) slippery slope

Rhetorical fallacies, when used with savvy, can be very convincing. It is worth knowing about them to do well on the AP English Language and Composition Exam and to become a critical reader and listener.

Don't become a victim of clever rhetorical tactics!

In the next chapter, we will discuss rhetorical modes, or patterns of exposition. This is an important topic because it will outline ready-made tactics and methods for writing your free-response essays.

The answers to the above questions are: (B), (C), (A), (B), and (D). If you didn't get them right, go back and review those rhetorical terms.

REFLECT

Respond to the following questions:

- For which topics discussed in this chapter do you feel you have achieved sufficient mastery to answer multiple-choice questions correctly?

- For which topics discussed in this chapter do you feel you have achieved sufficient mastery to discuss effectively in an essay?

- For which topics discussed in this chapter do you feel you need more work before you can answer multiple-choice questions correctly?

- For which topics discussed in this chapter do you feel you need more work before you can discuss effectively in an essay?

- What parts of this chapter are you going to re-review?

- Will you seek further help, outside of this book (such as a teacher, tutor, or AP Central), on any of the topics in this chapter—and, if so, on which ones?

Chapter 10
Basic Rhetorical Modes

WHAT ARE RHETORICAL MODES?

The rhetorical modes (or patterns) contained in this chapter are worth studying for two reasons. First, they will provide you with ready-made approaches for writing your essays on the exam, and second, the multiple-choice questions on the test also often include some of the rhetorical mode terminology.

As you prepare for the exam by taking practice tests, you'll see that 40 minutes is not much time in which to write a sophisticated essay, and the shortcuts you'll learn in this chapter will be invaluable in helping you write a great essay in the allotted time. However, you do not need to cram and memorize all the material in this section. If you read and understand the explanations and just make sure you retain the basics, you'll be comfortable enough with the process to do well on the exam.

Another important point to remember is that, more often than not, rhetorical modes are used in combination. Breaking them up into individual components is a somewhat arbitrary process—but for our purposes, it makes the material easier to understand. Let's begin.

EXAMPLE OR ILLUSTRATION

Our first rhetorical mode consists of using specific examples to illustrate an idea. Now, this may seem like a pretty simple idea, but one of the most common mistakes students make when writing their AP English Language and Composition essays is to use poor examples. Remember that all examples are not created equal. If you use poor illustrative examples, your ideas will be communicated much less clearly and effectively than if you'd used solid, appropriate ones. In writing these essays, your principal goal is clarity.

Read the following passage based on *Candide*, and as you do so, evaluate the effectiveness of the examples that it uses.

> Pangloss is correct when he claims that everything is for the best in the best of all possible worlds. First of all, we are seeing more and more technological innovation every year. Computer technology, in particular, has helped us in many ways, and break-throughs in medicine have helped raise the life expectancy significantly. Furthermore, in most cities, there are bustling restaurants and great nightlife. Finally, travel has become affordable for most people, and paradises like Aruba and Hawaii await us all!

Surely you agree that the examples are not convincing, but you should also understand that they are not even relevant. Implicit in the examples chosen is the reduction of the best of all possible worlds to the writer's own tiny corner. A better approach would be something as follows:

> Pangloss is correct when he claims that everything is for the best in the best of all possible worlds. First of all, the

challenges that we have faced or are facing have inspired some of our most important scientific advances. Great famines have led scientists to exciting new agricultural discoveries, such as drought-resistant crops; great droughts have inspired engineers to develop cost-effective desalination plants. In essence, the evils in the world have been necessary stimulants for changes for the better. Furthermore, advances in medicine are no longer restricted to the wealthy nations of the world, and there is reason to hope that coordinated efforts to help developing countries will become more effective; take, for example, the international relief efforts to help the people whose homes were destroyed by the recent tsunami. Not only will the victims have better and safer homes now, but also the cooperation among the developed nations will translate into a better, safer world. Indeed, everything is for the best.

While the second essay may be naive, at least it does its best to substantiate an untenable position. Without any doubt, the examples in the second passage are much more appropriate for the argument than those that were used in the first passage.

Just as it is important to choose relevant, convincing examples to substantiate your own ideas, it is essential to constantly evaluate the examples that others use in their attempts to explain or to convince.

Tricksters, dogmatists, and charlatans usually illustrate their positions with scanty, inappropriate details. Be critical.

Laundry List for Example (Illustration)

- Use examples that your reader (the person who reads your essays) will identify with and understand. Do not assume that the AP reader has seen the latest teen cult film or knows any pop culture icons younger than Britney Spears.

- Draw your examples from "real life," "real" culture (literature, art, classical music, and so on), and well-known folklore.

- Make sure the example really does illustrate your point. Don't use a fancy example just to show off your knowledge; find ones that really work!

- Introduce your examples using transitions, such as, *for example, for instance, case in point,* and *consider the case of.*

- A single example that is perfectly representative can serve to illustrate your point.

- A series of short, less-perfect (but still relevant) examples, can, by their accumulation, serve to illustrate your point.

- The ideal approach is to construct a well-developed, representative example supported by several shorter examples.

- Remember that you are in control of what you write. As you brainstorm, discard examples that may disprove your point. Your AP essays will have little or nothing to do with your beliefs or with a balanced examination of an issue. You will be defending a point of view (argumentative essay) or explaining something (expository essay)—don't feel like you have to be fair to all sides of an argument; your aim is to get your point across.

- Quality is more important than quantity; poorly chosen examples detract significantly from your presentation.

Sample Question

Write a thoughtful and carefully constructed essay in which you use specific examples to defend, challenge, or qualify the assertion that Hollywood movies are a reflection of a decaying society.

Drill: Reflect on How You Could Use Examples to Address the Following Topics

As you read each of the topics listed below, make a list of five examples you could use to support them. Are your examples all relevant? Do they support just this side of the argument? Treat each as the basis for your thesis statement in a practice free-response question.

TOPIC 1:   High schools unwittingly encourage students to cheat.

TOPIC 2:   Studying the humanities is important.

TOPIC 3:   Respecting diversity reveals much about a person.

CLASSIFICATION

How do you classify things? Well, you probably start by dividing up whatever you have into groups according to certain characteristics. For example, if you wanted to explain "new music" to someone, you might divide the artists into groups by type (female vocalists, male vocalists, and bands) and classify the groups by genre (heavy metal, punk rock, alternative, and so on). This would make the material easier for someone to understand because it would be organized. In other words: *We classify to more easily analyze and explain.*

When you place things into categories on the AP English Language and Composition Exam, avoid creating classifications that overlap. For example, it would not make sense to classify your favorite foods in the following way: sweets, barbecued meats, vegetables, and chocolates; logically, the last group is a smaller subset of the first group.

All of this boils down to the following: Classification is nearly the same thing as organization. And organization is important. As you know by now, the directions in the Free-Response section of the AP English Language and Composition Exam request that you write "a well-organized essay." It may seem obvious that the test writers would request this of you—but then you'd be surprised how poorly organized many of the AP essays that students write are. Classify before you write.

There is almost always more than one way to classify things. Right now, you may group your teachers as being either cool or uncool. Later, it's more likely that you'll classify them according to what they helped you learn: The new categories may be teachers who inspired you, teachers who taught you the most, teachers who taught you about life, and teachers who should not have been teachers.

Aristotle liked to classify, and he did so quite often. Some of classifications have stood the test of time, including the one you see below, which is the beginning of Part 6 of an essay entitled "Categories."

> Quantity is either discrete or continuous (…). Instances
> of discrete quantities are number and speech; instances
> of continuous quantities are lines, surfaces, solids, and,
> *Line* besides these, time and place.
> 5   In the case of the parts of a number, there is no common
> boundary at which they join. For example: two fives make
> ten, but the two fives have no common boundary, but are
> separate; the parts three and seven also do not join at any
> boundary. Nor, to generalize, would it ever be possible in
> 10 the case of number that there should be a common bound-
> ary among the parts; they are always separate. Number,
> therefore, is a discrete quantity.
>   The same is true of speech. That speech is a quantity
> is evident: for it is measured in long and short syllables.
> 15 I mean here that speech which is vocal. Moreover, it is a
> discrete quantity for its parts have no common boundary.
> There is no common boundary at which the syllables join,
> but each is separate and distinct from the rest.
>   A line, on the other hand, is a continuous quantity, for it
> 20 is possible to find a common boundary at which its parts
> join. In the case of the line, this common boundary is the
> point; in the case of the plane, it is the line, for the parts of
> the plane have also a common boundary. Similarly you can
> find a common boundary in the case of the parts of a solid,
> 25 namely either a line or a plane.
>   Space and time also belong to this class of quantities.
> Time, past, present, and future, forms a continuous whole.
> Space, likewise, is a continuous quantity; for the parts of
> a solid occupy a certain space, and these have a common
> 30 boundary; it follows that the parts of space also, which are
> occupied by the parts of the solid, have the same common
> boundary as the parts of the solid. Thus, not only time, but
> space also, is a continuous quantity, for its parts have a
> common boundary.

Here, Aristotle's division of quantity into two categories (discrete and continuous) makes sense. The examples that he uses to illustrate the nature of his categories reveal a great deal about his interests: time, space, language, and mathematics. This is a well-organized passage; the categories are well-defined and Aristotle has clearly explained why the members of each category have been put in their categories.

Laundry List for Classification

- Remember that when you're asked to analyze and explain something, classification will be very useful.

- Make sure you have a central idea (thesis).

- Sort your information into meaningful groups. Are there enough elements in each group to allow you to write a convincing, useful paragraph? Sometimes you'll find that you need to combine categories.

- Make sure you have a manageable number of categories—three or four. Remember that you have only about 40 minutes to plan and execute each essay.

- Make sure the categories (or the elements in the categories) do not overlap.

- Before writing, make sure the categories and central idea (thesis) are a good fit. Sometimes you'll want to modify your thesis statement based on the categories that you've found.

- As you write, do not justify your classification unless this is somehow necessary to address a very bizarre free-response question. Justify your thesis, not your categories.

Sample Question

Write a short essay in which you analyze the different methods a teacher uses to convey information to his or her class.

Drill: Reflect on How You Could Use Classification to Address the Following Topics

As you read each of the topics, think about how you would organize your essay in terms of classification. Come up with a possible thesis (central idea), and plan how you could categorize the information you have on these topics into three or four meaningful divisions.

TOPIC 1:   Television commercials

TOPIC 2:   Movies

TOPIC 3:   Students

TOPIC 4:   Cars

COMPARISON AND CONTRAST

You compare and contrast every day. When you note similarities between objects, people, characteristics, and even actions, you're making comparisons. When you note the differences, you're using a rhetorical mode called contrast.

It is very likely that you will have to use comparison and contrast when writing at least one of your essays for the free-response section of the AP test. Sometimes you'll use this mode merely *to explain*—especially when you're comparing something unfamiliar with something well known; other times, you will use comparison and contrast *to argue* in favor of one of the two elements.

> Keep in mind that to compare and contrast two elements, they need to have enough commonalities to justify comparison or contrast. It may be interesting to compare and contrast a baseball team from the National League and another from the American League, but it would be less pertinent (although potentially very entertaining) to compare and contrast one of those baseball teams with your neighbor's poker club.

To write a successful compare-and-contrast essay for the AP English Language and Composition Exam, you must first select the points of comparison (and contrast) and present them. Does this sound familiar? In other words, you must start by *classifying* them.

> The most common mistake people make when comparing and contrasting is to present a discussion of one of the elements first (in one paragraph), and then discuss the other element afterward (in a second paragraph). Do not do this.

Here is an example of a good method for comparing and contrasting.

Comparison and contrast of my favorite classes	
AP English	**AP Art History**
Involves essay writing, which I love	Involves essay writing
Teacher writes intriguing questions	Teacher writes intriguing questions
Most writing done in class	Most writing done out of class
Interesting reading	Interesting reading
A variety of books	A textbook
No pictures in books	Lots of pictures in book
Teacher is old	Teacher is young
Teacher tells bad jokes	Teacher is funny
Teacher is grumpy	Teacher is good-natured

Ideally, when you turned this into an essay you would not write the first half of your essay about AP English, and the second half about AP Art History. Using the information you collected in the outline above, ideally you would spend your first paragraph discussing the role of writing in both classes, spend your second paragraph discussing aspects of the reading in the two classes, and spend your third paragraph discussing the teachers. Integration is key in comparison and contrast.

Here is a real example, taken from Charles Darwin's *The Descent of Man,* of a passage that uses comparison and contrast.

My object in this chapter is to show that there is no fundamental difference between man and the higher mammals in their mental faculties. Each division of the subject might
Line have been extended into a separate essay but must here be
5 treated briefly. As no classification of the mental powers has been universally accepted, I shall arrange my remarks in the order most convenient for my purpose; and will select those facts which have struck me most, with the hope that they may produce some effect on the reader (…).
10 As man possesses the same senses as the lower animals, his fundamental intuitions must be the same. Man has also some few instincts in common, as that of self-preservation, sexual love, the love of the mother for her new-born offspring, the desire possessed by the latter to suck, and
15 so forth. But man, perhaps, has somewhat fewer instincts than those possessed by the animals which come next to him in the series. The orangutan in the Eastern islands and the chimpanzee in Africa, build platforms on which they sleep; and, as both species follow the same habit, it might
20 be argued that this was due to instinct, but we cannot feel sure that it is not the result of both animals having similar wants, and possessing similar powers of reasoning (…).
The lower animals, like man, manifestly feel pleasure and pain, happiness and misery. Happiness is never better
25 exhibited than by young animals, such as puppies, kittens, lambs, etc., when playing together, like our own children. Even insects play together, as has been described by that excellent observer, P. Huber, who saw ants chasing and pretending to bite each other, like so many puppies. The fact
30 that the lower animals are excited by the same emotions as ourselves is so well established, that it will not be necessary to weary the reader by many details. Terror acts in the same manner on them as on us, causing the muscles to tremble, the heart to palpitate, the sphincters to be relaxed,
35 and the hair to stand on end. Suspicion, the offspring of fear, is eminently characteristic of most wild animals (…).

Interestingly, Darwin extends this rhetorical mode of comparison and contrast over entire chapters of his famous work. Notice the rhetorical statements of comparison he uses (for example, "the lower animals, like man" or "like our own children"); Darwin does not leave it up to us to draw comparisons—he points out virtually all of them with examples. Speaking of examples (the first rhetorical mode that we discussed), notice that in the case of this passage, the two rhetorical modes of examples and comparison/contrast are used together.

It's Up to You

Don't rely upon the grader to form connections between your examples. Explain everything thoroughly!

Laundry List for Comparison and Contrast

- When comparing and contrasting A and B, find common elements (which will become your examples) from both.

- Do not write about A in one paragraph and B in another.

- Do your best to combine common elements into a limited number of groups—three, if possible—and write a paragraph about each group.

- Do not attempt to justify your groups or your examples; simply present them.

Sample Question

Write an essay in which you compare and contrast the careers and lifestyles of professional musicians and doctors. Be sure to include examples.

Drill: Reflect on How You Could Use Comparison and Contrast to Address the Following Topics

For each topic, make a list like the one above (AP English versus AP Art History). First, write down several similarities and differences. Then organize these similarities and differences in a logical manner; try to sort them out so that you have about three or four central ideas, which would translate into about three or four separate compare and contrast paragraphs. Do not attempt to answer the question by addressing one choice and then the other in separate paragraphs.

TOPIC 1:   Two of your friends

TOPIC 2:   Two teachers at your school

TOPIC 3:   Two singers or bands

TOPIC 4:   New York and Los Angeles (even if you haven't been to either)

TOPIC 5:   The experience of traveling to the mountains and the experience of traveling to the ocean

ANALOGY

Although analogies are not that useful in argumentative writing, they *are* useful in expository writing—this means that analogies will be useful when you write your expository essay for this test.

Analogies are sometimes used to explain things that are difficult to understand by comparing them with things that are easier to understand. Let's say that you want to explain how a well-run corporation works. You might explain that it functions like a football team. In both cases there are owners or stockholders. In the corporation, there's a CEO, who is similar to the coach of a football team. The CEO directs the managers (or vice presidents), just as the coach directs the assistant coaches; these work directly with the employees—the players. When an employee doesn't heed directions, the success of the enterprise is put at risk, just like when a player fails to execute a block or a tackle. The most important thing about using analogies is that you choose one that will be readily understood by your audience.

Think of an **analogy** as a comparison used to explain something.

In this case, if the reader knows nothing about football, this analogy may do more harm than good.

You can also use an analogy to explain something that's abstract by comparing it with something that's concrete. Throughout history, people have used analogies to explain their god or gods. Christians explain their god, for example, through analogy. They say that their god is like a father who loves his children and, thus, both punishes and rewards them. The only difference is that they consider their god's judgment to be perfect. They believe that their god is like a father in that both are good, but that the difference is that their god is *perfectly* good.

The most famous philosophical analogy serves as the basis for Plato's "allegory of the cave." The analogy purportedly evolved from a conversation between Socrates and Glaucon.

> Imagine human beings living in an underground cave;
> here they have been from their childhood, and they have
> their legs and necks chained so that they cannot move and
> *Line* can only see before them, being prevented by the chains
> 5 from turning round their heads. Above and behind them,
> a fire is blazing at a distance, and between the fire and the
> prisoners there is a raised way; and there is a low wall built
> along the way, like the screen which marionette players
> have to hide them and over which they show the puppets.
> 10 Men are passing along the wall (and screened by the
> wall) and are carrying all sorts of things and animals made
> of wood and stone and various materials that appear over
> the wall. Some of them are talking, others are silent.
> Like ourselves, they see only their own shadows, or the
> 15 shadows of one another, or the shadows of the things and
> animals, which the fire throws on the opposite wall of the
> cave.
> And if the human beings were able to converse with one
> another, would they not suppose that they were naming
> what was actually before them (even though they were
> 20 seeing only shadows of those things)?
> And suppose further that the prison had an echo which
> came from the other side, would they not be sure to fancy
> when one of the passers-by spoke that the voice which they
> heard came from the passing shadow?
> 25 To them, I said, the truth would be literally nothing but
> the shadows of the images.

This is only part of the analogy, but you probably get the idea. Socrates uses this analogy to explain that we think that we see things just as they really are in our world, but that we are seeing only reflections of a greater truth, an abstraction that we fail to grasp. The cave is our world; the shadows are the objects and people that we "see." We are like the prisoners, for we are not free to see what creates the shadows; the truth, made up of ideal forms, is out in the light.

Laundry List for Analogy

- Use analogy for expository writing (explanation).

- Do not use analogy for argumentative writing (argumentation).

- Use analogy to explain something difficult to understand or that is abstract.

- Make sure your audience will readily understand your "simple" or concrete subject.

Sample Question

Write an essay in which you explain the process of applying to college. Use analogy when appropriate.

Drill: Reflect on How You Could Use Analogy to Address the Following Topics

As you read each topic, think of it as the basis for the thesis of an expository essay. Come up with a simpler subject that you can use as an analogy for this more complex topic. Write down a basic plan for an essay.

TOPIC 1:   The way your school functions

TOPIC 2:   The benefits of honesty

MOVING ON...

In this chapter we discussed three rhetorical modes: example, classification, and comparison and contrast (analogy falls under this last category). Make sure you are familiar with the laundry lists in this chapter. If you get into good habits now when using these rhetorical modes, you'll be much better off on test day!

Further proving how useful these modes will be, we guarantee that both your expository and argumentative essay questions will fit into some combination of these modes.

Of course, remember to plan your essay before you begin writing. It often helps to write your thesis statement along with this plan so that you can keep in mind whether the parts of your plan are relevant to your central idea. This will ensure that you write the best organized, most coherent essay you can.

Now that we've covered the three basic rhetorical modes, let's move on to review a few complex modes in the next chapter.

REFLECT

Respond to the following questions:

- For which topics discussed in this chapter do you feel you have achieved sufficient mastery to answer multiple-choice questions correctly?

- For which topics discussed in this chapter do you feel you have achieved sufficient mastery to discuss effectively in an essay?

- For which topics discussed in this chapter do you feel you need more work before you can answer multiple-choice questions correctly?

- For which topics discussed in this chapter do you feel you need more work before you can discuss effectively in an essay?

- What parts of this chapter are you going to re-review?

- Will you seek further help, outside of this book (such as a teacher, tutor, or AP Central), on any of the topics in this chapter—and, if so, on which ones?

Chapter 11
Complex
Rhetorical
Modes

In this chapter, we'll discuss a few more—and more complex—rhetorical modes, including process analysis, cause-and-effect, definition, description, narration, and induction and deduction. As was the case with the rhetorical modes you learned about in the last chapter, it will be extremely beneficial to you to know all you can about these modes on test day. It will not only help you recognize when these modes are used in the sample passages, but also enable you to use them in your essays.

So let's jump right in.

PROCESS ANALYSIS

Process analysis is a rhetorical mode that's used by writers when they want to explain either how to do something or how something was done. When your science teacher hands you instructions for a lab, she is giving you a rather dry sheet of process analysis that says, "first do this; then do that; then examine the data; then explain such-and-such." When you write your lab report, you're also indulging in process analysis, saying, "first we did this; then we did that; then we examined the data; then we determined such-and-such." If you like to follow recipes when you cook, then you've already been exposed to process analysis. However, process analyses used in writing generally aren't as dry as recipes or how-to manuals; they usually have a few examples to spice them up a little.

Process analysis can be an effective way of relating an experience. Take, for example, this now famous passage about "dumpster diving."

> I learned to scavenge gradually, on my own. Since then I have initiated several companions into the trade. I have learned that there is a predictable series of stages a person
> *Line* goes through in learning to scavenge.
> 5   At first the new scavenger is filled with disgust and self-loathing. He is ashamed of being seen and may lurk around, trying to duck behind things, or he may try to dive at night. (In fact, most people instinctively look away from a scavenger. By skulking around, the novice calls attention
> 10 to himself and arouses suspicion. Diving at night is ineffective and needlessly messy.)
>   Every grain of rice seems to be a maggot. Everything seems to stink. He can wipe the egg yolk off the found can, but he cannot erase the stigma of eating garbage out of his
> 15 mind.
>   That stage passes with experience. The scavenger finds a pair of running shoes that fit and look and smell brand-new. He finds a pocket calculator in perfect working order. He finds pristine ice cream, still frozen, more than he can eat
> 20 or keep. He begins to understand: people do throw away perfectly good stuff, a lot of perfectly good stuff.
>   At this stage, Dumpster shyness begins to dissipate. The diver, after all, has the last laugh. He is finding all manner of good things which are his for the taking. Those who
> 25 disparage his profession are the fools, not he.

Mnemonics
If you're having trouble remembering rhetorical modes, make some flashcards and memorize them like vocabulary words.

He may begin to hang onto some perfectly good things
for which he has neither a use nor a market. Then he begins
to take note of the things which are not perfectly good but
are nearly so. He mates a Walkman with broken earphones
30 and one that is missing a battery cover. He picks up things
which he can repair.
At this stage he may become lost and never recover.
Dumpsters are full of things of some potential value to
someone and also of things which never have much intrin-
35 sic value but are interesting. All the Dumpster divers I have
known come to the point of trying to acquire everything
they touch. Why not take it, they reason, since it is all free.

Excerpt from "On Dumpster Diving" by Lars Eighner
from *Travels with Lizbeth* (St. Martin's Press)

Here's a good example of process analysis in writing. Although the material is organized in chronological stages, the author inserts explanatory examples and personal
commentary that make the passage more lively. In this passage, the author is not
instructing the reader on how to scavenge for food in Dumpsters; rather, he is
explaining the psychological evolution of a homeless scavenger—based on his own
experience—and illustrating the excesses of a consumerist society.

Laundry List for Process Analysis

> Remember that process analysis is a rhetorical mode that serves to organize
> something in a step-by-step manner, and it can serve both scientific and
> literary needs.

- Sequence is chronological and usually fixed—think of recipes.

- When you use this device, make sure the stages of the process are clear, by
  using transitions (e.g., *first, next, after two days, finally*).

- Make sure your terminology is appropriate for the reader. For example, the
  person who will read your essays probably does not know much about the
  embryonic development of frogs, so you should avoid using too-specialized
  terms like *Spemann organizer* or *Nieuwkoop center*.

- Verify that every step is clear; an error or omission in an intermediate step may
  make the rest of the process analysis very confusing. If you were describing
  how to braid hair, and wrote the following instructions: "First, comb or brush
  your hair so that it is untangled and manageable to work with. Next, take
  the far-right section of hair and put it over the middle section and under the
  far-left section." This could be confusing to your reader because you never said
  to divide the hair into three sections before starting the actual braiding process.

Sample Question

Write a short essay in which you describe the process of how you selected the colleges to which you applied (or are going to apply to).

Drill: Reflect on How You Could Use Process Analysis to Address the Following Topics

Try making a numbered list with a few examples. Make sure you have included all the necessary steps and have used appropriate language and terminology for your reader. Remember to use transition words when you write the essay.

TOPIC 1: How decisions are made at your school

TOPIC 2: How to get through your high school successfully

TOPIC 3: How to choose and keep close friends

CAUSE AND EFFECT

You just saw how process analysis is a useful rhetorical mode for explaining how to do things or how things were done; the rhetorical mode known as **cause and effect** explains *why things should be* or *should have been done*. In a sense, cause and effect explains the processes responsible for the process. You've probably received at least some rudimentary process analysis about how to use a computer at some point (first, turn on the computer; then launch your browser; log on to your IM; select someone else who is logged in…), but you probably don't know *why* all that works.

Some cause-and-effect relationships are easy to describe. For instance, read the example below from *Candide*'s Dr. Pangloss.

> "It is demonstrable," said Pangloss, "that things cannot
> be otherwise than as they are; for as all things have been
> created for some end, they must necessarily be created
> *Line* for the best end. Observe, for instance, the nose is formed
> 5 for spectacles; therefore we wear spectacles. The legs
> are visibly designed for stockings; accordingly we wear
> stockings. Stones were made to be hewn and to construct
> castles; therefore My Lord has a magnificent castle, for the
> greatest baron in the province ought to be the best lodged.
> 10 Swine were intended to be eaten; therefore we eat pork all
> the year round."

In this passage, Pangloss is using a series of cause-and-effect relationships to prove his point, that "things cannot be otherwise than as they are." This rhetorical mode is everywhere, however. You see examples of this rhetorical mode all around you.

On this exam, the causes and effects that you choose to explore will depend on what you're asked to explain. You may have to use cause and effect in your essays, possibly in combination with one or more other rhetorical modes; you may also see a few questions in the multiple-choice section that deal with how the author uses cause and effect to make a point. When making critical decisions, writers will often consider both the immediate and the long-term effects; when analyzing an important event, writers will often examine both the immediate and the underlying causes.

Laundry List for Cause and Effect

If you were writing about the poor average of AP English Language and Composition test scores at your school, you could go about it in two ways. First, you could examine some *immediate* causes: Ms. What's-Her-Name retired and was replaced by a teacher who had no experience teaching and no background in English, we didn't have a good review book for the exam, or the exam is administered in Room Z during school band practice. Alternatively, you could examine some *underlying* causes for the poor exam scores: The superintendent of schools changed hiring policies (so a terrible teacher was hired); last year, funds for buying books were diverted to buying new lockers for the football team (so we had no good review book); and the room that the school band normally practices in was flooded when a pipe broke.

- Do not confuse the relating of mere circumstances with a cause-and-effect relationship. For example, it is not logical to assume that socialism in Chile necessarily caused socialism in Argentina.

- Turn your causal relationships into causes and effects by using carefully chosen examples. Remember that not all causal relationships are causes and effects. However, careful use of evidence and examples can turn causal relationships into causes and effects.

- Make sure to carefully address each step in a series of causal relationships; if you don't, you risk losing your reader. Imagine the attendance secretary when she hears, "I'm sorry I'm late. We had a fire, so I had to find my cat." A better (clearer) explanation would have been: "I'm sorry I'm late. This morning at 4:00 A.M. there was an electrical fire in the garage; fortunately, there was an alarm that woke my dad, who put out the fire, but when he opened the garage door, my cat ran outside. I think it was frightened so it ran up a tree. I decided to climb up the tree and get the cat but I fell, and my mother had to take me to the emergency room."

Sample Question

Write an essay in which you examine the possible causes and effects of violence in the United States today.

Drill: Reflect on How You Could Use Cause and Effect to Address the Following Topics

TOPIC 1:   Academic dishonesty in high schools

TOPIC 2:   The fear of terrorism in the United States

TOPIC 3:   The changing face of ethnic America

DEFINITION

You are probably familiar with definitions; you see them every time you look up a word in the dictionary. Hopefully when you write, you try to make sure your reader understands the words that you use.

When writing your essays for the AP English Language and Composition Exam, if you happen to leave a key term unexplained or explained vaguely, even a carefully crafted essay will fall apart. This is especially true of very specialized terminology and obscure words. For example, if you are explaining a wonderful new tradition at your school and define it by synonym, you may write, "Basically, it's a Mexican *feis*." If your readers are Irish, this would be all right; if your readers were from just about anywhere else, you would need to define *feis* by putting it in a **category** (defining it in terms everyone will understand): "a *feis* is a competition for Irish dance, song, and instrumental music." Then, you could explain your project: "We want to do the same thing with traditional Mexican dance, song. and music."

> For the AP exam, we have to consider *definition* in its meaning as a rhetorical mode.

In this case, a paragraph—or an entire essay—is devoted to the definition of a term. Here, for example, is a paragraph that defines *feis* (pronounced "fesh").

> A *feis* is a day of competition in Irish dancing, music,
> and song. Perhaps you were wondering where all the
> Irish dancers from *Lord of the Dance* came from. All first
> Line performed at a *feis* and honed their skills through compe-
> 5 titions at various levels. A *feis* is a living legacy of Irish
> culture; it is where beginners, trying to remember their left
> from right, unknowingly dance the ancient steps of Ireland
> and pass this legacy on to the next generation. On the more

practical side, a *feis* is to Irish performers what a soccer
10   game is to athletes the world over. Competitions are organized by ability (Beginner, Advanced Beginner, Novice,
Open, Preliminary Championships, and Championships)
and by age (Under 6, Under 7, etc). At a typical *feis*, there
might be as many as 2,500 dancers.

The passage begins with a straightforward definition, but the definition is extended
and rhetorical modes are mixed. You noted, I'm sure, the *analogy* to a soccer game;
then, there is an inchoate (imperfectly formed) stab at *classification* (the divisions
in the competition). You could even argue that the mention of *Lord of the Dance*
serves as a kind of *example*. The rhetorical mode of *definition* can be used simply to
explain a word or concept, but typically the author using it also wants to interest
the reader in what's being explained.

Let's take a look at another good example of definition.

The *Palio* is a horse race that's held twice each year
in Siena, Italy: on July 2nd in honor of the Madonna
of Provenzano, and on August 16th in honor of the
Line   Assumption of the Virgin. But saying that the Palio is just
5   another horse race would be like calling the Superbowl
just another football game. The Palio is not just a race. It is
blood, sweat, and tears; it is part competition and part festi-
val. According to some, it is the world's craziest horse race;
according to others, it is Italy's most honored tradition. One
10   thing is clear to everyone, however: the Palio represents the
tradition, culture, and soul of Siena. The actual race lasts
only about a minute, but those moments represent an entire
year's worth of anticipation and preparation.

Again, the passage begins with a simple definition; but here, too, we have an
example of another rhetorical mode—analogy (to the Super Bowl).

However, the author of this passage uses an important additional tactic, known
as *definition by negation*. You should be aware of this rhetorical device and use
it where appropriate. In the passage above, the negation is partial—the Palio is,
indeed, a race, but it is not "just a race." Most negations work in that manner; definition by negation is usually used to impress upon the reader the importance of the
item under discussion or create a distinction between the item under discussion
and the item with which it is being "negatively" compared. For instance, you may
write, "Madonna is not a pop singer; she's a phenomenon, a true diva, a multital-
ented musical ambassador, and savvy businesswoman." Perhaps this statement is
true, but she's still a pop singer.

You may be able to use definition as a mode in your free-response essays, but most
likely, you will see definition used in the passages in the multiple-choice sections.
For example, you may be asked to answer a question that deals with how an author
uses definition to analyze a topic.

Laundry List for Definition

- Keep your reason for defining something in mind as you're writing.

- Define key terms according to what you know of your audience, in other words, the readers of the essays; you don't want to bore your reader by defining terms unnecessarily, nor do you want to perplex your reader by failing to define terms that may be obscure to your audience. Keep in mind that for you, your readers are the AP English Language and Composition Exam graders.

- Explain the background (history) when it is relevant to your definition.

- Define by negation when appropriate.

- Combine definition with any number of other rhetorical modes when applicable.

Sample Question

Write an essay in which you use definition to analyze the role of integrity in your life.

Drill: Reflect on How You Could Use Definition to Address the Following Topics

First define each word by category; then, define each word by negation.

WORD 1: Hip-hop

WORD 2: Success

WORD 3: Love

WORD 4: Cool

DESCRIPTION

Description can help make expository or argumentative writing lively and interesting and hold the reader's interest, which is vital, of course. Think of how many essays those test graders have to read every day; as we mentioned in the techniques chapters, a large part of scoring well on the free-response section is keeping your audience interested.

Oftentimes description serves as the primary rhetorical mode for an entire essay—or even an entire book. It's typically used to communicate a scene, a specific place, or a person to the reader. Although writers tend to concentrate most on the visual aspects of descriptions, descriptions can be used to appeal to any of the reader's senses.

Objective: Based on facts

Subjective: Based on feelings or opinions

It is important to keep in mind that sometimes description can be objective; in these cases, the author is not describing something in a sentimental or otherwise subjective way—he or she is merely stating the facts. As an example of this, take a look at Charles Darwin's depiction of Valparaíso, the chief seaport in Chile, in *Voyage of the Beagle*.

<blockquote>

The town is built at the very foot of a range of hills, about 1,600 feet high, and rather steep. From its position, it consists of one long, straggling street, which runs paral-

Line lel to the beach, and wherever a ravine comes down, the

5   houses are piled up on each side of it. The rounded hills, being only partially protected by very scanty vegetation, are worn into numberless little gullies, which expose a singularly bright red soil. From this cause, and from the low whitewashed houses with tile roofs, the view reminded me

10 of St. Cruz in Tenerife. In a northwesterly direction there are some fine glimpses of the Andes, but these mountains appear much grander when viewed from the neighboring hills: the great distance at which they are situated can then more readily be perceived.

</blockquote>

This type of objective description tends to be drier than more subjective description. The degree of objectivity exhibited above probably doesn't thrill you—nor will it thrill the AP readers.

Fortunately, unlike most other rhetorical modes, description allows for a significant degree of subjectivity. In most descriptions, the writer attempts to communicate personal impressions of something or someone, and to do so it is necessary to draw on the powers of figurative writing; simile, metaphor, and personification are the most common.

Here is another description of a city: Nathaniel Hawthorne's impressions of Florence. The description comes not from one of Hawthorne's novels, but from one of the notebooks that he kept during his travels in Europe.

<blockquote>

By and by, we had a distant glimpse of Florence, showing its great dome and some of its towers out of a sidelong valley, as if we were between two great waves of the tumul-

Line tuous sea of hills, while, far beyond, rose in the distance

5   the blue peaks of three or four of the Apennines, just on the remote horizon. There being a haziness in the atmosphere, however, Florence was little more distinct to us than the Celestial City was to Christian and Hopeful, when they spied at it from the Delectable Mountains.

10   Florence at first struck me as having the aspect of a very new city in comparison with Rome; but, on closer acquaintance, I find that many of the buildings are antique and massive, though still the clear atmosphere, the bright sunshine, the light, cheerful hues of the stucco, and—as

15   much as anything else, perhaps—the vivacious character of the human life in the streets, take away the sense of its being an ancient city.

    As we returned home over the Arno River, crossing the Ponte di Santa Trinitá, we were struck by the beautiful

20   scene of the broad, calm river, with the palaces along its

</blockquote>

shores repeated in it, on either side, and the neighboring
bridges, too, just as perfect in the tide beneath as in the air
above—a city of dream and shadow so close to the actual
one. God has a meaning, no doubt, in putting this spiritual
25   symbol continually beside us.
      Along the river, on both sides, as far as we could see,
there was a row of brilliant lamps, which, in the far
distance, looked like a cornice of golden light; and this
also shone as brightly in the river's depths. The lilies of
30   the evening, in the quarter where the sun had gone down,
were very soft and beautiful, though not so gorgeous as
thousands that I have seen in America. But I believe I must
fairly confess that the Italian sky, in the daytime, is bluer
and brighter than our own, and that the atmosphere has a
35   quality of showing objects to better advantage. It is more
than mere daylight; the magic of moonlight is somehow
mixed up with it, although it is so transparent a medium of
light.

This is a much more personal vision of a city. Hawthorne uses one simile to give us
a better visual image of the countryside around Florence ("as if we were between
two great waves of the tumultuous sea of hills"), and another to communicate the
effect of the gas lamps ("like a cornice of golden light"); and he employs a metaphor ("a city of dream and shadow") to evoke his impression of the reflections in
the river. In fact, virtually all of the description serves to communicate or explain
Hawthorne's impressions of the city; here, the writer wishes to evoke and is not
interested in scientific exactitude.

Keep in mind that this rhetorical device allows you a certain amount of freedom
of language, but it also allows you certain liberties in organization. In Hawthorne's
passage, for example, the author put down in writing his impressions in whatever order they came to him. In more objectively written descriptions, however, it
often makes sense to think spatially when writing a visual description. You might
describe a scene from left to right or front to back, for example; you might start a
description of a person with the head (and end with the feet).

In the following passage, Fyodor Dostoyevsky gives us both a spatial description
and a barrage of sensory impressions.

          In the first place, on entering this house, one passes into
      a very bare hall, and thence along a passage to a mean
      staircase. The reception room, however, is bright, clean,
      and spacious, and is lined with redwood and metalwork.
Line
5   But the scullery you would not care to see; it is greasy,
      dirty, and odoriferous, while the stairs are in rags, and
      the walls so covered with filth that the hand sticks fast
      wherever it touches them. Also, on each landing there is a
      medley of boxes, chairs, and dilapidated wardrobes; while
10   the windows have had most of their panes shattered, and
      everywhere stand washtubs filled with dirt, litter, eggshells,
      and fish bladders. The smell is abominable. In short, the
      house is not a nice one.
          As to the disposition of the rooms, I have described

15   it to you already. True, they are convenient enough, yet
every one of them has an atmosphere. I do not mean that
they smell badly so much as that each of them seems to
contain something which gives forth a rank, sickly sweet
odor. At first the impression is an unpleasant one, but a

20   couple of minutes will suffice to dissipate it, for the reason
that everything here smells—people's clothes, hands, and
everything else—and one grows accustomed to the rank-
ness. Canaries, however, soon die in this house. A naval
officer here has just bought his fifth. Birds cannot live long

25   in such an air. Every morning, when fish or beef is being
cooked, and washing and scrubbing are in progress, the
house is filled with steam. Always, too, the kitchen is full
of linen hanging out to dry; and since my room adjoins that
apartment, the smell from the clothes causes me not a little

30   annoyance. However, one can grow used to anything.

Note that Dostoyevsky's description first takes us through the ground floor and leads us up the staircase. Unlike the previous passages, this one appeals to our tactile ("so covered with filth that the hand sticks") and, even more prominently, olfactory senses. Choice of detail is important, and the choice of fish bladders, for example, conveys wonderfully the disgusting sights and smell. This is great writing—not only is the description effective, it's also humorous, thanks to the short comment at the end of each paragraph.

Laundry List for Description

- When possible, call on all five senses: visual, auditory, olfactory (smell), gustatory (taste), and tactile.

- Place the most striking examples at the beginnings and ends of your paragraphs (or essay) for maximum effect.

- Show, don't tell, using anecdotes and examples.

- Use concrete nouns and adjectives; nouns, not adjectives, should dominate.

- Concentrate on details that will convey the sense you're trying to get across most effectively. (Remember the fish bladders!)

- Employ figures of speech, especially similes, metaphors, and personification, when appropriate.

- When describing people, try to focus on distinctive mannerisms; if possible, you should go beyond physical appearance.

- Direct discourse (using dialogue or quotations) can be revealing and useful.

- A brief illustrative anecdote is worth a thousand words. Instead of simply using a general statement ("My friend Kai is a very generous person"), use an example ("My friend Kai is known for his generosity; the whole school knows about the time that he spent an entire weekend volunteering at a homeless shelter").

- To the extent possible, use action verbs. You could write, "The delightful aroma of chocolate chip cookies baking in the oven *crept around the corner and filled the den* with its sweetness" instead of just "The baking chocolate chip cookies *smelled* sweet."

Sample Question

Write an essay in which you describe your local shopping mall. Remember that you are not limited to physical descriptions.

Drill: Reflect on How You Could Use Description to Address the Following Topics

First decide the general feeling you'd like to convey, and second begin to list some specifics; don't forget examples or anecdotes. When describing people, go beyond just the physical.

TOPIC 1:   A party

TOPIC 2:   Your parents

TOPIC 3:   A natural disaster (seen from personal experience or on television)

TOPIC 4:   Your favorite place to relax

TOPIC 5:   The campus of your school

NARRATION

A narrative is a story in which pieces of information are arranged in chronological order. Narration can be an effective expository technique. Decades after her experience in a Japanese internment camp, Jeanne Wakatsuki Houston decided to narrate her experiences before, during, and immediately after imprisonment. She did not want to tell the story just for the story's sake; she wanted to relay her experience to the public to exorcize personal demons and to raise public awareness about this period in history. Here is a passage from this personal narrative. The passage describes the period after the Wakatsuki family had lost their house in Ocean Park, California, when they were forced into detention.

> My own family, after three years of mess hall living,
> collapsed as an integrated unit. Whatever dignity or feeling
> of filial strength we may have known before December
Line 1941 was lost, and we did not recover it until many years
> 5   after the war, not until after Papa died and we began to
> come together, trying to fill the vacuum his passing left in
> all our lives.
>   The closing of the camps, in the fall of 1945, only

aggravated what had begun inside. Papa had no money then
10 and could not get work. Half of our family had already
moved to the East Coast, where jobs had opened up for
them. The rest of us were relocated into a former defense
workers' housing project in Long Beach. In that small
apartment there never was enough room for all of us to
15 sit down for a meal. We ate in shifts, and I yearned all the
more for our huge round table in Ocean Park.
     Soon after we were released I wrote a paper for a
seventh-grade journalism class, describing how we used to
hunt grunion before the war. The whole family would go
20 down to Ocean Park Beach after dark, when the grunion
were running, and build a big fire on the sand. I would
watch Papa and my older brothers splash through the
moonlit surf to scoop out the fish, then we'd rush back to
the house where Mama would fry them up and set the siz-
25 zling pan on the table, with soy sauce and horseradish, for
a midnight meal. I ended the paper with this sentence: "The
reason I want to remember this is because I know we'll
never be able to do it again."

You may be asked to use personal narrative when writing your essays on the AP
English Language and Composition test; and you will certainly be asked to *analyze*
narratives that employ this rhetorical mode.

In the following passage, Booker T. Washington uses narrative to explain how his
view on education developed. Watch for changes between the first- and third-
person style of narration.

          When a mere boy, I saw a young colored man, who had
     spent several years in school, sitting in a common cabin in
     the South, studying a French grammar. I noted the poverty,
Line the untidiness, the want of system, and thrift that existed
  5 about the cabin, notwithstanding his knowledge of French
     and other academic subjects. Another time, when riding on
     the outer edges of a town in the South, I heard the sound of
     a piano coming from a cabin of the same kind. Contriving
     some excuse, I entered and began a conversation with the
10 young colored woman who was playing, and who had
     recently returned from a boarding-school, where she had
     been studying instrumental music among other things.
     Despite the fact that her parents were living in a rented
     cabin, eating poorly cooked food, surrounded with poverty,
15 and having almost none of the conveniences of life, she had
     persuaded them to rent a piano for four or five dollars per
     month. Many such instances as these, in connection with
     my own struggles, impressed upon me the importance of
     making a study of our needs as a race, and applying the
20 remedy accordingly.
          Some one may be tempted to ask, Has not the negro
     boy or girl as good a right to study a French grammar and
     instrumental music as the white youth? I answer, Yes, but

25 in the present condition of the negro race in this country
there is need of something more. Perhaps I may be forgiven
for the seeming egotism if I mention the expansion of my
own life partly as an example of what I mean. My earliest
recollection is of a small one-room log hut on a large slave
plantation in Virginia. After the close of the war, while
30 working in the coal-mines of West Virginia for the support of my mother, I heard in some accidental way of the
Hampton Institute.

  When I learned that it was an institution where a black
boy could study, could have a chance to work for his board,
35 and at the same time be taught how to work and to realize
the dignity of labor, I resolved to go there. Bidding my
mother good-by, I started out one morning to find my way
to Hampton, though I was almost penniless and had no
definite idea where Hampton was. By walking, begging
40 rides, and paying for a portion of the journey on the steam-
cars, I finally succeeded in reaching the city of Richmond,
Virginia. I was without money or friends. I slept under a
sidewalk, and by working on a vessel next day I earned
money to continue my way to the institute, where I arrived
45 with a surplus of fifty cents. At Hampton I found the opportunity—in the way of buildings, teachers, and industries
provided by the generous—to get training in the class-room
and by practical touch with industrial life, to learn thrift,
economy, and push. I was surrounded by an atmosphere of
50 business, Christian influence, and a spirit of self-help that
seemed to have awakened every faculty in me, and caused
me for the first time to realize what it meant to be a man
instead of a piece of property.

  While there I resolved that when I had finished the course
55 of training I would go into the far South, into the Black Belt
of the South, and give my life to providing the same kind of
opportunity for self-reliance and self-awakening that I had
found provided for me at Hampton.

Notice that in the first paragraph, the narration slips briefly into the third person—Washington is telling the story of the girl, not his own. Likewise, Washington presents the story of the boy studying French from his point of view. In these two instances, Washington switches from first to third person with ease, so that the transition is optimally effective and unnoticeable. The second paragraph effortlessly transitions to a personal anecdote, which is continued in the third paragraph. The final paragraph justifies the narrative: Washington's life story leads to his commitment to establish his own institute—called the Tuskegee Normal and Industrial Institute—deep in the South.

> Sometimes you'll see questions on the essay section of the AP exam that will ask you to relate someone else's experience to illustrate a point. In essence, you'll be asked to write a narrative in the third person, but choose wisely. For example, if you're asked to "relate an experience where someone you know (directly or indirectly) overcame incredible obstacles to reach a goal," you wouldn't want to narrate the story of your cat, who managed to catch an elusive mouse.

Laundry List for Narration

- When possible, structure the events in chronological order.

- Make your story complete: make sure you have a beginning, middle, and end.

- Provide a realistic setting (typically at the beginning). Notice how Booker T. Washington provides a setting in this passage with just a few details: "a young colored man," "a common cabin in the South," "the poverty, the untidiness, the want of system, and thrift that existed about the cabin."

- Whenever possible, use action verbs; for example, write "the fighters *tumbled* to the ground," rather than "there *were* fallen soldiers on the ground."

- Provide concrete and specific details.

- Show, don't tell. This is another way of saying that you should use anecdotes and examples whenever possible.

- Establish a clear point of view—if it's clear who is narrating and why, then it will be easier to choose relevant details.

- Include appropriate amounts of direct discourse (dialogue or quotations).

Sample Question

"A college education is not necessary for success." Relate an experience of someone you know (directly or indirectly) that defends, challenges, or qualifies this statement.

Drill: Reflect on How You Could Use Narration to Address the Following Topics

Think of a personal experience (or an experience of someone you know) that pertains to the topic. Determine how you would best describe this experience. Come up with a few anecdotes or examples.

TOPIC 1:   Danger when eating becomes an obsession

TOPIC 2:   Hardship is a necessary part of our education

INDUCTION AND DEDUCTION

You will probably find that the rhetorical modes of induction and deduction are most useful when you're writing the argumentative essay, although they will be helpful on the rhetorical analysis essay too.

Induction is a process in which specific examples are used to reach a general conclusion. If you took the AP European History Exam and did not like the experience, and then took the AP Calculus Exam and did not like the experience, you might arrive at the following general conclusion: AP exams are always an unpleasant experience. If, when you were young, you found that you didn't like broccoli, asparagus, or cabbage, your parents might have concluded that you didn't like vegetables. In both cases, the conclusion would be of questionable value because there is not enough evidence to justify the generalization.

Assume that you want to argue that your English teacher is in a bad mood every time the Boston Red Sox lose a game to the New York Yankees. You could substantiate that generalization by recalling certain tantrums that he or she threw and comparing those days with the dates of Red Sox losses. This would substantiate your claim but not prove it, especially if you didn't even know if your teacher saw the games. After all, what if something else happened to coincide with the games and was the real cause of his or her bad temper, such as traffic jams on the way home from school?

We tend to believe in generalizations arrived at through induction, whether they can actually be proved. The Food and Drug Administration, for example, has to follow the inductive reasoning of scientists; just because a certain drug produced the desired results—and didn't produce an undesirable result, such as death— 20,000 experimental cases does not prove that the same results will occur when 20,000,000 people take the drug.

Deduction involves the use of a generalization to draw a conclusion about a specific case. For example, if you read in the morning paper that all schools in your county would be closed that day because of inclement weather, you could conclude that you won't have to go to school. You just used deductive reasoning.

Laundry List for Induction and Deduction

- Induction proceeds from the specific to a generalization. For example, your classmate Ricky plays on the school's football and basketball teams, and he has ice hockey posters all over his bedroom at home. You could conclude that Ricky likes all sports in general.

- Make sure you have sufficient evidence to support your claim.

- Deduction is the process of applying a generalization to a specific case. For example, your cousin Jennifer told you that she hates dancing and loud music. From this, you could safely say that she probably wouldn't want to come with you to the hot new nightclub opening this weekend.

- Make sure your generalization has sufficient credibility before applying it to specific cases. For example, it would be an unfair generalization to assume that all baseball players use or have used anabolic steroids.

Sample Question

Write a short essay in which you analyze the following statement: *Contemporary films are a reflection of today's values.*

Drill: Reflect on How You Could Use Induction to Substantiate the Following Theses

THESIS 1: Academic honesty is alive and well.

THESIS 2: High schools don't really care about their mission to educate.

THESIS 3: Computer games have beneficial effects.

THESIS 4: Children generally demonstrate more wisdom than their parents.

In this chapter we looked at a few more rhetorical modes that will be extremely useful to you on test day. Remember that these can be used in combination with each other *and,* further complicating matters, in combination with the modes in the previous chapter. Hopefully, these modes have given you some ideas about how you can structure your essays into coherent works that the test readers will understand and maybe even enjoy.

Here we are at the end of the review section of the book. You are now ready to take the practice tests; you may be dreading these now, but we know that once you begin, you'll see that you know a lot more than you think you do! If you've worked through the book up to this point and complete these practice exams, you'll certainly be ready for test day.

Good luck!

REFLECT

Respond to the following questions:

- For which topics discussed in this chapter do you feel you have achieved sufficient mastery to answer multiple-choice questions correctly?

- For which topics discussed in this chapter do you feel you have achieved sufficient mastery to discuss effectively in an essay?

- For which topics discussed in this chapter do you feel you need more work before you can answer multiple-choice questions correctly?

- For which topics discussed in this chapter do you feel you need more work before you can discuss effectively in an essay?

- What parts of this chapter are you going to re-review?

- Will you seek further help, outside of this book (such as a teacher, tutor, or AP Central), on any of the topics in this chapter—and, if so, on which ones?

Part VI
Practice Test 2

Practice Test 2

AP® English Language and Composition Exam

SECTION I: Multiple-Choice Questions

DO NOT OPEN THIS BOOKLET UNTIL YOU ARE TOLD TO DO SO.

At a Glance

Total Time
1 hour
Number of Questions
55
Percent of Total Grade
45%
Writing Instrument
Pencil required

Instructions

Section I of this examination contains 55 multiple-choice questions. Fill in only the ovals for numbers 1 through 55 on your answer sheet.

Indicate all of your answers to the multiple-choice questions on the answer sheet. No credit will be given for anything written in this exam booklet, but you may use the booklet for notes or scratch work. After you have decided which of the suggested answers is best, completely fill in the corresponding oval on the answer sheet. Give only one answer to each question. If you change an answer, be sure that the previous mark is erased completely. Here is a sample question and answer.

<u>Sample Question</u>

Chicago is a
(A) state
(B) city
(C) country
(D) continent
(E) village

<u>Sample Answer</u>

Ⓐ ● Ⓒ Ⓓ Ⓔ

Use your time effectively, working as quickly as you can without losing accuracy. Do not spend too much time on any one question. Go on to other questions and come back to the ones you have not answered if you have time. It is not expected that everyone will know the answers to all the multiple-choice questions.

About Guessing

Many candidates wonder whether or not to guess the answers to questions about which they are not certain. Multiple choice scores are based on the number of questions answered correctly. Points are not deducted for incorrect answers, and no points are awarded for unanswered questions. Because points are not deducted for incorrect answers, you are encouraged to answer all multiple-choice questions. On any questions you do not know the answer to, you should eliminate as many choices as you can, and then select the best answer among the remaining choices.

GO ON TO THE NEXT PAGE.

This page intentionally left blank.

ENGLISH LANGUAGE AND COMPOSITION
SECTION I
Time—1 hour

Directions: This part consists of selections from prose works and questions on their content, form, and style. After reading each passage, choose the best answer to each question and completely fill in the corresponding oval on the answer sheet.

Note: Pay particular attention to the requirement of questions that contain the words NOT, LEAST, or EXCEPT.

Questions 1-11. Read the following passage carefully before you choose your answers.

(The following passage is from Samuel Johnson's Life of Sir Thomas Browne, *1756.)*

His exuberance of knowledge, and plenitude of ideas, sometimes obstruct the tendency of his reasoning and the clearness of his decisions: on whatever subject he employed
Line his mind, there started up immediately so many images
5 before him, that he lost one by grasping another. His memory supplied him with so many illustrations, parallel or dependent notions, that he was always starting into collateral considerations; but the spirit and vigour of his pursuit always gives delight; and the reader follows him, without reluctance,
10 through his mazes, in themselves flowery and pleasing, and ending at the point originally in view.
"To have great excellencies and great faults, *'magnæ virtutes nec minora vitia,'* is the poesy," says our author, "of the best natures." This poesy may be properly applied to
15 the style of Browne; it is vigorous, but rugged; it is learned, but pedantick; it is deep, but obscure; it strikes, but does not please; it commands, but does not allure; his tropes are harsh, and his combinations uncouth.
He fell into an age in which our language began to lose
20 the stability which it had obtained in the time of Elizabeth; and was considered by every writer as a subject on which he might try his plastick skill, by moulding it according to his own fancy. Milton, in consequence of this encroaching license, began to introduce the Latin idiom: and Browne,
25 though he gave less disturbance to our structures in phraseology, yet poured in a multitude of exotick words; many, indeed, useful and significant, which, if rejected, must be supplied by circumlocution, such as commensality, for the state of many living at the same table; but many superfluous,
30 as a paralogical, for an unreasonable doubt; and some so obscure, that they conceal his meaning rather than explain it, as arthritical analogies, for parts that serve some animals in the place of joints.
His style is, indeed, a tissue of many languages; a
35 mixture of heterogeneous words, brought together from distant regions, with terms originally appropriated to one art, and drawn by violence into the service of another. He must, however, be confessed to have augmented our philosophical diction; and, in defence of his uncommon words and
40 expressions, we must consider, that he had uncommon

sentiments, and was not content to express, in many words, that idea for which any language could supply a single term.
But his innovations are sometimes pleasing, and his temerities happy: he has many "verba ardentia" forcible
45 expressions, which he would never have found, but by venturing to the utmost verge of propriety; and flights which would never have been reached, but by one who had very little fear of the shame of falling.

1. The reader can infer from the first paragraph that some critics have

   (A) chastised Browne for his inability to reason
   (B) lauded Browne's frequent linear explanations
   (C) complained about Browne's lack of clarity
   (D) compared Browne with Shakespeare
   (E) compared the author of the passage with Browne

2. In context, "poesy" (line 13) most nearly means

   (A) poetry
   (B) inspiration for writing
   (C) sentimental thoughts
   (D) flowery writing
   (E) poetic dreaming

3. In context, the phrase *magnæ virtutes nec minora vitia* (lines 12-13) most nearly means which of the following?

   (A) Poetry is best when it embodies both excellence and failure.
   (B) Great excellencies are impossible without great faults.
   (C) Both excellence and weakness are often found in great people.
   (D) Our best nature is found in poesy.
   (E) Browne's style is both vigorous and rugged.

GO ON TO THE NEXT PAGE.

4. In the second paragraph, the author

   (A) is openly critical of Browne's style
   (B) hints that Browne's writing is pedantic
   (C) justifies the strength of Browne's style
   (D) argues in favor of a reexamination of Browne's style
   (E) suggests that Browne's writing is too facile

5. The author modifies the strict parallelism of "it is vigorous, but rugged; it is learned, but pedantick; it is deep, but obscure; it strikes, but does not please; it commands, but does not allure; his tropes are harsh, and his combinations uncouth" (lines 15-18) to

   (A) better define his point of view
   (B) keep the reader off balance
   (C) maintain a sense of imbalance
   (D) show more respect for Browne's accomplishments
   (E) to obfuscate his real opinions

6. According to the author, Browne lived at a time of significant

   (A) linguistic experimentation
   (B) literary conservatism
   (C) linguistic stability
   (D) metaphorical license
   (E) impoverishment of the English language

7. In lines 24-33 ("Browne, though he gave less disturbance…in the place of joints"), the author classifies Browne's diction in a manner that proceeds from

   (A) interesting, to captivating, to intriguing
   (B) appropriate, to inappropriate, to superfluous
   (C) interesting, to intriguing, to disappointing
   (D) useful, to unhelpful, to deleterious
   (E) appropriate, to inappropriate, to intriguing

8. The author posits that Browne's unusual diction can be tied to his desire

   (A) to mystify his readers
   (B) to develop English phraseology
   (C) to enrich the English language
   (D) to set himself apart from other authors of his time
   (E) to express exactly his unusual thoughts

9. According to the author, Browne's style is marked by

   (A) heteroclite diction
   (B) homogeneous words
   (C) mundane vocabulary
   (D) humorous phrases
   (E) heterogeneous tropes

10. Which of the following best summarizes the passage?

    (A) an impartial reconsideration of Browne's style
    (B) a scathing critique by a rival
    (C) a manifesto by one of Browne's colleagues
    (D) a comparative study of Milton and Browne
    (E) a virulent polemic

11. The author's tone in this passage is best described as

    (A) sarcastic and doctrinaire
    (B) analytical and scholarly
    (C) expository and harsh
    (D) indulgent and condescending
    (E) capricious and sentimental

GO ON TO THE NEXT PAGE.

Questions 12-20. Read the following passage carefully before you choose your answers.

(The following passage is excerpted from an article by Virginia Woolf that was first published in 1919.)

But is it upon the heroines that we would cast a final glance. "I have always been finding out my religion since I was a little girl," says Dorothea Casaubon. "I used to pray
Line
5 so much—now I hardly ever pray. I try not to have desires merely for myself." She is speaking for them all. That is their problem. They cannot live without religion, and they start out on the search for one when they are little girls. Each has the deep feminine passion for goodness, which makes the place where she stands in aspiration and agony the heart
10 of the book—still and cloistered like a place of worship, but that she no longer knows to whom to pray. In learning they seek their goal; in the ordinary tasks of womanhood; in the wider service of their kind. They do not find what they seek, and we cannot wonder. The ancient consciousness
15 of woman, charged with suffering and sensibility, and for so many ages dumb, seems in them to have brimmed and overflowed and uttered a demand for something— they scarcely know what—for something that is perhaps incompatible with the facts of human existence. George
20 Eliot had far too strong an intelligence to tamper with those facts, and too broad a humour to mitigate the truth because it was a stern one. Save for the supreme courage of their endeavour, the struggle ends, for her heroines, in tragedy, or in a compromise that is even more melancholy. But their
25 story is the incomplete version of the story that is George Eliot herself. For her, too, the burden and the complexity of womanhood were not enough; she must reach beyond the sanctuary and pluck for herself the strange bright fruits of art and knowledge. Clasping them as few women have ever
30 clasped them, she would not renounce her own inheritance— the difference of view, the difference of standard—nor accept an inappropriate reward. Thus we behold her, a memorable figure, inordinately praised and shrinking from her fame, despondent, reserved, shuddering back into the arms of
35 love as if there alone were satisfaction and, it might be, justification, at the same time reaching out with "a fastidious yet hungry ambition" for all that life could offer the free and inquiring mind and confronting her feminine aspirations with the real world of men. Triumphant was the issue for
40 her, whatever it may have been for her creations, and as we recollect all that she dared and achieved, how with every obstacle against her—sex and health and convention—she sought more knowledge and more freedom till the body, weighted with its double burden, sank worn out, we must lay
45 upon her grave whatever we have it in our power to bestow of laurel and rose.

12. The author's attitude toward George Eliot is best described as one of

(A) idolatrous devotion
(B) profound admiration
(C) feigned intimacy
(D) qualified enthusiasm
(E) reasoned objectivity

13. According to the speaker, George Eliot's heroines are "cloistered" (line 10) because they are

(A) in a church
(B) essentially alone
(C) in a monastery
(D) imprisoned in cloisters
(E) lost in prayer

14. In context, "the facts of human existence" (line 19)

(A) restrict both men and women
(B) restrict women only
(C) are only applicable to Eliot's heroines
(D) pertain to any literary character
(E) pertain to men only

15. "Save for" (line 22) most nearly means

(A) except for
(B) saving
(C) safe for
(D) guarding against
(E) keeping in mind

16. The "differences" mentioned in line 31 pertain to Eliot's

(A) profession
(B) class
(C) upbringing
(D) education
(E) gender

17. According to the speaker, Eliot

(A) enjoyed excellent health
(B) suffered from her independence and knowledge
(C) was prevented from attaining fame by men
(D) was very unlike the heroines of her books
(E) repudiated her feminine nature

GO ON TO THE NEXT PAGE.

18. In the sentence beginning "Thus we behold her" (lines 32-39), the speaker employs all of the following EXCEPT

    (A) apposition
    (B) hyperbole
    (C) personification
    (D) relative clauses
    (E) parallelism

19. It is reasonable to assume that the phrase "a fastidious yet hungry ambition" (lines 36-37)

    (A) is spoken by one of Eliot's heroines
    (B) comes from one of the speaker's literary works
    (C) is borrowed from one of Eliot's critics
    (D) is not to be taken seriously
    (E) does not represent the speaker's point of view

20. Generally, the style of the entire passage is best defined as

    (A) effusive and disorganized
    (B) pedantic and terse
    (C) sympathetic and concrete
    (D) abstract and metaphysical
    (E) intellectual and cynical

GO ON TO THE NEXT PAGE.

Questions 21-29. Read the following passage carefully before you choose your answers.

The following passage is from The Souls of Black Folk, *by American sociologist W. E. B. Du Bois, published in 1903.)*

And yet, being a problem is a strange experience—peculiar even for one who has never been anything else, save perhaps in babyhood and in Europe. It is in the early
Line days of rollicking boyhood that the revelation first bursts
5 upon one, all in a day, as it were. I remember well when the shadow swept across me. I was a little thing, away up in the hills of New England, where the dark Housatonic winds between Hoosac and Taghkanic to the sea. In a wee wooden schoolhouse, something put it into the boys' and girls' heads
10 to buy gorgeous visiting-cards—ten cents a package—and exchange. The exchange was merry, till one girl, a tall newcomer, refused my card—refused it peremptorily, with a glance. Then it dawned upon me with a certain suddenness that I was different from the others; or like, mayhap, in heart
15 and life and longing, but shut out from their world by a vast veil. I had thereafter no desire to tear down that veil, to creep through; I held all beyond it in common contempt, and lived above it in a region of blue sky and great wandering shadows. That sky was bluest when I could beat my mates
20 at examination-time, or beat them at a foot-race, or even beat their stringy heads. Alas, with the years all this fine contempt began to fade; for the worlds I longed for, and all their dazzling opportunities, were theirs, not mine. But they should not keep these prizes, I said; some, all, I would wrest
25 from them. Just how I would do it I could never decide: by reading law, by healing the sick, by telling the wonderful tales that swam in my head—some way. With other black boys the strife was not so fiercely sunny: their youth shrunk into tasteless sycophancy, or into silent hatred of the pale
30 world about them and mocking distrust of everything white; or wasted itself in a bitter cry, Why did God make me an outcast and a stranger in mine own house? The shades of the prison-house closed round about us all: walls strait and stubborn to the whitest, but relentlessly narrow, tall, and
35 unscalable to sons of night who must plod darkly on in resignation, or beat unavailing palms against the stone, or steadily, half hopelessly, watch the streak of blue above.

21. The phrase "being a problem is a strange experience" (line 1) contributes to the unity of the passage in which of the following ways?

(A) As a contrast to the author's relationship with his schoolmates
(B) As a condemnation of racial prejudice
(C) As a parallel to the universal sense of Black alienation
(D) As an indication of the author's own sense of racial disharmony
(E) As a satirical comment on the author's own shortcomings

22. In this passage, the anecdote of the visiting-cards serves as

(A) an epiphany for the speaker
(B) a moment of triumph for the speaker
(C) a revelation for the reader
(D) a turning point for the school
(E) a chance for redemption for the speaker

23. After presenting the incident of the visiting-cards, the speaker controls the rest of the passage by employing

(A) repeated appeals to authority
(B) a series of euphemisms
(C) a series of analogies
(D) two extended metaphors
(E) self-deprecating humor

24. In line 17, the word "it" refers to

(A) "world" (line 15)
(B) "veil" (line 16)
(C) "creep" (line 17)
(D) "contempt" (line 17)
(E) "sky" (line 18)

25. The speaker uses the word "beat" three times in lines 19-21 in order to

(A) appeal to the audience's moral sensibilities about race relations
(B) underscore his contempt of his peer group at that time
(C) establish a contrast between the first two uses of the word and the third use
(D) rely on a universal principle for future racial interactions
(E) analyze the power dynamics inherent in sociological interactions

GO ON TO THE NEXT PAGE.

26. The "sons of night" (line 35) are

    (A) evil young men
    (B) African American boys
    (C) sons of evil parents
    (D) lost souls
    (E) prisoners

27. One can infer from the passage all of the following EXCEPT that

    (A) the speaker considered himself inferior to his white peers
    (B) the speaker considered himself superior to his African American peers
    (C) the other African American boys treated their white peers with deference
    (D) the speaker was superior to his white peers in many ways
    (E) the speaker felt isolated from both white and African American peers

28. The speaker's contempt wanes and is replaced by

    (A) a commitment to become a famous professional
    (B) a pledge to beat his peers in athletic contests
    (C) a helpless rage against society
    (D) a spirit of revenge
    (E) actions that eventually lead him to prison

29. The tone of this passage can NOT be described as

    (A) self-aware
    (B) decisive
    (C) fervent
    (D) reflective
    (E) laudatory

GO ON TO THE NEXT PAGE.

Questions 30-40. Read the following passage carefully before you choose your answers.

(The following passage is from the Lincoln-Douglas Debates of 1858.)

Now, I hold that Illinois had a right to abolish and prohibit slavery as she did, and I hold that Kentucky has the same right to continue and protect slavery that Illinois
Line had to abolish it. I hold that New York had as much right to
5 abolish slavery as Virginia has to continue it, and that each and every State of this Union is a sovereign power, with the right to do as it pleases upon this question of slavery, and upon all its domestic institutions. Slavery is not the only question which comes up in this controversy. There is a far
10 more important one to you, and that is, what shall be done with the free negro? We have settled the slavery question as far as we are concerned; we have prohibited it in Illinois forever, and in doing so, I think we have done wisely, and there is no man in the State who would be more strenuous in
15 his opposition to the introduction of slavery than I would; but when we settled it for our selves, we exhausted all our power over that subject. We have done our whole duty, and can do no more. We must leave each and every other State to decide for itself the same question. In relation to the policy to be
20 pursued toward the free negroes, we have said that they shall not vote; whilst Maine, on the other hand, has said that they shall vote. Maine is a sovereign State, and has the power to regulate the qualifications of voters within her limits. I would never consent to confer the right of voting and of citizenship
25 upon a negro, but still I am not going to quarrel with Maine for differing from me in opinion. Let Maine take care of her own negroes, and fix the qualifications of her own voters to suit herself, without interfering with Illinois, and Illinois will not interfere with Maine. So with the State of New York.
30 She allows the negro to vote provided he owns two hundred and fifty dollars' worth of property, but not otherwise. While I would not make any distinction whatever between a negro who held property and one who did not, yet if the sovereign State of New York chooses to make that distinction
35 it is her business and not mine, and I will not quarrel with her for it. She can do as she pleases on this question if she minds her own business, and we will do the same thing. Now, my friends, if we will only act conscientiously and rigidly upon this great principle of popular sovereignty,
40 which guarantees to each State and Territory the right to do as it pleases on all things, local and domestic, instead of Congress interfering, we will continue at peace one with another. Why should Illinois be at war with Missouri, or Kentucky with Ohio, or Virginia, with New York, merely
45 because their institutions differ? Our fathers intended that our institutions should differ. They knew that the North and the South, having different climates, productions, and interests, required different institutions. This doctrine of Mr. Lincoln, of uniformity among the institutions of the different
50 States, is a new doctrine, never dreamed of by Washington, Madison, or the framers of this government. Mr. Lincoln and

the Republican party set themselves up as wiser than these men who made this government, which has flourished for seventy years under the principle of popular sovereignty,
55 recognizing the right of each State to do as it pleased. Under that principle, we have grown from a nation of three or four millions to a nation of about thirty millions of people; we have crossed the Allegheny mountains and filled up the whole Northwest, turning the prairie into a garden, and
60 building up churches and schools, thus spreading civilization and Christianity where before there was nothing but savage barbarism. Under that principle we have become, from a feeble nation, the most powerful on the face of the earth, and if we only adhere to that principle, we can go forward
65 increasing in territory, in power, in strength, and in glory until the Republic of America shall be the north star that shall guide the friend of freedom throughout the civilized world. And why can we not adhere to the great principle of self-government upon which our institutions were originally
70 based? I believe that this new doctrine preached by Mr. Lincoln and his party will dissolve the Union if it succeeds. They are trying to array all the Northern States in one body against the South, to excite a sectional war between the free States and the slave States, in order that the one or the other
75 may be driven to the wall.

30. In this passage the speaker's purpose is to

    (A) analyze the causes of slavery
    (B) argue in favor of states' rights
    (C) criticize individual states
    (D) describe the advantages of a federal government
    (E) argue in favor of slavery

31. Which of the following best describes the tone of the passage?

    (A) mock enthusiasm
    (B) righteous indignation
    (C) well-reasoned polemic
    (D) objective rationalization
    (E) ironic detachment

GO ON TO THE NEXT PAGE.

32. In the first two sentences (lines 1-8), the speaker grounds his central idea on which of the following rhetorical strategies?

(A) inductive reasoning
(B) deductive reasoning
(C) description
(D) classification
(E) appeal to ignorance

33. In line 36, the word "it" most closely refers to

(A) "property" (line 33)
(B) "State" (line 34)
(C) "business" (line 35)
(D) "distinction" (line 34)
(E) "quarrel" (line 35)

34. The sentence that begins "Now, my friends, if we will..." (lines 38-43) contains all of the following EXCEPT

(A) a classification
(B) an appeal to a principle
(C) a call to action
(D) a definition
(E) an accusation

35. The author suggests that which of the following is true of Maine, Illinois, and New York?

(A) They have relatively liberal policies toward "negroes."
(B) They prove that popular sovereignty has been generally successful.
(C) They exemplify the principle of popular sovereignty.
(D) They create inconsistent laws for both "negroes" and citizens.
(E) They create laws concerned more with wealth than justice.

36. The speaker substantiates his central idea with

(A) clever anecdotes
(B) innovative symbols
(C) unusual paradoxes
(D) extended metaphors
(E) appeal to authority

37. From the passage, it appears that the speaker's personal view is that African Americans

(A) should be slaves and should not be allowed to hold property
(B) should not be slaves and should be allowed to vote
(C) should not be free but should be allowed to hold some property
(D) should be free but not allowed to vote
(E) should be allowed to hold property and to vote

38. The author implies that Abraham Lincoln's policies would have all of the following potential negative effects EXCEPT

(A) consolidating power
(B) hindering Westward expansion
(C) dissolving the Union
(D) initiating war
(E) hindering population growth

39. In the final lines of the passage, the speaker attempts to win over his audience by

(A) inspiring confidence
(B) shifting blame
(C) instilling fear
(D) reconciling differences
(E) overstating a problem

40. The development of the passage can best be described as the

(A) argument for a particular solution to a political problem
(B) rebuttal of those who challenge the authority of Congress
(C) explanation of the failings of a political opponent
(D) exploration of the various meanings of a universal principle
(E) comparison between two political entities

GO ON TO THE NEXT PAGE.

Practice Test 2 | 209

Questions 41-55. Read the following passage carefully before you choose your answers.

(This passage is excerpted from a recent work that examines popular conceptions of the history of medieval Spain.)

If you have read anything about medieval Spain, then you probably know about *convivencia*—the peaceful "coexistence" of Muslims, Christians, and Jews for nearly
Line eight hundred years on the Iberian peninsula. The story
5 is invariably told in the same way: "once upon a time,"[1] after the Muslim invasion of the Iberian peninsula in 711, a "culture of tolerance"[2] was created among Muslims, Christians, and Jews. Tolerant adherents of these three Abrahamic faiths shared philosophical and scientific
10 learning, translating previously unknown sources (especially the works of Aristotle) for the rest of Europe. "But," the author or narrator intones in his gravest voice, "this world too quickly vanished. Greed, fear, and intolerance swept it away. Puritanical judgments and absolutism snuffed out the
15 light of learning." Then the author or narrator laments the loss of this vanished world: "it was truly a bright light in what was largely a dark and ignorant medieval landscape. Its loss is one of the great tragedies in history."[3] This is almost always followed by a didactic—and dramatic—moral
20 about the relevance of medieval Spain for contemporary problems: "Humanity has never completely found the way back. Medieval Spain might help point the way."[4] This is a fairy tale for adults who, like children, know nothing about the actual (medieval) world it attempts to describe. The story
25 of *convivencia* fulfills the requirements of the genre, replete as it is with exotic journeys in faraway lands and epic battles between noble heroes and depraved villains. And like all fairy tales, this story of *convivencia* tells us much more about the world of storytelling in which it was created than about
30 the historical past or objective reality, on which **it** is only loosely based.

While some of the recent books on *convivencia* have gestured in the direction of scholarly discourse, more often than not, they cannot resist the temptation to indulge
35 our basest tendencies to Orientalism and exoticism. In nearly every popular recounting of *convivencia,* images of an Islamic *locus amoenus* abound: we hear of gardens, bath-houses, exotic fruits, and enchanting mosques. Chris Lowney, in *A Vanished World,* emphasized that "daily life
40 was transformed as exotic new species like cotton, figs, spinach, and watermelon burgeoned in fields nourished by new irrigation techniques." The "luxury and sophistication" of the Islamic city of Cordoba "undoubtedly surpassed anything found elsewhere in Europe." Maria Rosa Menocal's
45 syrupy confection, *The Ornament of the World,* simmers

under a thick layer of Orientalized cheese. Some of her chapter titles themselves suffice to prove the point, "The Palaces of Memory," "The Mosque and the Palm Tree," "A Grand Vizier, A Grand City," "The Gardens of Memory,"
50 and "Sailing Away, Riding Away." And when these authors describe Islam, it is with the wonderment and delight of a tourist. We, their audience, are supposed to share in their surprise—and in the delicious irony—that Islam was a peaceful, tolerant religion, while Christianity was
55 persecutory, cruel, and violent.

41. One purpose of the first paragraph is to

   (A) discount the importance of medieval history
   (B) reinforce a popular perception of medieval Spain
   (C) suggest that historical research will need to explore new sources
   (D) define *convivencia* for non-specialists
   (E) distinguish among the various historical accounts of medieval Spain

42. The primary purpose of the quotes in the first paragraph is to

   (A) emphasize the author's bewilderment with the narrative of medieval history offered by most historians of medieval Spain
   (B) reinforce the author's position that proponents of *convivencia* misinterpret their evidence by quoting directly from their works
   (C) suggest an alternate interpretation of the historical record
   (D) recount the conventional narrative of *convivencia* in the words of its historians
   (E) provide a comprehensive survey of the history of medieval Spain

43. The footnotes serve to

   (A) demonstrate the range of sources he cites
   (B) reveal that all the quotes are from the same source
   (C) provide documentation for the sources for his quotes
   (D) impress the reader with the technical expertise of the author
   (E) explain the complexity of the argument at hand

---

1 Maria Rosa Menocal, *Ornament of the World: How Muslims, Christians, and Jews Created a Culture of Tolerance in Medieval Spain* (New York: Little, Brown, 2002), 5.
2 The subtitle of Menocal's *Ornament of the World.*
3 Chris Lowney, *A Vanished World: Muslims, Christians, and Jews in Medieval Spain* (Oxford: Oxford University Press, 2005).
4 Lowney, *A Vanished World,* 14.

GO ON TO THE NEXT PAGE.

44. The content of the second footnote

    (A) undermines the claims made by Maria Rosa Menocal
    (B) provides a citation for more information about the subject
    (C) introduces information that will turn out to be essential to the main argument
    (D) informs the reader of the whereabouts of a certain text
    (E) clarifies the source of the expression used in the text

45. The word "contemporary" (line 20) most nearly means

    (A) artistic
    (B) current
    (C) similar
    (D) historical
    (E) global

46. In line 25, the word "genre" refers to

    (A) "fairy tale" (line 23)
    (B) "convivencia" (line 25)
    (C) "children" (line 23)
    (D) "it" (line 26)
    (E) "exotic journeys" (line 26)

47. Which of the following rhetorical devices is used in lines 22-24 ("This...describe")?

    (A) analogy
    (B) understatement
    (C) simile
    (D) classical allusion
    (E) hyperbole

48. Which one of the following characteristics of the scholarship on convivencia is most troublesome to the author?

    (A) Its inherent lack of documentary evidence
    (B) Its misleading emphasis on the importance of religion
    (C) Its lack of methodological rigor or complexity
    (D) Its preoccupation with Islamic historical trends
    (E) Its tendency to exaggerate historical reality

49. All of the following accurately describe the tone of the second paragraph EXCEPT

    (A) emphatic
    (B) acerbic
    (C) relieved
    (D) comic
    (E) vituperative

50. The word "gestured" (line 33) most nearly means

    (A) addressed incompletely
    (B) characterized dishonestly
    (C) questioned fully
    (D) transferred abruptly
    (E) figured expressively

51. Which of the following sentences best represents the author's main point in the passage?

    (A) "If you have read anything about medieval Spain, then you probably know about convivencia—the peaceful "coexistence" of Muslims, Christians, and Jews for nearly eight hundred years on the Iberian peninsula." (lines 1-4)
    (B) "And like all fairy tales, this story of convivencia tells us much more about the world of storytelling in which it was created than about the historical past or objective reality, on which it is only loosely based." (lines 27-31)
    (C) "While some of the recent books on convivencia have gestured in the direction of scholarly discourse, more often than not, they cannot resist the temptation to indulge our basest tendencies to Orientalism and exoticism." (lines 32-35)
    (D) "And when these authors describe Islam, it is with the wonderment and delight of a tourist." (lines 50-52)
    (E) "We, their audience, are supposed to share in their surprise—and in the delicious irony—that Islam was a peaceful, tolerant religion, while Christianity was persecutory, cruel, and violent." (lines 52-55)

52. The author's observation about Maria Rosa Menocal's *The Ornament of the World* (lines 44-46) is best described as an example of which of the following?

    (A) Alliteration
    (B) Metaphor
    (C) Allegory
    (D) Linguistic paradox
    (E) Personification

GO ON TO THE NEXT PAGE.

53. The speaker mentions the chapter titles in lines 47-50 as examples of which of the following?

   (A) Islamic history
   (B) Poetic imagery
   (C) Hyperbolic language
   (D) Orientalist excess
   (E) Failed metaphors

54. Which of the following best describes the rhetorical function of the phrase "and in the delicious irony" (line 53)?

   (A) It raises a question the author answered at the beginning of the second paragraph.
   (B) It alludes to a contention made in the first paragraph.
   (C) It reiterates the thesis of the passage as stated in the first paragraph.
   (D) It critiques the scholarly discourse of *convivencia*.
   (E) It extends the metaphorical language of the second paragraph.

55. The passage as a whole is best characterized as

   (A) a treatise on history
   (B) an ironic attack
   (C) a qualified dismissal
   (D) an analysis of historical evidence
   (E) a vituperative comparison

END OF SECTION I

AP® English Language and Composition Exam

SECTION II: Free-Response Questions

DO NOT OPEN THIS BOOKLET UNTIL YOU ARE TOLD TO DO SO.

At a Glance

Total Time
2 hours, plus a 15-minute reading period

Number of Questions
3

Percent of Total Grade
55%

Writing Instrument
Pen required

Instructions

Section II of this examination requires answers in essay form. To help you use your time well, the coordinator will announce the time at which each question should be completed. If you finish any question before time is announced, you may go on to the following question. If you finish the examination in less than the time allotted, you may go back and work on any essay question you want.

Each essay will be judged on its clarity and effectiveness in dealing with the requirements of the topic assigned and on the quality of the writing. After completing each question, you should check your essay for accuracy of punctuation, spelling, and diction; you are advised, however, not to attempt many longer corrections. Remember that quality is far more important than quantity.

Write your essays with a pen, preferably in black or dark blue ink. Be sure to write CLEARLY and LEGIBLY. Cross out any errors you make.

The questions for Section II are printed in the green insert. You are encouraged to use the green insert to make notes and to plan your essays, but be sure to write your answers in the pink booklet. Number each answer as the question is numbered in the examination. Do not skip lines. Begin each answer on a new page in the pink booklet.

GO ON TO THE NEXT PAGE.

ENGLISH LANGUAGE AND COMPOSITION
SECTION II
Reading Period—15 minutes
Time—2 hours

Question 1

(Suggested writing time—40 minutes. This question counts for one-third of the total essay section score.)

Directions: The following prompt is based on the accompanying six sources.

This question requires you to synthesize a variety of sources into a coherent, well-written essay. When you synthesize sources you refer to them to develop your position and cite them accurately. *Your argument should be central; the sources should support this argument. Avoid merely summarizing sources.*

Remember to attribute both direct and indirect citations.

Introduction

Countries define effective leadership in different ways. Some focus on fear and power, while others point to respect and propriety.

Assignment

Read the following sources (including the introductory information) carefully. **Then, in an essay that synthesizes at least three of the sources for support, take a position that defends, challenges, or qualifies the claim that authoritative leadership is more effective than collaborative leadership.**

You may refer to the sources by their titles (Source A, Source B, etc.) or by the descriptions in parentheses.

Source A   (Patton)
Source B   (Machiavelli)
Source C   (Plato)
Source D   (Confucius)
Source E   (David)
Source F   (Hobbes)

GO ON TO THE NEXT PAGE.

> **Source A**
>
> George S. Patton

The following is a quote from one of the most highly regarded generals in World War II.

"Don't tell people how to do things, tell them what to do and let them surprise you with their results."

GO ON TO THE NEXT PAGE.

Source B

Machiavelli, Niccolo. <u>The Prince</u>. 1513.

The following passage is excerpted from a famous treatise on leadership.

Upon this a question arises: whether it be better to be loved than feared or feared than loved? It may be answered that one should wish to be both, but, because it is difficult to unite them in one person, it is much safer to be feared than loved, when, of the two, either must be dispensed with...that prince who, relying entirely on [the] promises [of his subjects], has neglected other precautions, is ruined;... men have less scruple in offending one who is beloved than one who is feared, for love is preserved by the link of obligation which, owing to the baseness of men, is broken at every opportunity for their advantage; but fear preserves you by a dread of punishment which never fails.

Nevertheless a prince ought to inspire fear in such a way that, if he does not win love, he avoids hatred; because he can endure very well being feared whilst he is not hated, which will always be as long as he abstains from the property of his citizens and subjects and from their women...But when a prince is with his army, and has under control a multitude of soldiers, then it is quite necessary for him to disregard the reputation of cruelty, for without it he would never hold his army united or disposed to its duties.

GO ON TO THE NEXT PAGE.

Source C

Plato. <u>The Republic</u>. Translated by
Benjamin Jowett.

The following passage is an excerpt from Plato's best-known work.

I said: Until philosophers are kings, or the kings and princes of this world have the spirit and power of philosophy, and political greatness and wisdom meet in one (and those commoner natures who pursue either to the exclusion of the other are compelled to stand aside) cities will never have rest from their evils—nor will the human race, as I believe—and then only will this our State have a possibility of life and behold the light of day. Such was the thought, my dear Glaucon, which I would fain have uttered if it had not seemed too extravagant; for to be convinced that in no other State can there be happiness private or public is indeed a hard thing.

GO ON TO THE NEXT PAGE.

Source D

Confucius. The Analects. Translated by James Legge,
with alterations for clarity.

The following passage is excerpted from a collection of philosophical sayings and ideas.

13. The Master said, "If a prince can govern his kingdom with tolerance and propriety, what difficulty will he have? If he cannot govern it with that tolerance, how can there be propriety?"

18. The Master said, "In serving his parents, a son may remonstrate with them, but gently; when he sees that they do not incline to follow his advice, he shows an increased degree of reverence, but does not abandon his purpose; and should they punish him, he does not allow himself to murmur."

26. Ziyu said, "In serving a prince, frequent remonstrances lead to disgrace. Between friends, frequent reproofs make the friend-ship distant."

GO ON TO THE NEXT PAGE.

Source E

David, Jacques-Louis. <u>Napoleon Crossing the Alps</u>, oil
on canvas, c. 1800.

*The following painting shows Napoleon Bonaparte, the French Emperor, crossing the Alps to invade
Italy. The name at the lower left refers to Hannibal, the Carthaginian general who led elephants over
the Alps, posing the most serious threat the Roman Empire ever faced.*

GO ON TO THE NEXT PAGE.

Source F

Hobbes, Thomas. <u>Leviathan</u>. 1651. Updated to modern English.

The following passage is excerpted from a book concerning the structure of society and legitimate government.

The only way to erect such a Common Power [as can] make [the people] secure…is to confer all their power and strength upon one man…that may reduce all their wills, by plurality of voices, unto one will: which is as much as to say, to appoint one man…to represent them all. And every person to own, and acknowledge himself to be author of, whatever this Man shall do, or cause to be done, in those things which concern the common peace and safety; and therein to submit their wills, every one, to that Man's will, and their judgments, to that Man's judgment. This is more than consent…it is a covenant of every man with every man…as if every man should say to every man, "I authorize and give up my right of governing myself to this Man…on the condition that you give up your right to him, and authorize all his actions in like manner."…For by this authority, given him by every particular man in the common-wealth, he hath the use of so much power and strength conferred on him, that by terror thereof, he is enabled to form the wills of them all, to peace at home, and mutual aid against their enemies abroad.

GO ON TO THE NEXT PAGE.

Question 2

(Suggested time—40 minutes. This question counts for one-third of the total essay section score.)

The passage below is excerpted from one of Mark Twain's most famous essays, "Fenimore Cooper's Literary Offenses." At the time Twain wrote his essay, Cooper's novels were generally well liked and respected. Read the entire passage carefully. Then write an essay analyzing the rhetorical strategies that Twain uses to convey his attitude.

If Cooper had been an observer his inventive faculty would have worked better; not more interestingly, but more rationally, more plausibly. Cooper's proudest creations in
Line the way of "situations" suffer noticeably from the absence of
5 the observer's protecting gift. Cooper's eye was splendidly inaccurate. Cooper seldom saw anything correctly. He saw nearly all things as through a glass eye, darkly. Of course a man who cannot see the commonest little every-day matters accurately is working at a disadvantage when he is
10 constructing a "situation." In the *Deerslayer* tale Cooper has a stream which is fifty feet wide where it flows out of a lake; it presently narrows to twenty as it meanders along for no given reason, and yet when a stream acts like that it ought to be required to explain itself. Fourteen pages later the width
15 of the brook's outlet from the lake has suddenly shrunk thirty feet, and become "the narrowest part of the stream." This shrinkage is not accounted for. The stream has bends in it, a sure indication that it has alluvial banks and cuts them; yet these bends are only thirty and fifty feet long. If Cooper had
20 been a nice and punctilious observer he would have noticed that the bends were often nine hundred feet long than short of it.

Cooper made the exit of that stream fifty feet wide, in the first place, for no particular reason; in the second place,
25 he narrowed it to less than twenty to accommodate some Indians. He bends a "sapling" to form an arch over this narrow passage, and conceals six Indians in its foliage. They are "laying" for a settler's scow or ark which is coming up the stream on its way to the lake; it is being hauled against
30 the stiff current by rope whose stationary end is anchored in the lake; its rate of progress cannot be more than a mile an hour. Cooper describes the ark, but pretty obscurely. In the matter of dimensions "it was little more than a modern canal boat." Let us guess, then, that it was about one hundred and
35 forty feet long. It was of "greater breadth than common." Let us guess then that it was about sixteen feet wide. This leviathan had been prowling down bends which were but a third as long as itself, and scraping between banks where it only had two feet of space to spare on each side. We
40 cannot too much admire this miracle. A low-roofed dwelling occupies "two-thirds of the ark's length"—a dwelling ninety feet long and sixteen feet wide, let us say—a kind of

vestibule train. The dwelling has two rooms—each forty-five feet long and sixteen feet wide, let us guess. One of
45 them is the bedroom of the Hutter girls, Judith and Hetty; the other is the parlor in the daytime, at night it is papa's bedchamber. The ark is arriving at the stream's exit now, whose width has been reduced to less than twenty feet to accommodate the Indians—say to eighteen. There is a foot
50 to spare on each side of the boat. Did the Indians notice that there was going to be a tight squeeze there? Did they notice that they could make money by climbing down out of that arched sapling and just stepping aboard when the ark scraped by? No, other Indians would have noticed these things, but
55 Cooper's Indians never notice anything. Cooper thinks they are marvelous creatures for noticing, but he was almost always in error about his Indians. There was seldom a sane one among them.

The ark is one hundred and forty-feet long; the dwelling
60 is ninety feet long. The idea of the Indians is to drop softly and secretly from the arched sapling to the dwelling as the ark creeps along under it at the rate of a mile an hour, and butcher the family. It will take the ark a minute and a half to pass under. It will take the ninety-foot dwelling a minute to
65 pass under. Now, then, what did the six Indians do? It would take you thirty years to guess, and even then you would have to give it up, I believe. Therefore, I will tell you what the Indians did. Their chief, a person of quite extraordinary intellect for a Cooper Indian, warily watched the canal-boat
70 as it squeezed along under him and when he had got his calculations fined down to exactly the right shade, as he judged, he let go and dropped. And missed the boat! That is actually what he did. He missed the house, and landed in the stern of the scow. It was not much of a fall, yet it knocked
75 him silly. He lay there unconscious. If the house had been ninety-seven feet long he would have made the trip. The error lay in the construction of the house. Cooper was no architect.

There still remained in the roost five Indians. The boat
80 has passed under and is now out of their reach. Let me explain what the five did—you would not be able to reason it out for yourself. No. 1 jumped for the boat, but fell in the water astern of it. Then No. 2 jumped for the boat, but fell in the water still further astern of it. Then No. 3 jumped for

GO ON TO THE NEXT PAGE.

85   the boat, and fell a good way astern of it. Then No. 4 jumped
     for the boat, and fell in the water away astern. Then even No.
     5 made a jump for the boat—for he was a Cooper Indian.
     In that matter of intellect, the difference between a Cooper
     Indian and the Indian that stands in front of the cigar-shop
90   is not spacious. The scow episode is really a sublime burst
     of invention; but it does not thrill, because the inaccuracy
     of details throw a sort of air of fictitiousness and general
     improbability over it. This comes of Cooper's inadequacy as
     observer.

GO ON TO THE NEXT PAGE.

Question 3

(Suggested time—40 minutes. This question counts for one-third of the total essay section score.)

Read and think carefully about the following quotation. Then write an essay in which you defend, challenge, or qualify Voltaire's claim. Make sure to use appropriate evidence from literary, historical, or personal sources to develop your argument.

It is dangerous to be right in matters about which the established authorities are wrong.

—*Voltaire*

STOP

END OF EXAM

Practice Test 2:
Answers and Explanations

ANSWER KEY

1. C
2. B
3. C
4. A
5. A
6. A
7. D
8. E
9. A
10. A
11. B
12. B
13. B
14. B
15. A
16. E
17. B
18. D
19. A
20. C
21. D
22. A
23. D
24. B
25. C
26. B
27. A
28. A

29. E
30. B
31. C
32. A
33. D
34. A
35. C
36. E
37. D
38. E
39. C
40. A
41. D
42. D
43. C
44. E
45. B
46. A
47. C
48. E
49. C
50. A
51. B
52. B
53. D
54. E
55. B

EXPLANATIONS FOR THE MULTIPLE-CHOICE QUESTIONS

1. **C**   Remember that oftentimes AP questions will ask you to infer—to draw a conclusion based on what is said in the text.

    The best course of action to take when approaching this question is POE. Answer (B) is the only one that posits a positive answer (to "laud" means to praise), and it can be eliminated easily because of the word "linear." The final sentence of the first paragraph does laud Browne's writing, but the author suggests that the reading process is like going through a series of mazes. This is anything but straightforward—or linear. Later in the text, there is an oblique allusion to William Shakespeare ("the time of Elizabeth"), but there is nothing resembling a comparison between Browne and Shakespeare; eliminate (D). There is even less reason to suspect that there is any suggestion of a comparison between the author of the passage (Samuel Johnson, by the way) and Browne; so you can eliminate answer (E). Now you're down to two choices. The author criticizes the exuberance and lack of clarity that makes it difficult to understand his reasoning; he does not suggest that Browne reasons poorly (or not at all); thus, answer (A) is not correct. You're left with (C), which fits: The author complains about Browne's lack of clarity.

2. **B**   This question also requires you to use POE. The first answer should be suspect—it would be far too easy if they just expected you to equate "poesy" and "poetry." Remember that the author applies the poesy to Browne's style, which the author qualifies with a combination of positive and negative attributes. In essence, you must match the positive qualities ("excellencies") and negative ones ("faults") with one of the answers. None of the last three answers–all of which are tied to "poetry" to keep you leaning toward a simplistic answer–is appropriate. Browne says that greatness is connected to certain extremes (both good and bad) in an individual's character; the author of the passage suggests that the extremes of Browne's character help explain the eccentricities of his style.

    More often than not the correct answer will be similar, but not identical, to the answer that you come up with from reading the passage. Your goal is to identify the best answer, and (B) is the only plausible one.

3. **C**   You don't need to know Latin to answer this question! Check the context around it: "To have great excellencies and great faults…is the poesy of the best natures" (lines 12-14). So, the "best" people (with the best natures) have both "great excellencies and great faults." Choices (A) and (D) are trap answers, since the quote is about human nature, not poetry or poesy. The quote cannot refer only to Browne, so rule out (E). Choice (B) is very close, but is far more extreme than (C). Choice (C) is a safe answer since it says "often."

4. **A**   Here's another example where POE comes in handy. At first glance, answer (B) seems plausible, but the problem lies in the word "hints." The author does not hint; rather, he says outright that the style is pedantic. The author describes, but does not justify or argue, so (C) and (D) are out. Choice (E) can't be correct; Browne's style is many things (including complex), but it is definitely not facile (easy). True, there are some positive elements in the author's evaluation, but these are outweighed by the negative epithets: rugged, pedantic (overly bookish), obscure, harsh, and uncouth. This appears to be open criticism, so (A) is the best answer.

5. **A** The key to answering this question correctly is to recognize that the author establishes a clear parallel pattern: a sequence of positive qualifiers contrasted with related negative ones (this, but that). At the end of the sentence, however, the author combines two pejorative statements (this and that). This parallelism tips the balance toward the negative, revealing the author's point of view. Remember that the passage begins with Browne's own comment that suggests that greatness originates in a sort of balance between the great qualities and great faults. By adding on only faults at the end of the sentence describing Browne's style, the author of the passage shows that he sees more faults than "excellencies." Some of the answers are deliberately misleading. Both (B) and (C) pertain to "balance," although each has nothing to do with our answer. Choice (D) appears to function only as "filler." If you chose this answer, you should review the meaning of parallelism before going any further. Choice (E) is the exact opposite of the correct answer; "obfuscate" means to intentionally mislead.

6. **A** The first sentence of the third paragraph allows you to use POE to begin eliminating incorrect answer choices: "He fell into an age in which our language began to lose the stability…." Right away, you can eliminate answers (B), (C), and (E). You should be suspicious of (D) because of the word "metaphorical." Where does "metaphorical" come in? It doesn't, which is why (D) is not the correct answer. Browne lived in a time of linguistic experimentation, and the author of the passage takes the time to discuss this to put some of Browne's excesses in context.

7. **D** The author at first classifies Browne's use of vocabulary as "useful" then goes on to describe some of it as "superfluous" and then "obscure." You can use POE to eliminate all but the correct answer. The last word in the correct answer, "deleterious," may have given you problems; this word means "harmful." The idea that some of his vocabulary is, in fact, harmful to his writing is given in the lines that say that some words "conceal his meaning rather than explain it."

8. **E** For this question, all of the answers probably seemed plausible. Your first step should have been to find the appropriate part of the text. In the last paragraph, the author writes: "in defence of his uncommon words and expressions, we must consider that he had uncommon sentiments, and was not content to express, in many words, that idea for which any language could supply a single term." Thus, the author attributes Browne's unusual diction (word choice) to his desire to find the exact word that expresses his uncommon thoughts or feelings, instead of circuitously expressing them through the use of many words.

9. **A** This question does not ask anything new; in essence, it addresses the same content as the preceding question, but in a slightly different way while indirectly testing your knowledge of a couple of words. If you understand that "heteroclite diction" signifies the use of words that are unusual or unusually varied, you can probably pick out the correct answer immediately. If not, use POE. You can eliminate (D) right away. Hopefully, you are familiar with the word "homogeneous" and can eliminate choice (B), too. Even if you aren't sure about the meaning of "mundane" (ordinary, usual, worldly) or "trope" (similar in meaning to rhetorical figure, for example, metaphor), you will have narrowed your choices to three options and should guess and move on.

10. **A** This question is relatively straightforward; using POE would enable you to eliminate answers (B) and (D). You may have been tempted by (C), but you should have noticed that the author of the passage discusses Browne as though he were writing in the past; for example, the third paragraph begins, "He fell into an age in which our language began to lose the stability which it had obtained in the time of Elizabeth." Finally, if you know that polemic means "debate" and that "virulent polemic" means something like a "heated debate," then you can dismiss answer (E). If not, then you should have guessed and moved on.

11. **B** Remember that with this type of question, if you can determine that half of the answer is untrue, then you can eliminate the entire answer. Thus, the fact that "sarcastic" seems way off-base allows you to eliminate (A), the inappropriateness of "harsh" allows you to discard (C), and the use of "sentimental" (or "capricious") disqualifies (E). It may not seem unreasonable to claim that the author of the passage is somewhat condescending, but it would be inaccurate to say that he is indulgent; the author appears to genuinely appreciate and admire certain aspects of Browne's style. In fact, he analyzes the style in a scholarly manner, which is why (B) is the best answer.

12. **B** In the very last line, the author says that we should "bestow laurel and rose" upon George Eliot. This would have a positive connotation, so rule out "feigned" (C) and "reasoned objectivity" (E). "Qualified" means "with some possible exceptions or reservations" (not "qualified for the job"), so (D) is too negative. That leaves (A) and (B). Choice (B) is less extreme, so it is therefore our best answer.

13. **B** This question digs deeper into the relevance of the discussion of religion as it applies to the speaker's view of Eliot as a feminist writer (or as a writer about the feminine condition). Don't let the simile ("like a place of worship") mislead you. The speaker claims that at the heart of Eliot's novels the reader finds a young woman's struggle "in aspiration and agony" for "something that is perhaps incompatible with the facts of human existence." There is no statement about where the heroine might be physically, so answers (A), (C), and (D) should be eliminated right away. Answer (E) may have seemed plausible, but in fact, the heroine, as a woman in a world dominated by men, is shut off from "the real world" and forced into herself, not necessarily "lost in prayer." She is more precisely "essentially alone."

14. **B** The great fact of human existence in the context of this passage is that it's a man's world (remember that Eliot wrote in nineteenth-century England). The entire passage is about women and their place in "the human condition." Answer (C) may have tempted you, but "the facts of human existence" cannot be limited to these female protagonists. You may have felt that answer (A) was correct because human existence restricts both men and women in some way; however, the aspirations of the heroines are incompatible only with "the facts of human existence." In this context, the incompatibility pertains only to women.

15. **A** Every once in a while, the exam will surprise you with a question as easy as this one. "Save for," which you may have seen written before, is sometimes substituted for the phrase "except for."

16. **E** "The difference of [point of] view" and "the difference of standard" are Eliot's "inheritance." Like men, Eliot sought and achieved a significant grasp of art and culture, but, according to the speaker, she did not renounce the feminine qualities—the results of her gender—that made her different.

17. **B** At the end of the passage, the speaker calls Eliot's knowledge and freedom a "double burden" and suggests that the burden led directly to Eliot's death, in the phrase "sank worn out." Clearly, Eliot was not in good health, since she has died, and answer (A) can be eliminated. The other answer choices are very obviously incorrect; choice (C) is incorrect since Eliot was in fact famous. Choice (D) is also untrue according to the passage, and (E) is the opposite of what is stated in the passage. Choice (B) is the best answer.

18. **D** The best way to approach this type of question is to use POE. The apposition ("her, a memorable figure") appears almost at the beginning of the sentence, so (A) is not the correct answer. The claim that Eliot reached out "for all that life could offer" may be intended literally, but the statement is hyperbolic (it is an overstatement). As for choice (C), there is a clear example of personification when Eliot shrinks "back into the arms of love." One could also argue that there are multiple examples of not very noteworthy parallelism, but perhaps the most obvious one is the construction "reaching out with…confronting her feminine aspirations with." You may expect to find a relative clause in such a long periodic sentence, however, there is none, and the correct answer is (D).

19. **A** The question boils down to this: Who is speaking? Let's use POE. The speaker put the phrase in quotation marks to show that it is not hers; therefore, (B) is incorrect. If the speaker borrowed it from one of Eliot's critics, she would need to identify the citation somehow; (C), therefore, does not seem plausible. From context, it is clear that the reader should, indeed, take the phrase seriously, and the phrase does represent the speaker's point of view, which is why the phrase is there in the first place. So answers (D) and (E) can be eliminated. The entire text centers on Eliot's relationship to her feminine protagonists, and so it seems very probable (in this case, certain) that the speaker would integrate a phrase from one of Eliot's heroines. Choice (A) is the best answer.

20. **C** It would be difficult to accept either qualifier in (A), but "disorganized" is far too pejorative and couldn't possibly be appropriate for this passage. Answer (B) is far off the mark too, especially if you can discern between "scholarship" and "pedantry." Pedantic means "characterized by a narrow, often ostentatious concern for book learning and formal rules." You could probably dismiss both terms in answer (D), also; this passage cannot accurately be described as "metaphysical." Answer (E) is half right; the style could be called "intellectual," but there is no cynicism here. POE leaves us with "sympathetic and concrete." This answer may not be ideal, but it's the best choice available.

21. **D** The passage is written by an African American author (W. E. B. Du Bois) and deals with racism and its psychological effect on the author. We know this from lines 13-16 and the author's reference to "other black boys" in lines 27-28. Both the author and the other black boys feel estranged from the white society around them. The sense of "being a problem" is not a contrast (A), it is a comparison. There is no satire in this passage, so rule out (E). The author is not directly condemning racial prejudice (B); he is simply relating his own psychological perspective. Choice (C) is very tempting, but "universal" makes this answer too extreme. Choice (D) is the best answer.

22. **A** An epiphany is a sudden realization; in this passage, there is a rhetorical statement that announces the moment of epiphany: "Then it dawned upon me with a certain suddenness…." Even if you didn't know the meaning of epiphany, you could use POE to arrive at the correct answer. The author is definitely not describing the incident as a moment of triumph (B). Answer (C) is partly true because the moment is a revelation, but the epiphany is for the boy, not for the reader. The remaining answers have no grounding in the passage.

23. **D** The more obvious of the metaphors is the sky, which is extended by "dazzling," "sunny," and "streak of blue." The blue, dazzling, and sunny sky represents the world of opportunity that shines above the white children and, for a while, the author. As the child matures, he realizes the narrowness of his opportunities (the blue is reduced to a streak). The other metaphor is the house/prison with its straight, narrow, tall, and unscalable walls of stone; of course, this edifice is not a real prison, but the limiting restrictions of racism. You may have noticed that the walls of the prison are white.

You can eliminate the other answers with ease, unless you are not familiar with "euphemism," which means "a word or words that replace a crass, crude, or simply inappropriate word or phrase."

24. **B**   Questions like this can be challenging, but take your time to find out what the word "it" is actually referring to. In this case, the correct answer is (B): "veil." When Du Bois talks about holding "all beyond it in common contempt," he is not talking about a verb, so we can eliminate "creep" in answer (C). Similarly, "contempt" (D) and "sky" (E) come after the word "it" so they are less likely to be the correct answer and can be eliminated.

25. **C**   Du Bois does appeal to our moral sensibilities about race at various points in the text, but he does not specifically rely on the use of the "beat" to accomplish this goal, so we can eliminate answer (A). We also learn that "contempt" for his peer group never becomes a dominant emotion for him, even though he says he wants to "beat their stringy heads" (line 21), so answer (B) can be eliminated as well. Because (D) and (E) both reference abstract concepts not really mentioned in this passage, those answers are not correct. Thus, answer (C) is correct. Du Bois uses "beat" in the first two instances to mean "to defeat, overcome" and in the third instance "to hit, strike," which is a clever play on words. Watch how the authors of the AP exam test this particular feature of good writing.

26. **B**   This is a common AP exam phenomenon: Two questions so closely linked that you are more likely to get both right or both wrong. In light of the previous explanation, the "night" is used metonymically to suggest the color of the boys' skin. (In metonymy, one term is substituted for another term with which it is closely associated.) Therefore (B) is the correct answer.

27. **A**   You can eliminate (C), (D), and (E) with certainty. The author states that his comrades shrank into "sycophancy" (obsequiousness, or, in the vernacular, "brown-nosing"); he implies that he had moments of intellectual and physical triumph over his white peers; he also sets himself somewhat apart from his African American comrades ("other black boys"). Choosing between (A) and (B) is the tricky part. On the one hand, even though the author does finally include himself ("the shades of the prison-house closed around us all"), the author places himself above them by accusing the other black boys of being sycophants, and saying that only he wrested his share of opportunity. On the other hand, he suggests that he is superior to his white peers by saying that he could win his share of prizes and contests at school, he suggests that he could at least hold his own in professional life (law, medicine, literature), if given the opportunity.

28. **A**   The previous explanation hints at the answer to this question. The author's first reaction was to remain aloof and "above" the racism at school; however, he realizes that this attitude would do nothing to change one stark reality: that he would not be able to remain apart if he were to somehow "wrest from them" the opportunities open to white boys. He vows to succeed in a field restricted almost exclusively to white men: law, medicine, or literature.

29. **E**   Laudatory means "praiseworthy or congratulatory," and if you know this, the question is not too difficult. If you didn't know this, then POE will enable you to eliminate all of the answers except (E). Watch out for questions that say "EXCEPT" or "NOT"—in these questions, you're looking for the opposite of what you'd usually look for.

30. **B** This passage is from one of the famous Lincoln-Douglas debates; here, Douglas argues in favor of states' rights.

You should note that it is possible to eliminate several of the choices based on the verb used. The speaker presents an argument; he does not analyze (A), criticize (C), or describe (D). Douglas says directly that he is vehemently opposed to the idea of slavery in his home state of Illinois; he argues in favor of letting each state decide the issue for itself and goes on to claim that the greatness of the country rests on the sovereignty of the states to do so.

31. **C** You might not agree with what Douglas is saying in this passage, but he controls his tone carefully; remember, he is engaged in a debate at a time when people turned out in droves, expecting not colossal home runs, spectacular slam-dunks, hockey fights, or touchdown passes, but brilliantly conceived, expertly delivered rhetoric.

If you use POE, you can narrow it down to three choices by eliminating (A) and (E). Answer (D) may be alluring, but be careful not to apply a twenty-first-century point of view to nineteenth-century reality. It may be tempting to see Douglas's defense of states' rights as a mask for his true feelings on slavery or, at least, as a poor veil for a racist bias. However, none of that is appropriate to the task at hand. The tone is best described as the tone of a debate; in other words, the speaker attempts to step back and let the force of his words (the voice of reason, if you will) carry the day. Also, remember that polemic means "controversial argument."

32. **A** The speaker uses inductive reasoning (which is defined as reasoning derived from detailed facts, to form general principles) that goes something like this: You all agree that it was right for Illinois to vote as it chose and abolish slavery; thus, every state should be able to make its own choice on this issue. Moreover, every state should be able to make its own choices on just about everything.

33. **D** In this instance, the word "it" is referring to the choice of New York to make the distinction between "a negro who held property and one who did not" (line 33), so (D) is the closest answer choice. Each of the other answer choices points to a different antecedent and is therefore not correct.

34. **A** The long sentence in lines 38-43 accomplishes many of Douglas's goals at once. It appeals to the principle of "popular sovereignty" (line 39), defines the term (lines 39-41), accuses Congress of "interfering" (line 42), and encourages his readers to "act conscientiously and rigidly" (line 38). Thus, answer (A) is the correct answer because this question highlights the word "EXCEPT" in capital letters. There is no evidence of a classification taking place in this sentence.

35. **C** Check lines 18-37. The author shows that Maine and New York have very different laws regarding African Americans, and that Maine and Illinois are not "interfering" with each other. Lines 39-42 define popular sovereignty as a guarantee "to each State and Territory the right to do as it pleases on all things, local and domestic." This supports either choice (B) or (C). Choice (B) is too strong, since it uses the word "prove," and the author has not necessarily shown that the laws are "successful."

36. **E** The correct answer may not have been readily apparent, but using POE allows you to eliminate (A) through (D). Douglas uses no anecdotes, much less clever ones; likewise, there are no symbols, paradoxes, or metaphors. The authorities in this case are not only the other states (meaning the voters in the other states), but also the founding fathers: "Washington, Madison, or the framers of this government."

37. **D**   Douglas states his own opinion on slavery (his official opinion, at least) at the beginning of the passage ("there is no man in the State who would be more strenuous in his opposition to the introduction of slavery than I would"). Douglas also presents a clear position on voting: "I would never consent to confer the right of voting and of citizenship upon a negro…." Finally, there is a clear position on property: "I would not make any distinction whatever between a negro who held property and one who did not…." Of course, this implies that he would allow African Americans to have property, but he states that, propertied or not, they should not be able to vote. With this information, it is possible to answer the question with certainty; the correct answer is (D).

38. **E**   Use POE! The last paragraph claims that Abraham Lincoln's policies will bring about the end of America's greatness and plunge the nation into Civil War. The "new doctrine" (line 70) is in opposition to "popular sovereignty" (line 54) and thus would lead to a consolidation of power (A). Westward expansion (B) is suggested in lines 57-59, and the author states that popular sovereignty enabled such expansion (line 65-66), so Lincoln's "new doctrine" may hinder that. Choice (C) is explicitly stated in line 71. Choice (D) is also stated directly in line 73. Population (E) is mentioned in lines 56-57, but there is no direct link between Lincoln's policies and population growth.

39. **C**   In a way, this is simply a reprise of Question 36, but here Douglas pushes his scare tactic even further by saying that Lincoln and his party are deliberately infringing on states' rights to incite a civil war. We hope you were not fooled by (B). While it is true that Douglas is blaming the war (that hadn't yet begun) on Lincoln and his political party, he is not shifting any blame; nowhere does he imply that anyone was blaming or accusing Douglas and his party of trying to provoke a war, and to shift blame, Douglas would have to have had blame at some point.

40. **A**   In this passage, Douglas is arguing for the application of the doctrine of "popular sovereignty" against the claims of Abraham Lincoln, which is why answer (A) must be correct. He does not spend his time talking at length about Lincoln's failings, so (C) must be incorrect. Douglas offers a nuanced argument, but he does spend his time exploring "the various meanings" of a "universal principle," so answer (D) is out as well. Because Douglas actively criticizes Congress (in lines 46-47, for example), answer (B) cannot be correct either. Finally, choice (E) may be referring to the comparison of different states at the beginning of the passage, but this does not describe "the development of the passage as a whole," so we can eliminate this choice as well.

41. **D**   The first paragraph lays out the definition of *convivencia* ("coexistence" among Muslims, Christians, and Jews in medieval Spain), so answer (D) is correct. Choices (A) and (B) are incorrect because the author does not want to say that medieval history is unimportant, just that it is portrayed incorrectly in popular histories, which he hardly wants to "reinforce." Notice the way the test writers used words and phrases that sounded correct ("discount the importance of…" and "the popular perception of…"), but were not part of complete, correct answer choices. Remember that if an answer is slightly wrong, it is entirely wrong on the AP English Language test. Answers (C) and (E) don't appear in the passage, which does not discuss historical sources or have "various historical accounts."

42. **D**   The author strings together quotes from various authors in order to retell the traditional "fairy tale" of medieval *convivencia*, which he then goes on to attack. This is why answer (D) is correct. While the author is frustrated with the "narrative of medieval history offered by most historians of medieval Spain," he is not confused by the narrative, so we can eliminate choice (A). Though the author criticizes the works of others, he does not offer his own interpretation in this excerpt, so we can eliminate (C) as well. Answer (E) may be appealing in that the author does survey the story told by many scholars, but his account is hardly "comprehensive" in describing the entire "history of medieval Spain," so we can eliminate this choice as well. Answer choice (B) is incorrect, because while the author is interested in how the "proponents of *convivencia* misinterpret" history, he is less concerned with their understanding of evidence. Besides, that's not the primary reason he used quotes in this paragraph.

43. **C**   The primary purpose of the footnotes in the first paragraph is to document the sources for the expressions in quotes, thus answer (C) is correct. While footnotes certainly can "demonstrate the range of sources" (A) in a work, this is not the case here and answer (A) can be eliminated. Answer (D) is not likely to be true because that is a relatively shallow reason for including footnotes and not one that we can easily detect. In fact most of the wrong answers are too subjective and judgmental to be correct.

44. **E**   The second footnote clarifies that the expression "culture of tolerance" originates in the subtitle of Maria Rosa Menocal's book. While the author is interested in undermining the claims of Menocal, answer (A) is not correct. Neither are the other choices, which do not accurately portray the author's purposes for including this information here.

45. **B**   The word "contemporary" can have many meanings. If two people live at the same time, then they are considered contemporaries of one another. Contemporary art refers to the art scene of the past decade or so. In this case, the author uses contemporary to mean "current" problems, so answer (B) is correct.

46. **A**   "Genre" refers in this case directly to "fairy tale," so choice (A) is correct. The AP loves to embed these grammatical/vocabulary questions into the multiple-choice section. Remember to take your time re-reading a few lines above and a few lines below the sentence in which "genre" appears. Then, begin eliminating every word that you know does not relate to "genre" directly, such as "exotic journeys" (E) or "children" (C).

47. **C**   The author claims that the proponents of *convivencia* are promoting a fairy tale to a largely ignorant audience: "This is a fairy tale for adults who, like children, know nothing about the actual (medieval) world it attempts to describe." The phrase "like children" is a clear example of a simile—a metaphor that contains the words "like" or "as," so answer (C) is correct.

48. **E**   The author does not mention documentary evidence or methodology whatsoever, so we can eliminate answers (A) and (C) right away. He does claim that some scholars have distorted the relationship between Islam and Christianity during this period, but he does not do so in terms of answers (B) or (D), which are not precise. The author believes that *convivencia* exaggerates historical reality and distorts the history of medieval Spain into a fairy tale, so choice (E) is the correct answer.

49. **C** Don't forget the word "EXCEPT" (printed entirely in capital letters) or you will have trouble with this kind of question. Four of these answer choices must be accurate in describing the tone of the second paragraph and one will not. The author shifts his tone between sharp criticism of academic works and elaborate metaphors and humorous insults. He certainly does insist on some of his claims, so (A) is accurate and can be eliminated. "Acerbic" (B) means sharp or bitter, and accurately describes much of this paragraph, as does "vituperative" (E), which means harsh and abusive in its criticism. We can also eliminate these answer choices. At no point does the author express a distinct feeling of relief, so answer (C) must be correct.

50. **A** When we normally think of "gesture," we think of motions we make with our hands when we speak. This author is going beyond this literal sense to emphasize that the proponents of *convivencia* are only halfheartedly committed to scholarship on the subject. This is why "addressed incompletely" in choice (A) is correct. When you try each of the other answer choices in the sentence, they either make no sense ("transferred abruptly in the direction of scholarship") or change the meaning of the passage ("characterized dishonestly in the direction of scholarship"). Answer choice (E) draws from the literal meaning of "gesture" as we normally understand it.

51. **B** This question asks you identify the author's main point in this passage, which is that the proponents of *convivencia* have encouraged people to believe a "fairy tale" about medieval Spain rather than its real history. Answer choice (A) is merely the author's introduction of the concept of *convivencia*, while answers (D) and (E) are more like asides than the main point. While answer (C) is appealing, it is making a specific point about "Orientalism and exoticism" that the author sustains throughout the second paragraph, not the entire passage. Choice (B) emphasizes the disconnect the author identifies between *convivencia* as a myth and the historical record, which he does not believe supports *convivencia*.

52. **B** By calling *The Ornament of the World* a "syrupy confection" that "simmers under a thick layer of Orientalized cheese," the author uses a metaphor built around food imagery to attack the book as unserious. Thus (B) is correct. Remember that alliteration (A) is the repetition of the same sound at the beginning of a word and allegory (C) is an extended series of symbols in a story. There is not a directly paradoxical (contradictory) claim in the sentence, so we can eliminate (D). Finally, the author does not ascribe human characteristics to a non-human subject, so we can eliminate (E).

53. **D** As we saw in the previous question, the author directly states that the chapter titles of the *The Ornament of the World* emphasize the extent to which the book "simmers under a thick layer of Orientalized cheese," so (D) is correct. While the titles do refer to Islamic history (A) and use poetic images (B), the titles are not included to demonstrate either of these features. The author makes many accusations in this excerpt, but he does not accuse Menocal of hyperbole (C) or failed metaphors (E), so we can eliminate those answers as well.

54. **E** This is a challenging question. The author inserts "and in the delicious irony" as an aside in the final sentence of the second paragraph. Throughout the paragraph, he alluded to sickly sweet food products in the overly dramatic characterizations of *convivencia* he criticizes: "exotic fruits," "figs, spinach, and watermelon," "nourished," "syrupy confection," and "simmers under a thick layer of Orientalized cheese." This metaphorical language is extended by his choice of the word "delicious" here, so (E) is correct. The phrase is too short and too unimportant to do any of the tasks mentioned in the other four answer choices.

55. **B** This is a critique of a particular historical perspective, but it is hardly comprehensive or complete enough to be considered a "treatise," so we can eliminate answer (A). And while the author is certainly writing a "dismissal," he is not qualifying it in the sense of *limiting or restricting a critique*, so we can eliminate (C) because it is only partially correct. (Remember that when "qualified" appears on the AP English Language Exam, it rarely refers to "qualifications" or "credentials.") Because there is no "analysis" of evidence or "comparison" at work in the passage, both (D) and (E) can be eliminated as well. Answer choice (B) is correct because the author sustains an aggressive attack on a position while employing humor and irony throughout.

EXPLANATIONS FOR THE FREE-RESPONSE QUESTIONS

Question 1

Synthesis Essay

This sample essay is above average, but winds up being unnecessarily repetitive. The author does a good job of bringing in outside knowledge to round out information in the sources. However, he or she does not fully engage with the sources—he or she treats the David painting, in particular, as though its meaning was obvious and required no further explanation. The author lays out a very clear framework for his or her views on leadership, which also guides the structure of the essay. However, he or she does not attempt to engage two of the more difficult sources, the quotations from Plato and Confucius, which might not fit well into that framework. At the level of writing, this essay is solid; however, some of its sentences get away from the author and become unwieldy. Further, the essay becomes repetitive in the final paragraph, where the author relies more on repeating his or her thesis, rather than demonstrating it by use of the sources. Finally, the conclusion, while clear, is a little too pat. The author fails to acknowledge that leaders of all kinds have been successful in history or that his or her examples do not necessarily fall into his or her desired categories as clearly as he or she might like. Overall, this essay likely merits a 7.

There are perhaps as many approaches to leadership and governing as there are leaders and rulers. However, in general, these styles can be separated into two categories: collaborative leadership and authoritative leadership. Collaborative leaders view their subjects as allies with useful skills and viewpoints, who may have worthwhile insights and who can be trusted, even if they need direction. Authoritative leadership, however, considers followers to be untrustworthy unless closely supervised, and claims that one cannot befriend the common people; one can only overawe them. Of these two ways of ruling, the collaborative style produces better results, even though strong believers in authority are not able to trust that a collaborative process can work.

In The Prince, Niccolo Machiavelli laid out a handbook for an authoritative leadership style. He claimed that a ruler cannot put his faith in the common people, because they will always betray the leader when times are difficult. A prince who relies "entirely on... promises" will fail, because only "the dread of punishment" can ensure compliance. Thomas Hobbes, in Leviathan, makes a similar point: security for the people is so important that they themselves must embrace a tyrannical ruler. People cannot trust each other unless they set up some absolute authority, which, once it exists, is unquestionable, and can ensure safety by intimidation.

History gives the lie to the assertions of these political thinkers. Machiavelli wanted a prince to unify the Italian city-states through force of arms; no such person would come about until the 19th Century, and then it was a king whose main appeal was that he was a limited, constitutional monarch, rather than a dictator. Hobbes claimed that security could only be assured by government that overwhelmed the will of the people; but the most secure states today are the ones which are run by democracies that respond to people's complaints.

Instead, the most successful leaders in history have been collaborative ones: those who inspire greatness, rather than fear, in their followers, and who help their followers to achieve greatness without micromanaging them. For example, General George Patton's view on leadership was that the leader should trust his subordinates. By making sure not to restrain his subordinates' creativity, Patton became one of the most successful generals in World War II. Napoleon Bonaparte was another kind of collaborative leader. He definitely gave his subordinates clear orders and goals, but he "led from the trenches." He was directly involved in their struggles. His personal boldness and character inspired greatness in his followers. Without needing to intimidate his people, Napoleon succeeded where even the great general Hannibal failed, becoming one of the greatest rulers in history. This collaborative leadership style—trusting people to do the right thing—is characteristic of highly successful leaders in history, as well as the most important form of government in the modern world: democracy.

Question 2

Rhetorical Analysis Essay

The following sample is a slightly better than adequate response; the strong writing would probably carry it to a 7 or 8, despite the tenuous grasp of rhetorical strategies. It would be possible to question the student's assertion that Mark Twain's comment that "the scow episode is really a sublime burst of invention" proves that "he is a reasonable critic and not bent on purely insulting the popular author." Most likely, this represents more of Twain's sarcasm.

Mark Twain's well-known essay "Fenimore Cooper's Literary Offenses" seeks to mock both the work itself and its devoted readers. Though Twain's piece has a decidedly ironic tone and is not meant to be serious literary criticism, he employs a variety of rhetorical tactics to argue his point and persuade the audience that not only is Cooper's work flawed and ridiculous, but also that they are mislead in having enjoyed Cooper's writing. Twain uses rhetorical devices rooted in both language and content to convince the reader of the validity of his scathing conclusion about Cooper.

By subtle choices of persuasive writing, Twain conveys his meaning through his language. He uses the first person plural as his point of view to connect with the reader and to give an impression of a sympathetic guide alerting the reader to literary inadequacy. Instead of always presenting his evidence outright, Twain uses rhetorical questions to intensify his essay and to catch the reader's attention. By demanding "Did the Indians notice [...]?" he highlights the unrealistic nature of Cooper's work. In the final paragraph, he employs an anaphora, beginning several successive sentences with "Then No...." This repetitive wording emphasizes his message of Cooper's inadequacy. His phrasing plays a key role in convincing the reader of his point.

In addition, Twain's choice of evidence is clearly intended to strengthen his argument. He uses a simile, "He saw nearly all things as through a glass eye, darkly" to help the audience visualize and better comprehend his meaning. To dramatize his critique, Twain writes "It would take you thirty years to guess," an obvious hyperbole that vividly depicts the ridiculousness of Cooper's work. Throughout the essay, Twain relies on mathematical computations and logic to undermine Cooper's credibility, hoping that objective reasoning will sway his readers. Finally, in a concession to Cooper's competency, Twain admits that "the scow episode is really a sublime burst of invention" to illustrate that he is a reasonable critic and not bent on purely insulting the popular author.

Twain's wide range of rhetorical techniques serve to convince his audience in as many different ways as possible that he is a logical, credible critic and that his argument is valid.

Question 3

Argumentative Essay

The sample essay below serves as a great model, for it exudes an ease that can come only with great practice with the art of writing. There is a clear thesis and organizational structure. Quality replaces quantity, and the clarity is pristine. Remember that above all else, the AP reader craves clarity. The work might not earn a 9, but it would definitely receive an 8.

For as long as authority has existed, there have been those who have challenged it, rebelled against it, and even refused to acknowledge it. Institutions that hold great power—the government, the church, public opinion—have dictated what is right and wrong to those under their control. However, when an individual's personal convictions come into conflict with authority's established morality, persecution, isolation, and other such punishments often follow. Voltaire was correct in his assertion that "it is dangerous to be right" in opposition to the status quo, as demonstrated in history and literature.

As science developed during the Renaissance and humans began to have a more objective understanding of the world, the church held vehemently to its tenets and persecuted those who contradicted its teachings. Italian astronomer Galileo Galilei, whose observations played a pivotal role in our model for the solar system, was one such man who suffered greatly for his non-Christian hypotheses. Though Galileo's theories were indeed correct, the Church nonetheless suppressed his work and placed him under house arrest. Similarly, during the 1950s, McCarthyism swept America, as the government tried to root out "Communists." For the few who condemned the inherent immorality of McCarthy's campaign and tactics, the result was that they too would be blacklisted and effectively ruined. In contradicting the Church and the government, independent thinkers have suffered greatly for "being right" throughout history.

The dangers of questioning authority have not been neglected in world literature. In Milan Kundera's The Joke, the protagonist Ludvik is expelled from the university and the Communist Party for making comments derogatory to the Party. Though his criticisms would certainly be deemed valid by later generations, his correct thinking is rewarded with isolation and prison-like punishment in the military. Fighting against both the establishment and the majority, Arthur Miller's character John Proctor is indeed "right" that the Salem witch trials depicted in The Crucible are madness, and ruining the lives of innocent people. However, his unpopular beliefs only cause him danger as he, too, is soon labeled as a witch. These two protagonists, whose lone voices of reason decry the authorities' "wrong" stance, suffer great dangers as a result of their challenges to the establishment. Voltaire's claim has been continually confirmed by history and literature.

HOW TO SCORE PRACTICE TEST 2

Section I: Multiple-Choice

$$\underline{\hspace{3cm}} \times 1.2500 = \underline{\hspace{3cm}}$$

Number of Correct
(out of 55)

Weighted
Section I Score
(Do not round)

Section II: Free Response

(See if you can find a teacher or classmate to score your essays using the guidelines in Chapter 4.)

Question 1 $\underline{\hspace{3cm}} \times 3.0556 = \underline{\hspace{3cm}}$
(out of 9)   (Do not round)

Question 2 $\underline{\hspace{3cm}} \times 3.0556 = \underline{\hspace{3cm}}$
(out of 9)   (Do not round)

Question 3 $\underline{\hspace{3cm}} \times 3.0556 = \underline{\hspace{3cm}}$
(out of 9)   (Do not round)

AP Score Conversion Chart English Language and Composition	
Composite Score Range	AP Score
112-150	5
98-111	4
80-97	3
55-79	2
0-54	1

Sum = $\underline{\hspace{3cm}}$

Weighted Section II
Score (Do not round)

Composite Score

$$\underline{\hspace{3cm}} + \underline{\hspace{3cm}} = \underline{\hspace{3cm}}$$

Weighted
Section I Score

Weighted
Section II Score

Composite Score
(Round to nearest
whole number)

Completely darken bubbles with a No. 2 pencil. If you make a mistake, be sure to erase mark completely. Erase all stray marks.

1. YOUR NAME:
(Print)   Last   First   M.I.

SIGNATURE: _____ DATE: ___ / ___ / ___

HOME ADDRESS: _____
(Print)   Number and Street

_____
City   State   Zip Code

PHONE NO. : _____
(Print)

5. YOUR NAME

First 4 letters of last name				FIRST INIT	MID INIT
A	A	A	A	A	A
B	B	B	B	B	B
C	C	C	C	C	C
D	D	D	D	D	D
E	E	E	E	E	E
F	F	F	F	F	F
G	G	G	G	G	G
H	H	H	H	H	H
I	I	I	I	I	I
J	J	J	J	J	J
K	K	K	K	K	K
L	L	L	L	L	L
M	M	M	M	M	M
N	N	N	N	N	N
O	O	O	O	O	O
P	P	P	P	P	P
Q	Q	Q	Q	Q	Q
R	R	R	R	R	R
S	S	S	S	S	S
T	T	T	T	T	T
U	U	U	U	U	U
V	V	V	V	V	V
W	W	W	W	W	W
X	X	X	X	X	X
Y	Y	Y	Y	Y	Y
Z	Z	Z	Z	Z	Z

IMPORTANT: Please fill in these boxes exactly as shown on the back cover of your test book.

2. TEST FORM

_____

6. DATE OF BIRTH

Month	Day		Year	
JAN				
FEB				
MAR	0	0	0	0
APR	1	1	1	1
MAY	2	2	2	2
JUN	3	3	3	3
JUL		4	4	4
AUG		5	5	5
SEP		7	7	7
OCT		8	8	8
NOV		9	9	9
DEC				

3. TEST CODE   **4. REGISTRATION NUMBER**

0	A	0	0	0	0	0	0	0	0	0
1	B	1	1	1	1	1	1	1	1	1
2	C	2	2	2	2	2	2	2	2	2
3	D	3	3	3	3	3	3	3	3	3
4	E	4	4	4	4	4	4	4	4	4
5	F	5	5	5	5	5	5	5	5	5
6	G	6	6	6	6	6	6	6	6	6
7		7	7	7	7	7	7	7	7	7
8		8	8	8	8	8	8	8	8	8
9		9	9	9	9	9	9	9	9	9

7. SEX

MALE
FEMALE

The Princeton Review®
© TPR Education IP Holdings, LLC
FORM NO. 00001-PR

Section 1

Start with number 1 for each new section.
If a section has fewer questions than answer spaces, leave the extra answer spaces blank.

1. A B C D
2. A B C D
3. A B C D
4. A B C D
5. A B C D
6. A B C D
7. A B C D
8. A B C D
9. A B C D
10. A B C D
11. A B C D
12. A B C D
13. A B C D
14. A B C D
15. A B C D
16. A B C D
17. A B C D
18. A B C D
19. A B C D
20. A B C D
21. A B C D
22. A B C D
23. A B C D
24. A B C D
25. A B C D
26. A B C D
27. A B C D
28. A B C D
29. A B C D
30. A B C D

31. A B C D
32. A B C D
33. A B C D
34. A B C D
35. A B C D
36. A B C D
37. A B C D
38. A B C D
39. A B C D
40. A B C D
41. A B C D
42. A B C D
43. A B C D
44. A B C D
45. A B C D
46. A B C D
47. A B C D
48. A B C D
49. A B C D
50. A B C D
51. A B C D
52. A B C D
53. A B C D
54. A B C D
55. A B C D
56. A B C D
57. A B C D
58. A B C D
59. A B C D
60. A B C D

61. A B C D
62. A B C D
63. A B C D
64. A B C D
65. A B C D
66. A B C D
67. A B C D
68. A B C D
69. A B C D
70. A B C D
71. A B C D
72. A B C D
73. A B C D
74. A B C D
75. A B C D
76. A B C D
77. A B C D
78. A B C D
79. A B C D
80. A B C D
81. A B C D
82. A B C D
83. A B C D
84. A B C D
85. A B C D
86. A B C D
87. A B C D
88. A B C D
89. A B C D
90. A B C D

91. A B C D
92. A B C D
93. A B C D
94. A B C D
95. A B C D
96. A B C D
97. A B C D
98. A B C D
99. A B C D
100. A B C D
101. A B C D
102. A B C D
103. A B C D
104. A B C D
105. A B C D
106. A B C D
107. A B C D
108. A B C D
109. A B C D
110. A B C D
111. A B C D
112. A B C D
113. A B C D
114. A B C D
115. A B C D
116. A B C D
117. A B C D
118. A B C D
119. A B C D
120. A B C D

Completely darken bubbles with a No. 2 pencil. If you make a mistake, be sure to erase mark completely. Erase all stray marks.

1. YOUR NAME:
(Print)   Last   First   M.I.

SIGNATURE: _____ DATE: ___/___/___

HOME ADDRESS: _____
(Print)
          Number and Street
_____
          City   State   Zip Code

PHONE NO. : _____
(Print)

IMPORTANT: Please fill in these boxes exactly as shown on the back cover of your test book.

2. TEST FORM

6. DATE OF BIRTH

Month		Day		Year	
○ JAN					
○ FEB					
○ MAR	⓪	⓪	⓪	⓪	
○ APR	①	①	①	①	
○ MAY	②	②	②	②	
○ JUN	③	③	③	③	
○ JUL		④	④	④	
○ AUG		⑤	⑤	⑤	
○ SEP		⑦	⑦	⑦	
○ OCT		⑧	⑧	⑧	
○ NOV		⑨	⑨	⑨	
○ DEC					

3. TEST CODE   **4. REGISTRATION NUMBER**

⓪ Ⓐ ⓪ ⓪ ⓪ ⓪ ⓪ ⓪ ⓪ ⓪ ⓪ ⓪
① Ⓑ ① ① ① ① ① ① ① ① ① ①
② Ⓒ ② ② ② ② ② ② ② ② ② ②
③ Ⓓ ③ ③ ③ ③ ③ ③ ③ ③ ③ ③
④ Ⓔ ④ ④ ④ ④ ④ ④ ④ ④ ④ ④
⑤ Ⓕ ⑤ ⑤ ⑤ ⑤ ⑤ ⑤ ⑤ ⑤ ⑤ ⑤
⑥ Ⓖ ⑥ ⑥ ⑥ ⑥ ⑥ ⑥ ⑥ ⑥ ⑥ ⑥
⑦ ⑦ ⑦ ⑦ ⑦ ⑦ ⑦ ⑦ ⑦ ⑦
⑧ ⑧ ⑧ ⑧ ⑧ ⑧ ⑧ ⑧ ⑧ ⑧
⑨ ⑨ ⑨ ⑨ ⑨ ⑨ ⑨ ⑨ ⑨ ⑨

7. SEX
○ MALE
○ FEMALE

The Princeton Review®
© TPR Education IP Holdings, LLC
FORM NO. 00001-PR

5. YOUR NAME

First 4 letters of last name				FIRST INIT	MID INIT
Ⓐ	Ⓐ	Ⓐ	Ⓐ	Ⓐ	Ⓐ
Ⓑ	Ⓑ	Ⓑ	Ⓑ	Ⓑ	Ⓑ
Ⓒ	Ⓒ	Ⓒ	Ⓒ	Ⓒ	Ⓒ
Ⓓ	Ⓓ	Ⓓ	Ⓓ	Ⓓ	Ⓓ
Ⓔ	Ⓔ	Ⓔ	Ⓔ	Ⓔ	Ⓔ
Ⓕ	Ⓕ	Ⓕ	Ⓕ	Ⓕ	Ⓕ
Ⓖ	Ⓖ	Ⓖ	Ⓖ	Ⓖ	Ⓖ
Ⓗ	Ⓗ	Ⓗ	Ⓗ	Ⓗ	Ⓗ
Ⓘ	Ⓘ	Ⓘ	Ⓘ	Ⓘ	Ⓘ
Ⓙ	Ⓙ	Ⓙ	Ⓙ	Ⓙ	Ⓙ
Ⓚ	Ⓚ	Ⓚ	Ⓚ	Ⓚ	Ⓚ
Ⓛ	Ⓛ	Ⓛ	Ⓛ	Ⓛ	Ⓛ
Ⓜ	Ⓜ	Ⓜ	Ⓜ	Ⓜ	Ⓜ
Ⓝ	Ⓝ	Ⓝ	Ⓝ	Ⓝ	Ⓝ
Ⓞ	Ⓞ	Ⓞ	Ⓞ	Ⓞ	Ⓞ
Ⓟ	Ⓟ	Ⓟ	Ⓟ	Ⓟ	Ⓟ
Ⓠ	Ⓠ	Ⓠ	Ⓠ	Ⓠ	Ⓠ
Ⓡ	Ⓡ	Ⓡ	Ⓡ	Ⓡ	Ⓡ
Ⓢ	Ⓢ	Ⓢ	Ⓢ	Ⓢ	Ⓢ
Ⓣ	Ⓣ	Ⓣ	Ⓣ	Ⓣ	Ⓣ
Ⓤ	Ⓤ	Ⓤ	Ⓤ	Ⓤ	Ⓤ
Ⓥ	Ⓥ	Ⓥ	Ⓥ	Ⓥ	Ⓥ
Ⓦ	Ⓦ	Ⓦ	Ⓦ	Ⓦ	Ⓦ
Ⓧ	Ⓧ	Ⓧ	Ⓧ	Ⓧ	Ⓧ
Ⓨ	Ⓨ	Ⓨ	Ⓨ	Ⓨ	Ⓨ
Ⓩ	Ⓩ	Ⓩ	Ⓩ	Ⓩ	Ⓩ

Section   1   Start with number 1 for each new section.
If a section has fewer questions than answer spaces, leave the extra answer spaces blank.

1. Ⓐ Ⓑ Ⓒ Ⓓ
2. Ⓐ Ⓑ Ⓒ Ⓓ
3. Ⓐ Ⓑ Ⓒ Ⓓ
4. Ⓐ Ⓑ Ⓒ Ⓓ
5. Ⓐ Ⓑ Ⓒ Ⓓ
6. Ⓐ Ⓑ Ⓒ Ⓓ
7. Ⓐ Ⓑ Ⓒ Ⓓ
8. Ⓐ Ⓑ Ⓒ Ⓓ
9. Ⓐ Ⓑ Ⓒ Ⓓ
10. Ⓐ Ⓑ Ⓒ Ⓓ
11. Ⓐ Ⓑ Ⓒ Ⓓ
12. Ⓐ Ⓑ Ⓒ Ⓓ
13. Ⓐ Ⓑ Ⓒ Ⓓ
14. Ⓐ Ⓑ Ⓒ Ⓓ
15. Ⓐ Ⓑ Ⓒ Ⓓ
16. Ⓐ Ⓑ Ⓒ Ⓓ
17. Ⓐ Ⓑ Ⓒ Ⓓ
18. Ⓐ Ⓑ Ⓒ Ⓓ
19. Ⓐ Ⓑ Ⓒ Ⓓ
20. Ⓐ Ⓑ Ⓒ Ⓓ
21. Ⓐ Ⓑ Ⓒ Ⓓ
22. Ⓐ Ⓑ Ⓒ Ⓓ
23. Ⓐ Ⓑ Ⓒ Ⓓ
24. Ⓐ Ⓑ Ⓒ Ⓓ
25. Ⓐ Ⓑ Ⓒ Ⓓ
26. Ⓐ Ⓑ Ⓒ Ⓓ
27. Ⓐ Ⓑ Ⓒ Ⓓ
28. Ⓐ Ⓑ Ⓒ Ⓓ
29. Ⓐ Ⓑ Ⓒ Ⓓ
30. Ⓐ Ⓑ Ⓒ Ⓓ

31. Ⓐ Ⓑ Ⓒ Ⓓ
32. Ⓐ Ⓑ Ⓒ Ⓓ
33. Ⓐ Ⓑ Ⓒ Ⓓ
34. Ⓐ Ⓑ Ⓒ Ⓓ
35. Ⓐ Ⓑ Ⓒ Ⓓ
36. Ⓐ Ⓑ Ⓒ Ⓓ
37. Ⓐ Ⓑ Ⓒ Ⓓ
38. Ⓐ Ⓑ Ⓒ Ⓓ
39. Ⓐ Ⓑ Ⓒ Ⓓ
40. Ⓐ Ⓑ Ⓒ Ⓓ
41. Ⓐ Ⓑ Ⓒ Ⓓ
42. Ⓐ Ⓑ Ⓒ Ⓓ
43. Ⓐ Ⓑ Ⓒ Ⓓ
44. Ⓐ Ⓑ Ⓒ Ⓓ
45. Ⓐ Ⓑ Ⓒ Ⓓ
46. Ⓐ Ⓑ Ⓒ Ⓓ
47. Ⓐ Ⓑ Ⓒ Ⓓ
48. Ⓐ Ⓑ Ⓒ Ⓓ
49. Ⓐ Ⓑ Ⓒ Ⓓ
50. Ⓐ Ⓑ Ⓒ Ⓓ
51. Ⓐ Ⓑ Ⓒ Ⓓ
52. Ⓐ Ⓑ Ⓒ Ⓓ
53. Ⓐ Ⓑ Ⓒ Ⓓ
54. Ⓐ Ⓑ Ⓒ Ⓓ
55. Ⓐ Ⓑ Ⓒ Ⓓ
56. Ⓐ Ⓑ Ⓒ Ⓓ
57. Ⓐ Ⓑ Ⓒ Ⓓ
58. Ⓐ Ⓑ Ⓒ Ⓓ
59. Ⓐ Ⓑ Ⓒ Ⓓ
60. Ⓐ Ⓑ Ⓒ Ⓓ

61. Ⓐ Ⓑ Ⓒ Ⓓ
62. Ⓐ Ⓑ Ⓒ Ⓓ
63. Ⓐ Ⓑ Ⓒ Ⓓ
64. Ⓐ Ⓑ Ⓒ Ⓓ
65. Ⓐ Ⓑ Ⓒ Ⓓ
66. Ⓐ Ⓑ Ⓒ Ⓓ
67. Ⓐ Ⓑ Ⓒ Ⓓ
68. Ⓐ Ⓑ Ⓒ Ⓓ
69. Ⓐ Ⓑ Ⓒ Ⓓ
70. Ⓐ Ⓑ Ⓒ Ⓓ
71. Ⓐ Ⓑ Ⓒ Ⓓ
72. Ⓐ Ⓑ Ⓒ Ⓓ
73. Ⓐ Ⓑ Ⓒ Ⓓ
74. Ⓐ Ⓑ Ⓒ Ⓓ
75. Ⓐ Ⓑ Ⓒ Ⓓ
76. Ⓐ Ⓑ Ⓒ Ⓓ
77. Ⓐ Ⓑ Ⓒ Ⓓ
78. Ⓐ Ⓑ Ⓒ Ⓓ
79. Ⓐ Ⓑ Ⓒ Ⓓ
80. Ⓐ Ⓑ Ⓒ Ⓓ
81. Ⓐ Ⓑ Ⓒ Ⓓ
82. Ⓐ Ⓑ Ⓒ Ⓓ
83. Ⓐ Ⓑ Ⓒ Ⓓ
84. Ⓐ Ⓑ Ⓒ Ⓓ
85. Ⓐ Ⓑ Ⓒ Ⓓ
86. Ⓐ Ⓑ Ⓒ Ⓓ
87. Ⓐ Ⓑ Ⓒ Ⓓ
88. Ⓐ Ⓑ Ⓒ Ⓓ
89. Ⓐ Ⓑ Ⓒ Ⓓ
90. Ⓐ Ⓑ Ⓒ Ⓓ

91. Ⓐ Ⓑ Ⓒ Ⓓ
92. Ⓐ Ⓑ Ⓒ Ⓓ
93. Ⓐ Ⓑ Ⓒ Ⓓ
94. Ⓐ Ⓑ Ⓒ Ⓓ
95. Ⓐ Ⓑ Ⓒ Ⓓ
96. Ⓐ Ⓑ Ⓒ Ⓓ
97. Ⓐ Ⓑ Ⓒ Ⓓ
98. Ⓐ Ⓑ Ⓒ Ⓓ
99. Ⓐ Ⓑ Ⓒ Ⓓ
100. Ⓐ Ⓑ Ⓒ Ⓓ
101. Ⓐ Ⓑ Ⓒ Ⓓ
102. Ⓐ Ⓑ Ⓒ Ⓓ
103. Ⓐ Ⓑ Ⓒ Ⓓ
104. Ⓐ Ⓑ Ⓒ Ⓓ
105. Ⓐ Ⓑ Ⓒ Ⓓ
106. Ⓐ Ⓑ Ⓒ Ⓓ
107. Ⓐ Ⓑ Ⓒ Ⓓ
108. Ⓐ Ⓑ Ⓒ Ⓓ
109. Ⓐ Ⓑ Ⓒ Ⓓ
110. Ⓐ Ⓑ Ⓒ Ⓓ
111. Ⓐ Ⓑ Ⓒ Ⓓ
112. Ⓐ Ⓑ Ⓒ Ⓓ
113. Ⓐ Ⓑ Ⓒ Ⓓ
114. Ⓐ Ⓑ Ⓒ Ⓓ
115. Ⓐ Ⓑ Ⓒ Ⓓ
116. Ⓐ Ⓑ Ⓒ Ⓓ
117. Ⓐ Ⓑ Ⓒ Ⓓ
118. Ⓐ Ⓑ Ⓒ Ⓓ
119. Ⓐ Ⓑ Ⓒ Ⓓ
120. Ⓐ Ⓑ Ⓒ Ⓓ